Cannabis Codes of California

Omar Figueroa

Cannabis Codes of California, First Edition

©2017 Omar Figueroa, All rights reserved.

ISBN 978-0-9984215-0-6

Disclaimer

Colophon

This book was set in the Sabon typeface.

Preface

California cannabis law has greatly expanded in the past few years. Not only did California voters "legalize" cannabis for adults 21 and older with the passage of Proposition 64, known as the Adult Use of Marijuana Act (AUMA) in November of 2016, but the Legislature also created a new framework for medical cannabis regulations with several bills comprising the Medical Cannabis Regulation and Safety Act (MCRSA). California cannabis law keeps evolving; further legislative efforts to reconcile MCRSA and AUMA continue.

I am a practicing lawyer in California, and I saw an unmet need for a reference volume containing California's cannabis laws. (I compiled my own binder with AB 243, AB 266, SB 643, etc., like many of my colleagues have, and when that task was completed, I realized I needed to organize the contents of the bills by code and code section.) All of the relevant code sections pertaining to cannabis law in California have been arranged into this comprehensive reference work. Moreover, the relevant code sections can be easily found with the annotated table of contents, with detailed section descriptors summarizing the contents of each code section.

Why is such a book necessary in this day of free online access to California's Codes? Because Proposition 64 did not create a legal tabula rasa by repealing all former cannabis laws and establishing a new legal order. Instead, Proposition 64 changed and augmented the existing laws, making California cannabis laws even more byzantine than before.

It was not always this way. Cannabis was legal in California until 1913, when the Poison Act was amended to outlaw "narcotic preparations of hemp or loco-weed." (At that point, it was legal under federal law.) In the 1950's, possession was escalated to a felony with mandatory jail. The madness continued until 1976, when the Legislature decriminalized possession of small quantities of marijuana with the Moscone Act. Nevertheless, the cultivation of a single plant, and the sale or possession for sale of any amount, remained non-reducible felonies under California law for decades.

On November 5, 1996, California voters approved Proposition 215, the Compassionate Use Act (CUA), making California the first state in the United States to legalize the possession and cultivation of medical cannabis by patients and primary caregivers. For the first time in nearly a century, patients were allowed to use medical cannabis for the treatment of "cancer, anorexia, AIDS, chronic pain, spasticity, glaucoma, arthritis, migraine, or any other illness for which marijuana provides relief."

Senate Bill 420 was passed in 2003, and became effective on January 1, 2004, establishing a voluntary program for the issuance of official identification cards to qualified medical cannabis patients and caregivers. SB 420 also purported to establish default limits of no more than eight ounces of dried processed flowers per qualified patient and no more than six mature or 12 immature marijuana plants per qualified patient; these "limits" were subsequently struck down by the California Supreme Court as unconstitutional legislative amendments to Proposition 215, to the extent that they burden an accused's defense. SB 420 also established a medical defense for qualified patients and caregivers who associate "in order collectively or cooperatively to cultivate cannabis for medical purposes." The era of collectives and cooperatives was born.

In 2010, Governor Schwarzenegger signed Senate Bill 1449, which reclassified possession of up to 28.5 grams of marijuana from a no jail misdemeanor punishable by a $100 maximum fine, to an infraction with the same lenient penalties, but without the right to a jury trial afforded to misdemeanor defendants by the California Constitution.

The Medical Marijuana Regulation and Safety Act (with the unfortunate acronym MMRSA) was passed on September 11, 2015, and went into effect on January 1, 2016. It first consisted of three bills: SB 643, AB 266, and AB 243. They established a new regulatory agency, the Bureau of Medical Marijuana Regulation, created a regulatory framework with a dual licensing system requiring local permits and state licenses, and added a sunset clause to the collective and cooperative defense. Within the next year, more legislation was added, which resulted in numerous changes including a renamed Medical Cannabis Regulation and Safety Act (MCRSA) and Bureau of Medical Cannabis Regulation (BMCR).

On November 8, 2016, the California voters approved the Adult Use of Marijuana Act (AUMA), which officially went into effect the next day. AUMA partially legalized marijuana under state law by adults 21 and older, allowing adults to legally grow, possess, and use small quantities of marijuana for nonmedical purposes. It also reduced the severity of, and penalties for, many cannabis-related offenses, and established a regulatory framework for non-medical cannabis similar to the MCRSA framework. At this juncture, the laws governing medical and recreational cannabis are separate but similar, and the Legislature will attempt to reconcile them in the future.

The goal of this publication is to combine all of the relevant code sections related to cannabis law into a user-friendly guide that can be used by cannabis lawyers, scholars, and entrepreneurs to be able to research the law. We hope you find *Cannabis Codes of California* to be an indispensable tool in your legal library.

A Word About Legal Hierarchy

In order to get the most out of this resource, it's helpful to know the legal nomenclature of California's laws. Laws are contained in what are known as "Codes," which are organized by subject matter, such as the Business and Professions Code, or the Health and Safety Code. Codes are divided into "Titles," which are numbered and cover a broad area of law within that subject matter. Titles are further broken down into numbered "Divisions" which cover a narrow area of law within that Title. Divisions are broken down into "Parts," followed by "Chapters," then "Articles," and finally into individual "Sections." A law is most typically referred to in the California Courts by its Code name and Section number (for example, Health and Safety Code Section 11362.5).

Table of Contents

I. Business and Professions Code Sections

Part A: Medical Cannabis Regulation and Safety Act

Division 6. BUSINESS RIGHTS
Chapter 3. Trade Names and Designations

Article 3. Farm Names

Division 8. SPECIAL BUSINESS REGULATIONS
Chapter 3.5 Medical Cannabis Regulation and Safety Act.

Article 1. Definitions

Article 2. Administration

Article 3. Enforcement

Article 4. Licensing

Article 5. Medical Marijuana Regulation

Article 6. Licensed Cultivation Sites

Article 7. Licensed Distributors, Dispensaries, and Transporters

Article 7.5. Unique Identifier and Track and Trace Program

Article 8. Licensed Transporters

Article 9. Delivery

Article 10. Licensed Manufacturers and Licensed Laboratories

Article 11. Taxation

Article 13. Funding

Article 14. Reporting

Article 15. Privacy

Article 17. Penalties and Violations

Part B: Adult Use of Marijuana Act

Division 10. Marijuana

[Added to the Business and Professions Code by Proposition 64]

Chapter 1. General Provisions and Definitions

Chapter 2. Administration

Chapter 3. Enforcement

Chapter 4. Appeals

Chapter 5. Licensing

Chapter 6. Licensed Cultivation Sites

Chapter 7. Retailers and Distributors

Chapter 8. Distribution and Transport

Chapter 9. Delivery

Chapter 10. Manufacturers and Testing Laboratories

Chapter 11. Quality Assurance, Inspection, and Testing

Chapter 12. Packaging and Labeling

Chapter 13. Marijuana Products

Chapter 14. Protection of Minors

Chapter 15. Advertising and Marketing Restrictions

Chapter 16. Records

Chapter 17. Track and Trace System

Chapter 18. License Fees

Chapter 19. Annual Reports; Performance Audit

Chapter 20. Local Control

Chapter 21. Funding

II. Fish and Game Code Sections

III. Food and Agricultural Code Sections

IV. Government Code Sections

V. Health and Safety Code Sections

VI. Labor Code Sections

VII. Penal Code Sections

VIII. Revenue and Taxation Code Sections

IX. Vehicle Code Sections

X. Water Code Sections

XI. Helpful Charts

Part A. Medical Cannabis Regulation and Safety Act Charts

Part B. Adult Use of Marijuana Act Charts

I. Business and Professions Code Sections

Part A: Medical Cannabis Regulation and Safety Act

Business and Professions Code § 27

(MCRSA- SB 837, Effective June 27, 2016.)

(a) Each entity specified in subdivisions (c), (d), and (e) shall provide on the Internet information regarding the status of every license issued by that entity in accordance with the California Public Records Act (Chapter 3.5 (commencing with Section 6250) of Division 7 of Title 1 of the Government Code) and the Information Practices Act of 1977 (Chapter 1 (commencing with Section 1798) of Title 1.8 of Part 4 of Division 3 of the Civil Code). The public information to be provided on the Internet shall include information on suspensions and revocations of licenses issued by the entity and other related enforcement action, including accusations filed pursuant to the Administrative Procedure Act (Chapter 3.5 (commencing with Section 11340) of Part 1 of Division 3 of Title 2 of the Government Code) taken by the entity relative to persons, businesses, or facilities subject to licensure or regulation by the entity. The information may not include personal information, including home telephone number, date of birth, or social security number. Each entity shall disclose a licensee's address of record. However, each entity shall allow a licensee to provide a post office box number or other alternate address, instead of his or her home address, as the address of record. This section shall not preclude an entity from also requiring a licensee, who has provided a post office box number or other alternative mailing address as his or her address of record, to provide a physical business address or residence address only for the entity's internal administrative use and not for disclosure as the licensee's address of record or disclosure on the Internet.

(b) In providing information on the Internet, each entity specified in subdivisions (c) and (d) shall comply with the Department of Consumer Affairs' guidelines for access to public records.

(c) Each of the following entities within the Department of Consumer Affairs shall comply with the requirements of this section:

(1) The Board for Professional Engineers, Land Surveyors, and Geologists shall disclose information on its registrants and licensees.

(2) The Bureau of Automotive Repair shall disclose information on its licensees, including auto repair dealers, smog stations, lamp and brake stations, smog check technicians, and smog inspection certification stations.

(3) The Bureau of Electronic and Appliance Repair, Home Furnishings, and Thermal Insulation shall disclose information on its licensees and registrants, including major appliance repair dealers, combination dealers (electronic and appliance), electronic repair dealers, service contract sellers, and service contract administrators.

(4) The Cemetery and Funeral Bureau shall disclose information on its licensees, including cemetery brokers, cemetery salespersons, cemetery managers, crematory managers, cemetery authorities, crematories, cremated remains disposers, embalmers, funeral establishments, and funeral directors.

(5) The Professional Fiduciaries Bureau shall disclose information on its licensees.

(6) The Contractors' State License Board shall disclose information on its licensees and registrants in accordance with Chapter 9 (commencing with Section 7000) of Division 3. In addition to information related to licenses as specified in subdivision (a), the board shall also disclose information provided to the board by the Labor Commissioner pursuant to Section 98.9 of the Labor Code.

(7) The Bureau for Private Postsecondary Education shall disclose information on private postsecondary institutions under its jurisdiction, including disclosure of notices to comply issued pursuant to Section 94935 of the Education Code.

(8) The California Board of Accountancy shall disclose information on its licensees and registrants.

(9) The California Architects Board shall disclose information on its licensees, including architects and landscape architects.

(10) The State Athletic Commission shall disclose information on its licensees and registrants.

(11) The State Board of Barbering and Cosmetology shall disclose information on its licensees.

(12) The State Board of Guide Dogs for the Blind shall disclose information on its licensees and registrants.

(13) The Acupuncture Board shall disclose information on its licensees.

(14) The Board of Behavioral Sciences shall disclose information on its licensees, including licensed marriage and family therapists, licensed clinical social workers, licensed educational psychologists, and licensed professional clinical counselors.

(15) The Dental Board of California shall disclose information on its licensees.

(16) The State Board of Optometry shall disclose information regarding certificates of registration to practice optometry, statements of licensure, optometric corporation registrations, branch office licenses, and fictitious name permits of its licensees.

(17) The Board of Psychology shall disclose information on its licensees, including psychologists, psychological assistants, and registered psychologists.

(d) The State Board of Chiropractic Examiners shall disclose information on its licensees.

(e) The Structural Pest Control Board shall disclose information on its licensees, including applicators, field representatives, and operators in the areas of fumigation, general pest and wood destroying pests and organisms, and wood roof cleaning and treatment.

(f) The Bureau of Medical Cannabis Regulation shall disclose information on its licensees.

(g) "Internet" for the purposes of this section has the meaning set forth in paragraph (6) of subdivision (f) of Section 17538.

Business and Professions Code § 101

(MCRSA- SB 837, Effective June 27, 2016.)

The department is comprised of the following:

(a) The Dental Board of California.

(b) The Medical Board of California.

(c) The State Board of Optometry.

(d) The California State Board of Pharmacy.

(e) The Veterinary Medical Board.

(f) The California Board of Accountancy.

(g) The California Architects Board.

(h) The Bureau of Barbering and Cosmetology.

(i) The Board for Professional Engineers and Land Surveyors.

(j) The Contractors' State License Board.

(k) The Bureau for Private Postsecondary Education.

(l) The Bureau of Electronic and Appliance Repair, Home Furnishings, and Thermal Insulation.

(m) The Board of Registered Nursing.

(n) The Board of Behavioral Sciences.

(o) The State Athletic Commission.

(p) The Cemetery and Funeral Bureau.

(q) The State Board of Guide Dogs for the Blind.

(r) The Bureau of Security and Investigative Services.

(s) The Court Reporters Board of California.

(t) The Board of Vocational Nursing and Psychiatric Technicians.

(u) The Landscape Architects Technical Committee.

(v) The Division of Investigation.

(w) The Bureau of Automotive Repair.

(x) The Respiratory Care Board of California.

(y) The Acupuncture Board.

(z) The Board of Psychology.

(aa) The California Board of Podiatric Medicine.

(ab) The Physical Therapy Board of California.

(ac) The Arbitration Review Program.

(ad) The Physician Assistant Committee.

(ae) The Speech-Language Pathology and Audiology Board.

(af) The California Board of Occupational Therapy.

(ag) The Osteopathic Medical Board of California.

(ah) The Naturopathic Medicine Committee.

(ai) The Dental Hygiene Committee of California.

(aj) The Professional Fiduciaries Bureau.

(ak) The State Board of Chiropractic Examiners.

(al) The Bureau of Real Estate.

(am) The Bureau of Real Estate Appraisers.

(an) The Structural Pest Control Board.

(ao) The Bureau of Medical Cannabis Regulation.

(ap) Any other boards, offices, or officers subject to its jurisdiction by law.

Business and Professions Code § 144

(MCRSA- SB 837, Effective June 27, 2016.)

(a) Notwithstanding any other law, an agency designated in subdivision (b) shall require an applicant to furnish to the agency a full set of fingerprints for purposes of conducting criminal history record checks. Any agency designated in subdivision (b) may obtain and receive, at its discretion, criminal history information from the Department of Justice and the United States Federal Bureau of Investigation.

(b) Subdivision (a) applies to the following:

(1) California Board of Accountancy.

(2) State Athletic Commission.

(3) Board of Behavioral Sciences.

(4) Court Reporters Board of California.

(5) State Board of Guide Dogs for the Blind.

(6) California State Board of Pharmacy.

(7) Board of Registered Nursing.

(8) Veterinary Medical Board.

(9) Board of Vocational Nursing and Psychiatric Technicians.

(10) Respiratory Care Board of California.

(11) Physical Therapy Board of California.

(12) Physician Assistant Committee of the Medical Board of California.

(13) Speech-Language Pathology and Audiology and Hearing Aid Dispenser Board.

(14) Medical Board of California.

(15) State Board of Optometry.

(16) Acupuncture Board.

(17) Cemetery and Funeral Bureau.

(18) Bureau of Security and Investigative Services.

(19) Division of Investigation.

(20) Board of Psychology.

(21) California Board of Occupational Therapy.

(22) Structural Pest Control Board.

(23) Contractors' State License Board.

(24) Naturopathic Medicine Committee.

(25) Professional Fiduciaries Bureau.

(26) Board for Professional Engineers, Land Surveyors,
and Geologists.

(27) Bureau of Medical Cannabis Regulation.

(c) For purposes of paragraph (26) of subdivision (b), the term "applicant" shall be limited to an initial applicant who has never been registered or licensed by the board or to an applicant for a new licensure or registration category.

Business and Professions Code § 205.1

(MCRSA- SB 837, Effective June 27, 2016.)

Notwithstanding subdivision (a) of Section 205, the Medical Cannabis Regulation and Safety Act Fund is a special fund within the Professions and Vocations Fund, and is subject to subdivision (b) of Section 205.

Business and Professions Code § 2220.05

(MCRSA- SB 643, Effective January 1, 2016.)

(a) In order to ensure that its resources are maximized for the protection of the public, the Medical Board of California shall prioritize its investigative and prosecutorial resources to ensure that physicians and surgeons representing the greatest threat of harm are identified and disciplined expeditiously. Cases involving any of the following allegations shall be handled on a priority basis, as follows, with the highest priority being given to cases in the first paragraph:

(1) Gross negligence, incompetence, or repeated negligent acts that involve death or serious bodily injury to one or more patients, such that the physician and surgeon represents a danger to the public.

(2) Drug or alcohol abuse by a physician and surgeon involving death or serious bodily injury to a patient.

(3) Repeated acts of clearly excessive prescribing, furnishing, or administering of controlled substances, or repeated acts of prescribing, dispensing, or furnishing of controlled substances without a good faith prior examination of the patient and medical reason therefor. However, in no event shall a physician and surgeon prescribing, furnishing, or administering controlled substances for intractable pain consistent with lawful prescribing, including, but not limited to, Sections 725, 2241.5, and 2241.6 of this code and Sections 11159.2 and 124961 of the Health and Safety Code, be prosecuted for excessive prescribing and prompt review of the applicability of these provisions shall be made in any complaint that may implicate these provisions.

(4) Repeated acts of clearly excessive recommending of cannabis to patients for medical purposes, or repeated acts of recommending cannabis to patients for medical purposes without a good faith prior examination of the patient and a medical reason for the recommendation.

(5) Sexual misconduct with one or more patients during a course of treatment or an examination.

(6) Practicing medicine while under the influence of drugs or alcohol.

(b) The board may by regulation prioritize cases involving an allegation of conduct that is not described in subdivision (a). Those cases prioritized by regulation shall not be assigned a priority equal to or higher than the priorities established in subdivision (a).

(c) The Medical Board of California shall indicate in its annual report mandated by Section 2312 the number of temporary restraining orders, interim suspension orders, and disciplinary actions that are taken in each priority category specified in subdivisions (a) and (b).

Business and Professions Code § 2241.5

(MCRSA- SB 643, Effective January 1, 2016.)

(a) A physician and surgeon may prescribe for, or dispense or administer to, a person under his or her treatment for a medical condition dangerous drugs or prescription controlled substances for the treatment of pain or a condition causing pain, including, but not limited to, intractable pain.

(b) No physician and surgeon shall be subject to disciplinary action for prescribing, dispensing, or administering dangerous drugs or prescription controlled substances in accordance with this section.

(c) This section shall not affect the power of the board to take any action described in Section 2227 against a physician and surgeon who does any of the following:

(1) Violates subdivision (b), (c), or (d) of Section 2234 regarding gross negligence, repeated negligent acts, or incompetence.

(2) Violates Section 2241 regarding treatment of an addict.

(3) Violates Section 2242 or 2525.3 regarding performing an appropriate prior examination and the existence of a medical indication for prescribing, dispensing, or furnishing dangerous drugs or recommending medical cannabis.

(4) Violates Section 2242.1 regarding prescribing on the Internet.

(5) Fails to keep complete and accurate records of purchases and disposals of substances listed in the California Uniform Controlled Substances Act (Division 10 (commencing with Section 11000) of the Health and Safety Code) or controlled substances scheduled in the federal Comprehensive Drug Abuse Prevention and Control Act of 1970 (21 U.S.C. Sec. 801 et seq.), or pursuant to the federal Comprehensive Drug Abuse Prevention and Control Act of 1970. A physician and surgeon shall keep records of his or her purchases and disposals of these controlled substances or dangerous drugs, including the date of purchase, the date and records of the sale or disposal of the drugs by the physician and surgeon, the name and address of the person receiving the drugs, and the reason for the disposal or the dispensing of the drugs to the person, and shall otherwise comply with all state recordkeeping requirements for controlled substances.

(6) Writes false or fictitious prescriptions for controlled substances listed in the California Uniform Controlled Substances Act or scheduled in the federal Comprehensive Drug Abuse Prevention and Control Act of 1970.

(7) Prescribes, administers, or dispenses in violation of this chapter, or in violation of Chapter 4 (commencing with Section 11150) or Chapter 5 (commencing with Section 11210) of Division 10 of the Health and Safety Code.

(d) A physician and surgeon shall exercise reasonable care in determining whether a particular patient or condition, or the complexity of a patient's treatment, including, but not limited to, a current or recent pattern of drug abuse, requires consultation with, or referral to, a more qualified specialist.

(e) Nothing in this section shall prohibit the governing body of a hospital from taking disciplinary actions against a physician and surgeon pursuant to Sections 809.05, 809.4, and 809.5.

Business and Professions Code § 2242.1

(MCRSA- SB 643, Effective January 1, 2016.)

(a) No person or entity may prescribe, dispense, or furnish, or cause to be prescribed, dispensed, or furnished, dangerous drugs or dangerous devices, as defined in Section 4022, on the Internet for delivery to any person in this state, without an appropriate prior examination and medical indication, except as authorized by Section 2242.

(b) Notwithstanding any other provision of law, a violation of this section may subject the person or entity that has committed the violation to either a fine of up to twenty-five thousand dollars ($25,000) per occurrence pursuant to a citation issued by the board or a civil penalty of twenty-five thousand dollars ($25,000) per occurrence.

(c) The Attorney General may bring an action to enforce this section and to collect the fines or civil penalties authorized by subdivision (b).

(d) For notifications made on and after January 1, 2002, the Franchise Tax Board, upon notification by the Attorney General or the board of a final judgment in an action brought under this section, shall subtract the amount of the fine or awarded civil penalties from any tax refunds or lottery winnings due to the person who is a defendant in the action using the offset authority under Section 12419.5 of the Government Code, as delegated by the Controller, and the processes as established by the Franchise Tax Board for this purpose. That amount shall be forwarded to the board for deposit in the Contingent Fund of the Medical Board of California.

(e) If the person or entity that is the subject of an action brought pursuant to this section is not a resident of this state, a violation of this section shall, if applicable, be reported to the person's or entity's appropriate professional licensing authority.

(f) Nothing in this section shall prohibit the board from commencing a disciplinary action against a physician and surgeon pursuant to Section 2242 or 2525.3.

Business and Professions Code § 2525

(MCRSA- SB 643, Effective January 1, 2016.)

(a) It is unlawful for a physician and surgeon who recommends cannabis to a patient for a medical purpose to accept, solicit, or offer any form of remuneration from or to a facility issued a state license pursuant to Chapter 3.5 (commencing with Section 19300) of Division 8, if the physician and surgeon or his or her immediate family have a financial interest in that facility.

(b) For the purposes of this section, "financial interest" shall have the same meaning as in Section 650.01.

(c) A violation of this section shall be a misdemeanor punishable by up to one year in county jail and a fine of up to five thousand dollars ($5,000) or by civil penalties of up to five thousand dollars ($5,000) and shall constitute unprofessional conduct.

Business and Professions Code § 2525.1

(MCRSA- SB 643, Effective January 1, 2016.)

The Medical Board of California shall consult with the California Marijuana Research Program, known as the Center for Medicinal Cannabis Research, authorized pursuant to Section 11362.9 of the Health and Safety Code, on developing and adopting medical guidelines for the appropriate administration and use of medical cannabis.

Business and Professions Code § 2525.2

(MCRSA- SB 643, Effective January 1, 2016.)

An individual who possesses a license in good standing to practice medicine or osteopathy issued by the Medical Board of California or the Osteopathic Medical Board of California shall not recommend medical cannabis to a patient, unless that person is the patient's attending physician, as defined by subdivision (a) of Section 11362.7 of the Health and Safety Code.

Business and Professions Code § 2525.3

(MCRSA- SB 643, Effective January 1, 2016.)

Recommending medical cannabis to a patient for a medical purpose without an appropriate prior examination and a medical indication constitutes unprofessional conduct.

Business and Professions Code § 2525.4

(MCRSA- SB 643, Effective January 1, 2016.)

It is unprofessional conduct for any attending physician recommending medical cannabis to be employed by, or enter into any other agreement with, any person or entity dispensing medical cannabis.

Business and Professions Code § 2525.5

(MCRSA- SB 643, Effective January 1, 2016.)

(a) A person shall not distribute any form of advertising for physician recommendations for medical cannabis in California unless the advertisement bears the following notice to consumers:

NOTICE TO CONSUMERS: The Compassionate Use Act of 1996 ensures that seriously ill Californians have the right to obtain and use cannabis for medical purposes where medical use is deemed appropriate and has been recommended by a physician who has determined that the person's health would benefit from the use of medical cannabis. Recommendations must come from an attending physician as defined in Section 11362.7 of the Health and Safety Code. Cannabis is a Schedule I drug according to the federal Controlled Substances Act. Activity related to cannabis use is subject to federal prosecution, regardless of the protections provided by state law.

(b) Advertising for attending physician recommendations for medical cannabis shall meet all of the requirements in Section 651. Price advertising shall not be fraudulent, deceitful, or misleading, including statements or advertisements of bait, discounts, premiums, gifts, or statements of a similar nature.

Division 6. Business Rights

Chapter 3. Trade Names and Designations

Article 3. Farm Names

Business and Professions Code § 14460

(Added by Stats. 1941, Ch. 59.)

"Farm," as used in this article, includes ranch, estate and villa.

Business and Professions Code 14461

(Amended by Stats. 1999, Ch. 1000, Sec. 6. Effective January 1, 2000.)

Any farm owner or lessee in this state may register the name of his or her farm with the Secretary of State, and the Secretary of State shall issue a certificate setting forth the name and location of the farm and the name of the owner upon payment of the fee as set forth in subdivision (g) of Section 12193 of the Government Code.

Business and Professions Code § 14462

(Added by Stats. 1941, Ch. 59.)

Any person selling or marketing the products grown on a farm may use the name of the farm as a trade-mark on the products of the farm, in the same manner as provided for other trade-marks, and subject to the same rights and duties, as provided in this code.

Business and Professions Code § 14463

(Added by Stats. 1941, Ch. 59.)

Registration under this article shall have the same effect as the registration of a trade-mark.

Business and Professions Code § 14464

(Added by Stats. 1941, Ch. 59.)

When any name has been registered as the name of any farm, that name shall not be registered as the name of any other farm in this State, unless designating words have been prefixed or added thereto. The Secretary of State shall register such name only for the person entitled thereto.

Business and Professions Code § 14465

(Added by Stats. 1941, Ch. 59.)

Any person who registers as his own, any name already in use in this State, knowing that the name is already adopted as the name of a farm, or makes use of the name when regularly registered and in use by any other person entitled thereto under this article is guilty of a misdemeanor.

Division 8: Special Business Regulations

Chapter 3.5: Medical Cannabis Regulation and Safety Act

Article 1. Definitions

Business and Professions Code § 19300

(MCRSA- SB 837, Effective June 27, 2016.)

This act shall be known and may be cited as the Medical Cannabis Regulation and Safety Act.

Business and Professions Code § 19300.5

(MCRSA- SB 837, Effective June 27, 2016.)

For purposes of this chapter, the following definitions shall apply:

(a) "Accrediting body" means a nonprofit organization that requires conformance to ISO/IEC 17025 requirements and is a signatory to the International Laboratory Accreditation Cooperation Mutual Recognition Arrangement for Testing.

(b) "Applicant," for purposes of Article 4 (commencing with Section 19320), includes the following:

(1) Owner or owners of the proposed premises, including all persons or entities having ownership interest other than a security interest, lien, or encumbrance on property that will be used by the premises.

(2) If the owner is an entity, "owner" includes within the entity each person participating in the direction, control, or management of, or having a financial interest in, the proposed premises.

(3) If the applicant is a publicly traded company, "owner" means the chief executive officer or any person or entity with an aggregate ownership interest of 5 percent or more.

(c) "Batch" means a specific quantity of homogeneous medical cannabis or medical cannabis product and is one of the following types.

(1) "Harvest batch" means a specifically identified quantity of dried flower or trim, leaves, and other cannabis plant matter that is uniform in strain, harvested at the same time, and, if applicable, cultivated using the same pesticides and other agricultural chemicals, and harvested at the same time.

(2) "Manufactured cannabis batch" means either:

(A) An amount of cannabis concentrate or extract produced in one production cycle using the same extraction methods and standard operating procedures, and is from the same harvest batch.

(B) An amount of a type of manufactured cannabis produced in one production cycle using the same formulation and standard operating procedures.

(d) "Bureau" means the Bureau of Medical Cannabis Regulation within the Department of Consumer Affairs.

(e) "Cannabinoid" or "phytocannabinoid" means a chemical compound that is unique to and derived from cannabis.

(f) "Cannabis" means all parts of the plant Cannabis sativa Linnaeus, Cannabis indica, or Cannabis ruderalis, whether growing or not; the seeds thereof; the resin, whether crude or purified, extracted from any part of the plant; and every compound, manufacture, salt, derivative, mixture, or preparation of the plant, its seeds, or resin. "Cannabis" also means the separated resin, whether crude or purified, obtained from cannabis. "Cannabis" also means marijuana as defined by Section 11018 of the Health and Safety Code as enacted by Chapter 1407 of the Statutes of 1972. "Cannabis" does not include the mature stalks of the plant, fiber produced from the stalks, oil or cake made from the seeds of the plant, any other compound, manufacture, salt, derivative, mixture, or preparation of the mature stalks (except the resin extracted therefrom), fiber, oil, or cake, or the sterilized seed of the plant which is incapable of germination. For the purpose of this chapter, "cannabis" does not mean "industrial hemp" as defined by Section 81000 of the Food and Agricultural Code or Section 11018.5 of the Health and Safety Code.

(g) "Cannabis concentrate" means manufactured cannabis that has undergone a process to concentrate one or more active cannabinoids, thereby increasing the product's potency. Resin from granular trichomes from a cannabis plant is a concentrate for purposes of this chapter. A cannabis concentrate is not considered food, as defined by Section 109935 of the Health and Safety Code, or a drug, as defined by Section 109925 of the Health and Safety Code.

(h) "Certificate of accreditation" means a certificate issued by an accrediting body to a testing laboratory.

(i) "Chief" means Chief of the Bureau of Medical Cannabis Regulation within the Department of Consumer Affairs.

(j) "Commercial cannabis activity" includes cultivation, possession, manufacture, processing, storing, laboratory testing, labeling, transporting, distribution, delivery, or sale of medical cannabis or a medical cannabis product, except as set forth in Section 19319, related to qualifying patients and primary caregivers.

(k) "Cultivation" means any activity involving the planting, growing, harvesting, drying, curing, grading, or trimming of medical cannabis.

(l) "Cultivation site" means a location where medical cannabis is planted, grown, harvested, dried, cured, graded, or trimmed, or that does all or any combination of those activities.

(m) "Delivery" means the commercial transfer of medical cannabis or medical cannabis products from a dispensary, up to an amount determined by the bureau to a primary caregiver or qualified patient as defined in Section 11362.7 of the Health and Safety Code, or a testing laboratory. "Delivery" also includes the use by a dispensary of any technology platform owned and controlled by the dispensary, or independently licensed under this chapter, that enables qualified patients or primary caregivers to arrange for or facilitate the commercial transfer by a licensed dispensary of medical cannabis or medical cannabis products.

(n) "Dispensary" means a premises where medical cannabis, medical cannabis products, or devices for the use of medical cannabis or medical cannabis products are offered, either individually or in any combination, for retail sale, including an establishment that delivers, pursuant to Section 19340, medical cannabis and medical cannabis products as part of a retail sale.

(o) "Dispensing" means any activity involving the retail sale of medical cannabis or medical cannabis products from a dispensary.

(p) "Distribution" means the procurement, sale, and transport of medical cannabis and medical cannabis products between entities licensed pursuant to this chapter.

(q) "Distributor" means a person licensed under this chapter to engage in the business of purchasing medical cannabis from a licensed cultivator, or medical cannabis products from a licensed manufacturer, for sale to a licensed dispensary.

(r) "Dried flower" means all dead medical cannabis that has been harvested, dried, cured, or otherwise processed, excluding leaves and stems.

(s) "Edible cannabis product" means manufactured cannabis that is intended to be used, in whole or in part, for human consumption, including, but not limited to, chewing gum, but excluding products set forth in Division 15 (commencing with Section 32501) of the Food and Agricultural Code. An edible medical cannabis product is not considered food as defined by Section 109935 of the Health and Safety Code or a drug as defined by Section 109925 of the Health and Safety Code.

(t) "Fund" means the Medical Cannabis Regulation and Safety Act Fund established pursuant to Section 19351.

(u) "Identification program" means the universal identification certificate program for commercial medical cannabis activity authorized by this chapter.

(v) "Labeling" means any label or other written, printed, or graphic matter upon a medical cannabis product, or upon its container or wrapper, or that accompanies any medical cannabis product.

(w) "Labor peace agreement" means an agreement between a licensee and a bona fide labor organization that, at a minimum, protects the state's proprietary interests by prohibiting labor organizations and members from engaging in picketing, work stoppages, boycotts, and any other economic interference with the applicant's business. This agreement means that the applicant has agreed not to disrupt efforts by the bona fide labor organization to communicate with, and attempt to organize and represent, the applicant's employees. The agreement shall provide a bona fide labor organization access at reasonable times to areas in which the applicant's employees work, for the purpose of meeting with employees to discuss their right to representation, employment rights under state law, and terms and conditions of employment. This type of agreement shall not mandate a particular method of election or certification of the bona fide labor organization.

(x) "Licensee" means a person issued a state license under this chapter to engage in commercial cannabis activity.

(y) "Licensing authority" means the state agency responsible for the issuance, renewal, or reinstatement of the license.

(z) "Live plants" means living medical cannabis flowers and plants, including seeds, immature plants, and vegetative stage plants.

(aa) "Local license, permit, or other authorization" means an official document granted by a local jurisdiction that specifically authorizes a person to conduct commercial cannabis activity in the local jurisdiction.

(ab) "Lot" means a batch or a specifically identified portion of a batch.

(ac) "Manufactured cannabis" means raw cannabis that has undergone a process whereby the raw agricultural product has been transformed into a concentrate, an edible product, or a topical product.

(ad) "Manufacturer" means a person that conducts the production, preparation, propagation, or compounding of manufactured medical cannabis, as described in subdivision (ae), or medical cannabis products either directly or indirectly or by extraction methods, or independently by means of chemical synthesis or by a combination of extraction and chemical synthesis at a fixed location that packages or repackages medical cannabis or medical cannabis products or labels or relabels its container.

(ae) "Manufacturing site" means the premises that produces, prepares, propagates, or compounds manufactured medical cannabis or medical cannabis products, directly or indirectly, by extraction methods, independently by

means of chemical synthesis, or by a combination of extraction and chemical synthesis, and is owned and operated by a licensee for these activities.

(af) "Medical cannabis," "medical cannabis product," or "cannabis product" means a product containing cannabis, including, but not limited to, concentrates and extractions, intended to be sold for use by medical cannabis patients in California pursuant to the Compassionate Use Act of 1996 (Proposition 215), found at Section 11362.5 of the Health and Safety Code. For the purposes of this chapter, "medical cannabis" does not include "industrial hemp" as defined by Section 81000 of the Food and Agricultural Code or Section 11018.5 of the Health and Safety Code.

(ag) "Nursery" means a licensee that produces only clones, immature plants, seeds, and other agricultural products used specifically for the planting, propagation, and cultivation of medical cannabis.

(ah) "Person" means an individual, firm, partnership, joint venture, association, corporation, limited liability company, estate, trust, business trust, receiver, syndicate, or any other group or combination acting as a unit and includes the plural as well as the singular number.

(ai) "Primary caregiver" has the same meaning as that term is defined in Section 11362.7 of the Health and Safety Code.

(aj) "State license" or "license" means a state license issued pursuant to this chapter.

(ak) "Testing laboratory" means the premises where tests are performed on medical cannabis or medical cannabis products and that holds a valid certificate of accreditation.

(al) "Topical cannabis" means a product intended for external use. A topical cannabis product is not considered a drug as defined by Section 109925 of the Health and Safety Code.

(am) "Transport" means the transfer of medical cannabis or medical cannabis products from the permitted business location of one licensee to the permitted business location of another licensee, for the purposes of conducting commercial cannabis activity authorized pursuant to this chapter.

(an) "Transporter" means a person who holds a license by the bureau to transport medical cannabis or medical cannabis products in an amount above a threshold determined by the bureau between licensees that have been issued a license pursuant to this chapter.

Business and Professions Code § 19300.7

(MCRSA- SB 837, Effective June 27, 2016.)

**AB 2516 adds Type 1C, or "Specialty Cottage," as of January 1, 2018.

License classifications pursuant to this chapter are as follows:

(a) Type 1 = Cultivation; Specialty outdoor; Small.

(b) Type 1A = Cultivation; Specialty indoor; Small.

(c) Type 1B = Cultivation; Specialty mixed-light; Small.

(d) Type 2 = Cultivation; Outdoor; Small.

(e) Type 2A = Cultivation; Indoor; Small.

(f) Type 2B = Cultivation; Mixed-light; Small.

(g) Type 3 = Cultivation; Outdoor; Medium.

(h) Type 3A = Cultivation; Indoor; Medium.

(i) Type 3B = Cultivation; Mixed-light; Medium.

(j) Type 4 = Cultivation; Nursery.

(k) Type 6 = Manufacturer 1.

(l) Type 7 = Manufacturer 2.

(m) Type 8 = Testing laboratory.

(n) Type 10 = Dispensary; General.

(o) Type 10A = Producing Dispensary; No more than three retail sites.

(p) Type 11 = Distributor.

(q) Type 12 = Transporter.

Article 2. Administration

Business and Professions Code § 19302

(MCRSA- SB 837, Effective June 27, 2016.)

There is in the Department of Consumer Affairs the Bureau of Medical Cannabis Regulation, under the supervision and control of the director. The director shall administer and enforce the provisions of this chapter related to the bureau.

Business and Professions Code § 19302.1

(MCRSA- SB 837, Effective June 27, 2016.)

(a) The Governor shall appoint a chief of the bureau, subject to confirmation by the Senate, at a salary to be fixed and determined by the Director of Consumer Affairs with the approval of the Director of Finance. The chief shall serve under the direction and supervision of the director and at the pleasure of the Governor.

(b) Every power granted to or duty imposed upon the Director of Consumer Affairs under this chapter may be exercised or performed in the name of the director by a deputy or assistant director or by the chief, subject to conditions and limitations that the director may prescribe. In addition to every power granted or duty imposed with this chapter, the director shall have all other powers and duties generally applicable in relation to bureaus that are part of the Department of Consumer Affairs.

(c) The Director of Consumer Affairs may employ and appoint all employees necessary to properly administer the work of the bureau, in accordance with civil service laws and regulations. The Governor may also appoint a deputy chief and an assistant chief counsel to the bureau. These positions shall hold office at the pleasure of the Governor.

(d) The Department of Consumer Affairs shall have the sole authority to create, issue, renew, discipline, suspend, or revoke licenses for the transportation, storage unrelated to manufacturing activities, testing, distribution, and sale of medical cannabis within the state and to collect fees in connection with activities the bureau regulates. The bureau shall have the authority to create licenses in addition to those identified in this chapter that the bureau deems necessary to effectuate its duties under this chapter.

(e) The Department of Food and Agriculture shall administer the provisions of this chapter related to and associated with the cultivation of medical cannabis and will serve as lead agency for the purpose of fulfilling the requirements of the California Environmental Quality Act (Division 13 (commencing with Section 21000) of the Public Resources Code). The Department of Food and Agriculture shall have the authority to create, issue, renew, discipline, suspend, or revoke licenses for the cultivation of medical cannabis and to collect fees in connection with activities it regulates. The Department of Food and Agriculture shall have the authority to create licenses in addition to those identified in this chapter that it deems necessary to effectuate its duties under this chapter.

(f) The State Department of Public Health shall administer the provisions of this chapter related to and associated with the manufacturing of medical cannabis. The State Department of Public Health shall have the authority to create, issue, renew, discipline, suspend, or revoke licenses for the manufacturing of medical cannabis and medical cannabis products and to collect fees in connection with activities it regulates. The State Department of Public Health shall have the authority to create licenses in addition to those identified in this chapter that it deems necessary to effectuate its duties under this chapter.

Business and Professions Code § 19303

(MCRSA- SB 837, Effective June 27, 2016.)

Protection of the public shall be the highest priority for all licensing authorities in exercising its licensing, regulatory, and disciplinary functions under this chapter. Whenever the protection of the public is inconsistent with other interests sought to be promoted, the protection of the public shall be paramount.

Business and Professions Code § 19304

(MCRSA- SB 837, Effective June 27, 2016.)

(a) The licensing authorities shall make and prescribe rules and regulations as may be necessary or proper to carry out the purposes and intent of this chapter and to enable each licensing authority to exercise the powers and duties conferred upon it by this chapter, not inconsistent with any statute of this state, including particularly this chapter and Chapter 3.5 (commencing with Section 11340) of Part 1 of Division 3 of Title 2 of the Government Code.

For the performance of its duties, each licensing authority has the power conferred by Sections 11180 to 11191, inclusive, of the Government Code.

(b) Each licensing authority may adopt emergency regulations to implement this chapter.

(1) Each licensing authority may readopt any emergency regulation authorized by this section that is the same as, or substantially equivalent to, an emergency regulation previously adopted by this section. Any such readoption shall be limited to one time for each regulation.

(2) Notwithstanding any other law, the initial adoption of emergency regulations and the readoption of emergency regulations authorized by this section shall be deemed an emergency and necessary for the immediate preservation of the public peace, health, safety, or general welfare. The initial emergency regulations and the readopted emergency regulations authorized by this section shall be each submitted to the Office of Administrative Law for filing with the Secretary of State and shall remain in effect for no more than 180 days, by which time final regulations may be adopted.

Business and Professions Code § 19305

(MCRSA- SB 837, Effective June 27, 2016.)

Notice of any action of a licensing authority required by this chapter to be given may be signed and given by the director of the licensing authority or an authorized employee of the licensing authority and may be made personally or in the manner prescribed by Section 1013 of the Code of Civil Procedure, or in the manner prescribed by Section 124 of this code.

Business and Professions Code § 19306

(MCRSA- SB 837, Effective June 27, 2016.)

(a) The bureau may convene an advisory committee to advise the bureau and licensing authorities on the development of standards and regulations pursuant to this chapter, including best practices and guidelines to ensure qualified patients have adequate access to medical cannabis and medical cannabis products. The advisory committee members shall be determined by the chief.

(b) The advisory committee members may include, but not be limited to, representatives of the medical cannabis industry, representatives of medical cannabis cultivators, appropriate local and state agencies, appropriate local and state law enforcement, physicians, environmental and public health experts, and medical cannabis patient advocates.

Business and Professions Code § 19307

(MCRSA- SB 837, Effective June 27, 2016.)

A licensing authority may make or cause to be made such investigation as it deems necessary to carry out its duties under this chapter. A licensing authority may work with state and local law enforcement agencies on investigations and enforcement actions pertaining to licenses.

Business and Professions Code § 19308

(MCRSA- AB 266, Effective January 1, 2016.)

For any hearing held pursuant to this chapter, the director, or a licensing authority, may delegate the power to hear and decide to an administrative law judge. Any hearing before an administrative law judge shall be pursuant to the procedures, rules, and limitations prescribed in Chapter 5 (commencing with Section 11500) of Part 1 of Division 3 of Title 2 of the Government Code.

Business and Professions Code § 19309

(MCRSA- AB 266, Effective January 1, 2016.)

In any hearing before a licensing authority pursuant to this chapter, the licensing authority may pay any person appearing as a witness at the hearing at the request of the licensing authority pursuant to a subpoena, his or her actual, necessary, and reasonable travel, food, and lodging expenses, not to exceed the amount authorized for state employees.

Business and Professions Code § 19310

(MCRSA- SB 837, Effective June 27, 2016.)

A licensing authority may on its own motion at any time before a penalty assessment is placed into effect and without any further proceedings, review the penalty, but such review shall be limited to its reduction.

Article 3. Enforcement

Business and Professions Code § 19311

(MCRSA- SB 837, Effective June 27, 2016.)

Grounds for disciplinary action include, but are not limited to, the following:

(a) Failure to comply with the provisions of this chapter or any rule or regulation adopted pursuant to this chapter.

(b) Conduct that constitutes grounds for denial of licensure pursuant to Chapter 3 (commencing with Section 490) of Division 1.5.

(c) Any other grounds contained in regulations adopted by a licensing authority pursuant to this chapter.

(d) Failure to comply with any state law, except as provided for in this chapter or other California law.

(e) Failure to maintain safe conditions for inspection by a licensing authority.

(f) Failure to comply with any operating procedure submitted to the licensing authority pursuant to subdivision (b) of Section 19322.

Business and Professions Code § 19312

(MCRSA- SB 837, Effective June 27, 2016.)

(a) (1) Each licensing authority may suspend, revoke, place on probation with terms and conditions, or otherwise discipline licenses issued by that licensing authority and fine a licensee, after proper notice and hearing to the licensee, if the licensee is found to have committed any of the acts or omissions constituting grounds for disciplinary action.

(2) A licensing authority may revoke a license when a local agency has notified the licensing authority that a licensee or applicant within its jurisdiction is in violation of state rules and regulation relating to commercial cannabis activities, and the licensing authority, through an investigation, has determined that the violation is grounds for termination or revocation of the license.

(b) The disciplinary proceedings under this chapter shall be conducted in accordance with Chapter 5 (commencing with Section 11500) of Part 1 of Division 3 of Title 2 of the Government Code, and the director and agency head, as that term is defined in Section 11405.40 of the Government Code, of each licensing authority shall have all the powers granted therein.

(c) Each licensing authority may take disciplinary action and assess fines against its respective licensees for any violation of this chapter when the violation was committed by the licensee's agent or employee while acting on behalf of the licensee or engaged in commercial cannabis activity.

(d) A licensing authority may recover the costs of investigation and enforcement of a disciplinary proceeding pursuant to Section 125.3 of this code.

Business and Professions Code § 19313.5

(MCRSA- AB 266, Effective January 1, 2016.)

Upon suspension or revocation of a license, the licensing authority shall inform the bureau. The bureau shall then inform all other licensing authorities and the Department of Food and Agriculture.

Business and Professions Code § 19314

(MCRSA- AB 266, Effective January 1, 2016.)

All accusations against licensees shall be filed by the licensing authority within five years after the performance of the act or omission alleged as the ground for disciplinary action; provided, however, that the foregoing provision shall not constitute a defense to an accusation alleging fraud or misrepresentation as a ground for disciplinary action. The cause for disciplinary action in such case shall not be deemed to have accrued until discovery, by the licensing authority, of the facts constituting the fraud or misrepresentation, and, in such case, the accusation shall be filed within five years after such discovery.

Business and Professions Code § 19315

(MCRSA- SB 837, Effective June 27, 2016.)

(a) Nothing in this chapter shall be interpreted to supersede or limit existing local authority for law enforcement activity, enforcement of local zoning requirements or local ordinances, or enforcement of local license, permit, or other authorization requirements.

(b) Nothing in this chapter shall be interpreted to require a licensing authority to undertake local law enforcement responsibilities, enforce local zoning requirements, or enforce local licensing, permitting, or other authorization requirements.

(c) Nothing in this chapter shall be interpreted to supersede or limit state agencies from exercising their existing enforcement authority under the Fish and Game Code, the Water Code, the Food and Agricultural Code, or the Health and Safety Code.

Business and Professions Code § 19316

(MCRSA- AB 266, Effective January 1, 2016.)

(a) Pursuant to Section 7 of Article XI of the California Constitution, a city, county, or city and county may adopt ordinances that establish additional standards, requirements, and regulations for local licenses and permits for commercial cannabis activity. Any standards, requirements, and regulations regarding health and safety, testing, security, and worker protections established by the state shall be the minimum standards for all licensees statewide.

(b) For facilities issued a state license that are located within the incorporated area of a city, the city shall have full power and authority to enforce this chapter and the regulations promulgated by the bureau or any licensing authority, if delegated by the state. Notwithstanding Sections 101375, 101400, and 101405 of the Health and Safety Code or any contract entered into pursuant thereto, or any other law, the city shall further assume complete responsibility for any regulatory function relating to those licensees within the city limits that would otherwise be performed by the county or any county officer or employee, including a county health officer, without liability, cost, or expense to the county.

(c) Nothing in this chapter, or any regulations promulgated thereunder, shall be deemed to limit the authority or remedies of a city, county, or city and county under any provision of law, including, but not limited to, Section 7 of Article XI of the California Constitution.

Business and Professions Code § 19317

(MCRSA- AB 266, Effective January 1, 2016.)

(a) The actions of a licensee, its employees, and its agents that are (1) permitted pursuant to both a state license and a license or permit issued by the local jurisdiction following the requirements of the applicable local ordinances, and (2) conducted in accordance with the requirements of this chapter and regulations adopted pursuant to this chapter, are not unlawful under state law and shall not be an offense subject to arrest, prosecution, or other sanction under state law, or be subject to a civil fine or be a basis for seizure or forfeiture of assets under state law.

(b) The actions of a person who, in good faith, allows his or her property to be used by a licensee, its employees, and its agents, as permitted pursuant to both a state license and a local license or permit following the requirements of the applicable local ordinances, are not unlawful under state law and shall not be an offense subject to arrest, prosecution, or other sanction under state law, or be subject to a civil fine or be a basis for seizure or forfeiture of assets under state law.

Business and Professions Code § 19319

(MCRSA- SB 643, Effective January 1, 2016.)

(a) A qualified patient, as defined in Section 11362.7 of the Health and Safety Code, who cultivates, possesses, stores, manufactures, or transports cannabis exclusively for his or her personal medical use but who does not provide, donate, sell, or distribute cannabis to any other person is not thereby engaged in commercial cannabis activity and is therefore exempt from the licensure requirements of this chapter.

(b) A primary caregiver who cultivates, possesses, stores, manufactures, transports, donates, or provides cannabis exclusively for the personal medical purposes of no more than five specified qualified patients for whom he or she is the primary caregiver within the meaning of Section 11362.7 of the Health and Safety Code, but who does not receive remuneration for these activities except for compensation in full compliance with subdivision (c) of Section 11362.765 of the Health and Safety Code, is exempt from the licensure requirements of this chapter.

Article 4. Licensing

Business and Professions Code § 19320

(MCRSA- SB 837, Effective June 27, 2016.)

(a) All commercial cannabis activity shall be conducted between licensees, except as otherwise provided in this chapter.

(b) Licensing authorities administering this chapter may issue state licenses only to qualified applicants engaging in commercial cannabis activity pursuant to this chapter. Upon the date of implementation of regulations by the licensing authority, no person shall engage in commercial cannabis activity without possessing both a state license and a local permit, license, or other authorization. A licensee shall not commence activity under the authority of a state license until the applicant has obtained, in addition to the state license, a local license, permit, or other authorization from the local jurisdiction in which he or she proposes to operate, following the requirements of the applicable local ordinance.

(c) Each licensee shall obtain a separate license for each location where it engages in commercial medical cannabis activity. However, transporters only need to obtain licenses for each physical location where the licensee conducts business while not in transport or where any equipment that is not currently transporting medical cannabis or medical cannabis products permanently resides.

(d) Revocation of a local license, permit, or other authorization shall terminate the ability of a medical cannabis business to operate within that local jurisdiction until the local jurisdiction reinstates or reissues the local license, permit, or other authorization. Local authorities shall notify the bureau upon revocation of a local license, permit, or other authorization. The bureau shall inform relevant licensing authorities.

(e) Revocation of a state license shall terminate the ability of a medical cannabis licensee to operate within California until the licensing authority reinstates or reissues the state license.

(f) In addition to the provisions of this chapter, local jurisdictions retain the power to assess fees and taxes, as applicable, on facilities that are licensed pursuant to this chapter and the business activities of those licensees.

(g) Nothing in this chapter shall be construed to supersede or limit state agencies, including the Department of Food and Agriculture, the State Water Resources Control Board, and the Department of Fish and Wildlife, from establishing fees to support their medical cannabis regulatory programs.

Business and Professions Code § 19321

(MCRSA- SB 837, Effective June 27, 2016.)

(a) A license issued pursuant to this chapter shall be valid for 12 months from the date of issuance. The license shall be renewed annually. Each licensing authority shall establish procedures for the renewal of a license.

(b) Notwithstanding subdivision (b) of Section 19320, the premises or person that is operating in compliance with local zoning ordinances and other state and local requirements on or before January 1, 2018, may continue its operations until its application for licensure is approved or denied pursuant to this chapter only if (1) a completed application and all required documentation and approvals for licensure are submitted to the licensing authority no later than the deadline established by the licensing authority and (2) the applicant continues to operate in compliance with all local and state requirements, except possession of a state license pursuant to this chapter. In issuing licenses, the licensing authority shall prioritize any premises or person that can demonstrate to the authority's satisfaction that the premises or person was in operation and in good standing with the local jurisdiction by January 1, 2016.

(c) Issuance of a state license or a determination of compliance with local law by the licensing authority shall in no way limit the ability of the City of Los Angeles to prosecute any person or entity for a violation of, or otherwise enforce, Proposition D, approved by the voters of the City of Los Angeles on the May 21, 2013, ballot for the city, or the city's zoning laws. Nor may issuance of a license or determination of compliance with local law by the licensing authority be deemed to establish, or be relied upon, in determining satisfaction with the immunity requirements of Proposition D or local zoning law, in court or in any other context or forum.

Business and Professions Code § 19322

(MCRSA- SB 837, Effective June 27, 2016.)

(a) A person shall not submit an application for a state license issued by a

licensing authority pursuant to this chapter unless that person has received a license, permit, or authorization from the local jurisdiction. An applicant for any type of state license issued pursuant to this chapter shall do all of the following:

(1) Electronically submit to the Department of Justice fingerprint images and related information required by the Department of Justice for the purpose of obtaining information as to the existence and content of a record of state or federal convictions and arrests, and information as to the existence and content of a record of state or federal convictions and arrests for which the Department of Justice establishes that the person is free on bail or on his or her own recognizance, pending trial or appeal.

(A) The Department of Justice shall provide a response to the licensing authority pursuant to paragraph (1) of subdivision (p) of Section 11105 of the Penal Code.

(B) The licensing authority shall request from the Department of Justice subsequent notification service, as provided pursuant to Section 11105.2 of the Penal Code, for applicants.

(C) The Department of Justice shall charge the applicant a fee sufficient to cover the reasonable cost of processing the requests described in this paragraph.

(2) Provide documentation issued by the local jurisdiction in which the proposed business is operating certifying that the applicant is or will be in compliance with all local ordinances and regulations.

(3) Provide evidence of the legal right to occupy and use the proposed location. For an applicant seeking a cultivator, distributor, manufacturing, testing, transporter, or dispensary license, provide a statement from the owner of real property or their agent where the cultivation, distribution, manufacturing, testing, transport, or dispensing of commercial medical cannabis activities will occur, as proof to demonstrate the landowner has acknowledged and consented to permit cultivation, distribution, manufacturing, testing, transport, or dispensary activities to be conducted on the property by the tenant applicant.

(4) If the application is for a cultivator or a dispensary, provide evidence that the proposed location is located beyond at least a 600-foot radius from a school, as required by Section 11362.768 of the Health and Safety Code.

(5) Provide a statement, signed by the applicant under penalty of perjury, that the information provided is complete, true, and accurate.

(6) (A) For an applicant with 20 or more employees, provide a statement that the applicant will enter into, or demonstrate that it has already entered into, and abide by the terms of a labor peace agreement.

(B) For the purposes of this paragraph, "employee" does not include a supervisor.

(C) For purposes of this paragraph, "supervisor" means an individual having authority, in the interest of the licensee, to hire, transfer, suspend, lay off, recall, promote, discharge, assign, reward, or discipline other employees, or responsibility to direct them or to adjust their grievances, or effectively to recommend such action, if, in connection with the foregoing, the exercise of that authority is not of a merely routine or clerical nature, but requires the use of independent judgment.

(7) Provide the applicant's valid seller's permit number issued pursuant to Part 1 (commencing with Section 6001) of Division 2 of the Revenue and Taxation Code or indicate that the applicant is currently applying for a seller's permit.

(8) Provide any other information required by the licensing authority.

(9) For an applicant seeking a cultivation license, provide a statement declaring the applicant is an "agricultural employer," as defined in the Alatorre-Zenovich-Dunlap-Berman Agricultural Labor Relations Act of 1975 (Part 3.5 (commencing with Section 1140) of Division 2 of the Labor Code), to the extent not prohibited by law.

(10) Pay all applicable fees required for licensure by the licensing authority.

(11) Provide proof of a bond to cover the costs of destruction of medical cannabis or medical cannabis products if necessitated by a violation of licensing requirements.

(b) For applicants seeking licensure to cultivate, distribute, manufacture, test, or dispense medical cannabis or medical cannabis products, the application shall also include a detailed description of the applicant's operating procedures for all of the following, as required by the licensing authority:

(1) Cultivation.

(2) Extraction and infusion methods.

(3) The transportation process.

(4) Inventory procedures.

(5) Quality control procedures.

(6) Security protocols.

Business and Professions Code § 19323

(MCRSA- SB 837, Effective June 27, 2016.)

(a) A licensing authority shall deny an application if the applicant or the premises for which a state license is applied does not qualify for licensure under this chapter or the rules and regulations for the state license.

(b) A licensing authority may deny an application for licensure or renewal of a state license, or issue a conditional license, if any of the following conditions apply:

(1) Failure to comply with the provisions of this chapter or any rule or regulation adopted pursuant to this chapter, including but not limited to, any requirement imposed to protect natural resources, instream flow, and water quality pursuant to subdivision (a) of Section 19332.

(2) Conduct that constitutes grounds for denial of licensure pursuant to Chapter 2 (commencing with Section 480) of Division 1.5.

(3) The applicant has failed to provide information required by the licensing authority.

(4) The applicant or licensee has been convicted of an offense that is substantially related to the qualifications, functions, or duties of the business or profession for which the application is made, except that if the licensing authority determines that the applicant or licensee is otherwise suitable to be issued a license and granting the license would not compromise public safety, the licensing authority shall conduct a thorough review of the nature of the crime, conviction, circumstances, and evidence of rehabilitation of the applicant, and shall evaluate the suitability of the applicant or licensee to be issued a license based on the evidence found through the review. In determining which offenses are substantially related to the qualifications, functions, or duties of the

business or profession for which the application is made, the licensing authority shall include, but not be limited to, the following:

(A) A felony conviction for the illegal possession for sale, sale, manufacture, transportation, or cultivation of a controlled substance.

(B) A violent felony conviction, as specified in subdivision (c) of Section 667.5 of the Penal Code.

(C) A serious felony conviction, as specified in subdivision (c) of Section 1192.7 of the Penal Code.

(D) A felony conviction involving fraud, deceit, or embezzlement.

(5) The applicant, or any of its officers, directors, or owners, is a licensed physician making patient recommendations for medical cannabis pursuant to Section 11362.7 of the Health and Safety Code.

(6) The applicant or any of its officers, directors, or owners has been subject to fines or penalties for cultivation or production of a controlled substance on public or private lands pursuant to Section 12025 or 12025.1 of the Fish and Game Code.

(7) The applicant, or any of its officers, directors, or owners, has been sanctioned by a licensing authority or a city, county, or city and county for unlicensed commercial cannabis activities or has had a license revoked under this chapter in the three years immediately preceding the date the application is filed with the licensing authority.

(8) Failure to obtain and maintain a valid seller's permit required pursuant to Part 1 (commencing with Section 6001) of Division 2 of the Revenue and Taxation Code.

(9) The applicant or any of its officers, directors, owners, employees, or authorized agents have failed to comply with any operating procedure required pursuant to subdivision (b) of Section 19322.

(10) Conduct that constitutes grounds for disciplinary action pursuant to this chapter.

Business and Professions Code § 19324

(MCRSA- AB 643, Effective January 1, 2016.)

Upon the denial of any application for a license, the licensing authority shall notify the applicant in writing. Within 30 days of service of the notice, the applicant may file a written petition for a license with the licensing authority. Upon receipt of a timely filed petition, the licensing authority shall set the petition for hearing. The hearing shall be conducted in accordance with Chapter 5 (commencing with Section 11500) of Part 1 of Division 3 of Title 2 of the Government Code, and the director of each licensing authority shall have all the powers granted therein.

Business and Professions Code § 19325

(MCRSA- AB 643, Effective January 1, 2016.)

An applicant shall not be denied a state license if the denial is based solely on any of the following:

(a) A conviction or act that is substantially related to the qualifications, functions, or duties of the business or profession for which the application is made for which the applicant or licensee has obtained a certificate of rehabilitation pursuant to Chapter 3.5 (commencing with Section 4852.01) of Title 6 of Part 3 of the Penal Code.

(b) A conviction that was subsequently dismissed pursuant to Section 1203.4, 1203.4a, or 1203.41 of the Penal Code.

Article 5. Medical Marijuana Regulation

Business and Professions Code § 19326

(MCRSA- SB 837, Effective June 27, 2016.)

(a) A person other than a transporter shall not transport medical cannabis or medical cannabis products from one licensee to another licensee, unless otherwise specified in this chapter.

(b) (1) All cultivators, manufacturers, and licensees holding a producing dispensary license in addition to a cultivation or manufacturing license shall send all medical cannabis and medical cannabis products cultivated or manufactured to a distributor, as defined in Section 19300.5, for presale quality assurance and inspection by a distributor and for a batch testing by a testing laboratory prior to distribution to a dispensary.

(2) Notwithstanding paragraph (1), a cultivator shall not be required to send medical cannabis to a distributor if the medical cannabis is to be used, sold, or otherwise distributed by methods approved pursuant to this chapter by a manufacturer for further manufacturing.

(c) (1) Upon receipt of medical cannabis or medical cannabis products from a cultivator, manufacturer, or a licensee holding a producing dispensary license in addition to a cultivation or a manufacturing license, the distributor shall first inspect the product to ensure the identity and quantity of the product and ensure a random sample of the medical cannabis or medical cannabis product is tested by a testing laboratory.

(2) Upon issuance of a certificate of analysis by the testing laboratory that the product is fit for dispensing medical cannabis and medical cannabis products shall undergo a quality assurance review by the distributor prior to distribution to ensure the quantity and content of the medical cannabis or medical cannabis product, and for tracking and taxation purposes by the state.

(3) This section does not limit the ability of licensed cultivators, manufacturers, and dispensaries to directly enter into contracts with one another indicating the price and quantity of medical cannabis or medical cannabis products to be distributed. However, a distributor responsible for executing the contract is authorized to collect a fee for the services rendered, including, but not limited to, costs incurred by a testing laboratory, as well as applicable state or local taxes and fees.

(d) Medical cannabis and medical cannabis products shall be tested by a licensed testing laboratory, prior to dispensing, pursuant to Section 19344.

(e) This chapter shall not prohibit a licensee from performing testing on the licensee's premises for the purposes of quality assurance of the product in conjunction with reasonable business operations. On-site testing by the licensee shall not be certified by the Bureau of Medical Cannabis Regulation.

Business and Professions Code § 19327

(MCRSA- SB 837, Effective June 27, 2016.)

(a) A licensee shall keep accurate records of commercial cannabis activity.

(b) All records related to commercial cannabis activity shall be maintained for a minimum of seven years.

(c) Licensing authorities may examine the records of licensees and inspect the premises of a licensee as the licensing authority or a state or local agency deems necessary to perform its duties under this chapter. All inspections and examination of records shall be conducted during standard business hours of the licensed facility or at any other reasonable time. Licensees shall provide and deliver records to the licensing authority upon request.

(d) Licensees shall keep records identified by the licensing authorities on the premises of the location licensed.

(e) A licensee or its agent, or employee, that refuses, impedes, obstructs, or interferes with an inspection of the premises or records of the licensee pursuant to this section has engaged in a violation of this chapter.

(f) If a licensee, its agent, or an employee of a licensee fails to maintain or provide the records required pursuant to this section, the licensee may be subject to a citation and fine of thirty thousand dollars ($30,000) per individual violation.

Business and Professions Code § 19328

(MCRSA- SB 837, Effective June 27, 2016. **Repealed as of January 1, 2026 by its own provisions.)

(a) Except as provided in paragraphs (9) and (10), a licensee may only hold a state license in up to two separate license categories, as follows:

(1) Type 1, 1A, 1B, 2, 2A, or 2B licensees may also hold either a Type 6 or 7 state license.

(2) Type 6 or 7 licensees, or a combination thereof, may also hold either a Type 1, 1A, 1B, 2, 2A, or 2B state license.

(3) Type 6 or 7 licensees, or a combination thereof, may also hold a Type 10A state license.

(4) Type 10A licensees may also hold either a Type 6 or 7 state license, or a combination thereof.

(5) Type 1, 1A, 1B, 2, 2A, or 2B licensees, or a combination thereof, may also hold a Type 10A state license.

(6) Type 10A licensees may hold a Type 1, 1A, 1B, 2, 2A, or 2B state license, or a combination thereof.

(7) Type 11 licensees shall also hold a Type 12 state license, but shall not hold any other type of state license.

(8) Type 12 licensees may hold a Type 11 state license.

(9) A Type 10A licensee may hold a Type 6 or 7 state license and may also hold a 1, 1A, 1B, 2, 2A, 2B, 3, 3A, 3B, 4 or combination thereof if, under the 1, 1A, 1B, 2, 2A, 2B, 3, 3A, 3B, 4 or combination of licenses thereof, no more than four acres of total canopy size of cultivation by the licensee is occurring throughout the state during the period that the respective licenses are valid. All cultivation pursuant to this section shall comply with local ordinances. This paragraph shall become inoperative on January 1, 2026.

(10) All cultivators and manufacturers may hold a Type 12 transporter license. All cultivators and manufacturers who are issued Type 12 transporter licenses shall comply with the following:

(A) Cultivators shall only transport medical cannabis from a cultivation site to a manufacturer or a distributor.

(B) Manufacturers shall only transport medical cannabis and medical cannabis products as follows:

(i) Between a cultivation site and a manufacturing site.

(ii) Between a manufacturing site and a manufacturing site.

(iii) Between a manufacturing site and a distributor.

(b) Except as provided in subdivision (a), a person or entity that holds a state license is prohibited from licensure for any other activity authorized under this chapter, and is prohibited from holding an ownership interest in real property, personal property, or other assets associated with or used in any other license category.

(c) (1) In a jurisdiction that adopted a local ordinance, prior to July 1, 2015, requiring qualified businesses to cultivate, manufacture, and dispense medical cannabis or medical cannabis products, with all commercial cannabis activity being conducted by a single qualified business, upon licensure that business shall not be subject to subdivision (a) if it meets all of the following conditions:

(A) The business was cultivating, manufacturing, and dispensing medical cannabis or medical cannabis products on January 1, 2016, and has continuously done so since that date.

(B) The business has been in full compliance with all applicable local ordinances at all times prior to licensure.

(C) The business is registered with the State Board of Equalization for tax purposes.

(2) A business licensed pursuant to paragraph (1) is not required to conduct all cultivation or manufacturing within the bounds of a local jurisdiction, but all cultivation and manufacturing shall have commenced prior to January 1, 2016, and have been in full compliance with applicable local ordinances.

(d) This section shall remain in effect only until January 1, 2026, and as of that date is repealed.

Business and Professions Code § 19329

(MCRSA- AB 266, Effective January 1, 2016.)

A licensee shall not also be licensed as a retailer of alcoholic beverages pursuant to Division 9 (commencing with Section 23000).

Business and Professions Code § 19330

(MCRSA- AB 266, Effective January 1, 2016.)

This chapter and Article 2 (commencing with Section 11357) and Article 2.5 (commencing with Section 11362.7) of Chapter 6 of Division 10 of the Health and Safety Code shall not interfere with an employer's rights and obligations to maintain a drug and alcohol free workplace or require an employer to permit or accommodate the use, consumption, possession, transfer, display, transportation, sale, or growth of cannabis in the workplace or affect the ability of employers to have policies prohibiting the use of cannabis by employees and prospective employees, or prevent employers from complying with state or federal law.

Article 6. Licensed Cultivation Sites

Business and Professions Code § 19331

(MCRSA- AB 243, Effective January 1, 2016.)

The Legislature finds and declares all of the following:

(a) The United States Environmental Protection Agency has not established appropriate pesticide tolerances for, or permitted the registration and lawful use of, pesticides on cannabis crops intended for human consumption pursuant to the Federal Insecticide, Fungicide, and Rodenticide Act (7 U.S.C. 136 et seq.).

(b) The use of pesticides is not adequately regulated due to the omissions in federal law, and cannabis cultivated in California for California patients can and often does contain pesticide residues.

(c) Lawful California medical cannabis growers and caregivers urge the Department of Pesticide Regulation to provide guidance, in absence of federal guidance, on whether the pesticides currently used at most cannabis cultivation sites are actually safe for use on cannabis intended for human consumption.

Business and Professions Code § 19332

**(MCRSA- SB 837, Effective June 27, 2016- January 1, 2018.)

(a) The Department of Food and Agriculture shall promulgate regulations governing the licensing of indoor and outdoor commercial cultivation sites.

(b) The Department of Pesticide Regulation shall develop guidelines for the use of pesticides in the cultivation of cannabis and residue in harvested cannabis.

(c) The Department of Food and Agriculture shall serve as the lead agency for purposes of the California Environmental Quality Act (Division 13 (commencing with Section 21000) of the Public Resources Code) related to the licensing of cannabis cultivation.

(d) Pursuant to Section 13149 of the Water Code, the State Water Resources Control Board, in consultation with the Department of Fish and Wildlife and the Department of Food and Agriculture, shall ensure that individual and cumulative effects of water diversion and discharge associated with cultivation of cannabis do not affect the instream flows needed for fish spawning, migration, and rearing, and the flows needed to maintain natural flow variability.

(e) The Department of Food and Agriculture shall have the authority necessary for the implementation of the regulations it adopts pursuant to this chapter. The regulations shall do all of the following:

(1) Provide that weighing or measuring devices used in connection with the sale or distribution of medical cannabis are required to meet standards equivalent to Division 5 (commencing with Section 12001).

(2) Require that cannabis cultivation by licensees is conducted in accordance with state and local laws. Nothing in this chapter, and no regulation adopted by the department, shall be construed to supersede or limit the authority of the State Water Resources Control Board, regional water quality control boards, or the Department of Fish and Wildlife to implement and enforce their statutory obligations or to adopt regulations to protect water quality, water supply, and natural resources.

(3) Establish procedures for the issuance and revocation of unique identifiers for activities associated with a cannabis cultivation license, pursuant to Article 8 (commencing with Section 19337). All cannabis shall be labeled with the unique identifier issued by the Department of

Food and Agriculture.

(4) Prescribe standards, in consultation with the bureau, for the reporting of information as necessary related to unique identifiers, pursuant to Article 8 (commencing with Section 19337).

(f) The Department of Pesticide Regulation shall require that the application of pesticides or other pest control in connection with the indoor or outdoor cultivation of medical cannabis complies with Division 6 (commencing with Section 11401) of the Food and Agricultural Code and its implementing regulations.

(g) State cultivator license types issued by the Department of Food and Agriculture may include:

(1) Type 1, or "specialty outdoor," for outdoor cultivation using no artificial lighting of less than or equal to 5,000 square feet of total canopy size on one premises, or up to 50 mature plants on noncontiguous plots.

(2) Type 1A, or "specialty indoor," for indoor cultivation using exclusively artificial lighting of less than or equal to 5,000 square feet of total canopy size on one premises.

(3) Type 1B, or "specialty mixed-light," for cultivation using a combination of natural and supplemental artificial lighting at a maximum threshold to be determined by the licensing authority, of less than or equal to 5,000 square feet of total canopy size on one premises.

(4) Type 2, or "small outdoor," for outdoor cultivation using no artificial lighting between 5,001 and 10,000 square feet, inclusive, of total canopy size on one premises.

(5) Type 2A, or "small indoor," for indoor cultivation using exclusively artificial lighting between 5,001 and 10,000 square feet, inclusive, of total canopy size on one premises.

(6) Type 2B, or "small mixed-light," for cultivation using a combination of natural and supplemental artificial lighting at a maximum threshold to be determined by the licensing authority, between 5,001 and 10,000 square feet, inclusive, of total canopy size on one premises.

(7) Type 3, or "outdoor," for outdoor cultivation using no artificial lighting from 10,001 square feet to one acre, inclusive, of total canopy size on one premises. The Department of Food and Agriculture shall

limit the number of licenses allowed of this type.

(8) Type 3A, or "indoor," for indoor cultivation using exclusively artificial lighting between 10,001 and 22,000 square feet, inclusive, of total canopy size on one premises. The Department of Food and Agriculture shall limit the number of licenses allowed of this type.

(9) Type 3B, or "mixed-light," for cultivation using a combination of natural and supplemental artificial lighting at a maximum threshold to be determined by the licensing authority, between 10,001 and 22,000 square feet, inclusive, of total canopy size on one premises. The Department of Food and Agriculture shall limit the number of licenses allowed of this type.

(10) Type 4, or "nursery," for cultivation of medical cannabis solely as a nursery. Type 4 licensees may transport live plants, if the licensee also holds a Type 12 transporter license issued pursuant to this chapter.

Business and Professions Code § 19332

**(MCRSA- Amended by AB 2516, Effective January 1, 2018.)

(a) The Department of Food and Agriculture shall promulgate regulations governing the licensing of indoor and outdoor commercial cultivation sites.

(b) The Department of Pesticide Regulation shall develop guidelines for the use of pesticides in the cultivation of cannabis and residue in harvested cannabis.

(c) The Department of Food and Agriculture shall serve as the lead agency for purposes of the California Environmental Quality Act (Division 13 (commencing with Section 21000) of the Public Resources Code) related to the licensing of cannabis cultivation.

(d) Pursuant to Section 13149 of the Water Code, the State Water Resources Control Board, in consultation with the Department of Fish and Wildlife and the Department of Food and Agriculture, shall ensure that individual and cumulative effects of water diversion and discharge associated with cultivation of cannabis do not affect the instream flows needed for fish spawning, migration, and rearing, and the flows needed to maintain natural flow variability.

(e) The Department of Food and Agriculture shall have the authority necessary for the implementation of the regulations it adopts pursuant to this chapter. The regulations shall do all of the following:

(1) Provide that weighing or measuring devices used in connection with the sale or distribution of medical cannabis are required to meet standards equivalent to Division 5 (commencing with Section 12001).

(2) Require that cannabis cultivation by licensees is conducted in accordance with state and local laws. Nothing in this chapter, and no regulation adopted by the Department of Food and Agriculture, shall be construed to supersede or limit the authority of the State Water Resources Control Board, regional water quality control boards, or the Department of Fish and Wildlife to implement and enforce their statutory obligations or to adopt regulations to protect water quality, water supply, and natural resources.

(3) Establish procedures for the issuance and revocation of unique identifiers for activities associated with a cannabis cultivation license, pursuant to Article 8 (commencing with Section 19337). All cannabis shall be labeled with the unique identifier issued by the Department of Food and Agriculture.

(4) Prescribe standards, in consultation with the bureau, for the reporting of information as necessary related to unique identifiers, pursuant to Article 8 (commencing with Section 19337).

(f) The Department of Pesticide Regulation shall require that the application of pesticides or other pest control in connection with the indoor or outdoor cultivation of medical cannabis complies with Division 6 (commencing with Section 11401) of the Food and Agricultural Code and its implementing regulations.

(g) State cultivator license types issued by the Department of Food and Agriculture may include:

(1) Type 1, or "specialty outdoor," for outdoor cultivation using no artificial lighting of less than or equal to 5,000 square feet of total canopy size on one premises, or up to 50 mature plants on noncontiguous plots.

(2) Type 1A, or "specialty indoor," for indoor cultivation using exclusively artificial lighting of between 501 and 5,000 square feet of total canopy size on one premises.

(3) Type 1B, or "specialty mixed-light," for cultivation using a combination of natural and supplemental artificial lighting at a maximum

threshold to be determined by the licensing authority, of between 2,501 and 5,000 square feet of total canopy size on one premises.

(4) Type 1C, or "specialty cottage," for cultivation using a combination of natural and supplemental artificial lighting at a maximum threshold to be determined by the licensing authority, of 2,500 square feet or less of total canopy size for mixed-light cultivation, up to 25 mature plants for outdoor cultivation, or 500 square feet or less of total canopy size for indoor cultivation, on one premises.

(5) Type 2, or "small outdoor," for outdoor cultivation using no artificial lighting between 5,001 and 10,000 square feet, inclusive, of total canopy size on one premises.

(6) Type 2A, or "small indoor," for indoor cultivation using exclusively artificial lighting between 5,001 and 10,000 square feet, inclusive, of total canopy size on one premises.

(7) Type 2B, or "small mixed-light," for cultivation using a combination of natural and supplemental artificial lighting at a maximum threshold to be determined by the licensing authority, between 5,001 and 10,000 square feet, inclusive, of total canopy size on one premises.

(8) Type 3, or "outdoor," for outdoor cultivation using no artificial lighting from 10,001 square feet to one acre, inclusive, of total canopy size on one premises. The Department of Food and Agriculture shall limit the number of licenses allowed of this type.

(9) Type 3A, or "indoor," for indoor cultivation using exclusively artificial lighting between 10,001 and 22,000 square feet, inclusive, of total canopy size on one premises. The Department of Food and Agriculture shall limit the number of licenses allowed of this type.

(10) Type 3B, or "mixed-light," for cultivation using a combination of natural and supplemental artificial lighting at a maximum threshold to be determined by the licensing authority, between 10,001 and 22,000 square feet, inclusive, of total canopy size on one premises. The Department of Food and Agriculture shall limit the number of licenses allowed of this type.

(11) Type 4, or "nursery," for cultivation of medical cannabis solely as a nursery. Type 4 licensees may transport live plants, if the licensee also holds a Type 12 transporter license issued pursuant to this chapter.

Business and Professions Code § 19332.2

(MCRSA- SB 837, Effective June 27, 2016.)

(a) An application for a license for indoor or outdoor cultivation shall identify the source of water supply.

(1) (A) If water will be supplied by a retail water supplier, as defined in Section 13575 of the Water Code, the application shall identify the retail water supplier.

(B) Paragraphs (2) and (3) shall not apply to any water subject to subparagraph (A) unless the retail water supplier has 10 or fewer customers, the applicant receives 10 percent or more of the water supplied by the retail water supplier, 25 percent or more of the water delivered by the retail water supplier is used for cannabis cultivation, or the applicant and the retail water supplier are affiliates, as defined in Section 2814.20 of Title 23 of the California Code of Regulations.

(2) If the water supply includes a diversion within the meaning of Section 5100 of the Water Code, the application shall identify the point of diversion and maximum amount to be diverted.

(3) If water will be supplied from a groundwater extraction not subject to paragraph (2), the application shall identify the location of the extraction and the maximum amount to be diverted for cannabis cultivation in any year.

(b) An application for a license issued by the Department of Food and Agriculture before January 1, 2020, shall include one of the following:

(1) A copy of a registration, permit, or license issued under Part 2 (commencing with Section 1200) of Division 2 of the Water Code that covers the diversion.

(2) A copy of a statement of water diversion and use, filed with the State Water Resources Control Board before July 1, 2017, that covers the diversion and specifies the amount of water used for cannabis cultivation.

(3) A copy of a pending application for a permit to appropriate water, filed with the State Water Resources Control before July 1, 2017.

(4) Documentation, submitted to the State Water Resources Control

Board before July 1, 2017, establishing that the diversion is subject to subdivision (a), (c), (d) or (e) of Section 5101 of the Water Code.

(5) Documentation, submitted to the State Water Resources Control Board before July 1, 2017, establishing that the diversion is authorized under a riparian right and that no diversion occurred after January 1, 2010, and before January 1, 2017.

(c) An application for a cultivation license issued after December 31, 2019, shall include one of the following:

(1) A copy of a registration, permit, or license issued under Part 2 (commencing with Section 1200) of Division 2 of the Water Code that covers the diversion.

(2) A copy of a statement of water diversion and use, filed with the State Water Resources Control Board, that covers the diversion.

(3) Documentation, submitted to the State Water Resources Control Board, establishing that the diversion is subject to subdivision (a), (c), (d) or (e) of Section 5101 of the Water Code.

(4) Documentation, submitted to the State Water Resources Control Board, establishing that the diversion is authorized under a riparian right and that no diversion occurred in any calendar year between January 1, 2010, and the calendar year in which the application is submitted.

(d) The Department of Food and Agriculture shall include in any license for cultivation requirements for compliance with applicable principles, guidelines, and requirements established under Section 13149 of the Water Code.

(e) The Department of Food and Agriculture shall include in any license for cultivation any relevant mitigation requirements the Department of Food and Agriculture identifies as part of its approval of the final environmental documentation for the cannabis cultivation licensing program as requirements that should be included in a license for cultivation. Chapter 3.5 (commencing with Section 11340) of Part 1 of Division 3 of Title 2 of the Government Code does not apply to the identification of these mitigation measures.

(f) Every license for cultivation shall include a condition that the license shall not be effective until the licensee has complied with Section 1602 of the Fish and Game Code or receives written verification from the Department of Fish and Wildlife that a streambed alteration agreement is not required.

(g) The Department of Food and Agriculture shall consult with the State Water Resources Control Board and the Department of Fish and Wildlife in the implementation of this section.

Business and Professions Code § 19332.5

(MCRSA- SB 837, Effective June 27, 2016.)

(a) Not later than January 1, 2020, the Department of Food and Agriculture shall make available a certified organic designation and organic certification program for medical cannabis cultivation, if permitted under federal law and the National Organic Program (Section 6517 of the federal Organic Foods Production Act of 1990 (7 U.S.C. Sec. 6501 et seq.)), and Article 7 (commencing with Section 110810) of Chapter 5 of Part 5 of Division 104 of the Health and Safety Code.

(b) The Department of Food and Agriculture may establish appellations of origin for cannabis grown in California.

(c) It is unlawful for medical cannabis to be marketed, labeled, or sold as grown in a California county when the medical cannabis was not grown in that county.

(d) It is unlawful to use the name of a California county in the labeling, marketing, or packaging of medical cannabis products unless the product was grown in that county.

Business and Professions Code § 19333

(MCRSA- AB 243, Effective January 1, 2016.)

An employee engaged in commercial cannabis cultivation activity shall be subject to Wage Order 4-2001 of the Industrial Welfare Commission.

Article 7. Licensed Distributors, Dispensaries, and Transporters

Business and Professions Code § 19334

(MCRSA- AB 243, Effective January 1, 2016.)

(a) State licenses to be issued by the Department of Consumer Affairs are as follows:

(1) "Dispensary," Type 10 license as defined in this chapter. This license shall allow for delivery pursuant to Section 19340.

(2) "Distributor," Type 11 license for the distribution of medical cannabis and medical cannabis products from manufacturer to dispensary. A distributor licensee shall hold a Type 12 or transporter license. Each location where product is stored for the purposes of distribution must be individually licensed. A distributor licensee shall not hold a license in a cultivation, manufacturing, dispensing, or testing license category and shall not own, or have an ownership interest in, premises licensed in those categories other than a security interest, lien, or encumbrance on property that is used by a licensee. A distributor shall be bonded and insured at a minimum level established by the licensing authority.

(3) "Producing dispensary," Type 10A for dispensers who have no more than three licensed dispensary facilities and wish to hold either a cultivation or manufacturing license or both. This license shall allow for delivery where expressly authorized by local ordinance. Each dispensary must be individually licensed.

(4) "Transport," Type 12 license for transporters of medical cannabis or medical cannabis products between licensees. A Type 12 licensee shall be bonded and insured at a minimum level established by the licensing authority.

(b) The bureau shall establish minimum security requirements for the commercial transportation, storage, and delivery of medical cannabis and medical cannabis products.

(c) The State Department of Public Health shall establish minimum security requirements for the storage of medical cannabis products at the manufacturing site.

(d) A licensed dispensary shall implement sufficient security measures to both deter and prevent unauthorized entrance into areas containing medical cannabis or medical cannabis products and theft of medical cannabis or medical cannabis products at the dispensary. These security measures shall include, but not be limited to, all of the following:

(1) Preventing individuals from remaining on the premises of the dispensary if they are not engaging in activity expressly related to the operations of the dispensary.

(2) Establishing limited access areas accessible only to authorized dispensary personnel.

(3) Storing all finished medical cannabis and medical cannabis products in a secured and locked room, safe, or vault, and in a manner as to prevent diversion, theft, and loss, except for limited amounts of cannabis used for display purposes, samples, or immediate sale.

(e) A dispensary shall notify the licensing authority and the appropriate law enforcement authorities within 24 hours after discovering any of the following:

(1) Significant discrepancies identified during inventory. The level of significance shall be determined by the bureau.

(2) Diversion, theft, loss, or any criminal activity pertaining to the operation of the dispensary.

(3) Diversion, theft, loss, or any criminal activity by any agent or employee of the dispensary pertaining to the operation of the dispensary.

(4) The loss or unauthorized alteration of records related to medical cannabis or medical cannabis products, registered qualifying patients, primary caregivers, or dispensary employees or agents.

(5) Any other breach of security.

Article 7.5. Unique Identifier and Track and Trace Program

Business and Professions Code § 19335

(MCRSA- AB 243, Effective January 1, 2016.)

(a) The Department of Food and Agriculture, in consultation with the bureau, shall establish a track and trace program for reporting the movement of medical cannabis items throughout the distribution chain that utilizes a unique identifier pursuant to Section 11362.777 of the Health and Safety Code and secure packaging and is capable of providing information that captures, at a minimum, all of the following:

(1) The licensee receiving the product.

(2) The transaction date.

(3) The cultivator from which the product originates, including the associated unique identifier, pursuant to Section 11362.777 of the Health and Safety Code.

(b) (1) The Department of Food and Agriculture, in consultation with the State Board of Equalization, shall create an electronic database containing the electronic shipping manifests to facilitate the administration of the track and trace program, which shall include, but not be limited to, the following information:

(A) The quantity, or weight, and variety of products shipped.

(B) The estimated times of departure and arrival.

(C) The quantity, or weight, and variety of products received.

(D) The actual time of departure and arrival.

(E) A categorization of the product.

(F) The license number and the unique identifier pursuant to Section 11362.777 of the Health and Safety Code issued by the licensing authority for all licensees involved in the shipping process, including, but not limited to, cultivators, manufacturers, transporters, distributors, and dispensaries.

(2) (A) The database shall be designed to flag irregularities for all licensing authorities in this chapter to investigate. All licensing authorities pursuant to this chapter may access the database and share information related to licensees under this chapter, including social security and individual taxpayer identifications notwithstanding Section 30.

(B) The Department of Food and Agriculture shall immediately inform the bureau upon the finding of an irregularity or suspicious finding related to a licensee, applicant, or commercial cannabis activity for investigatory purposes.

(3) Licensing authorities and state and local agencies may, at any time, inspect shipments and request documentation for current inventory.

(4) The bureau shall have 24-hour access to the electronic database administered by the Department of Food and Agriculture. The State Board of Equalization shall have read access to the electronic database for the purpose of taxation and regulation of medical cannabis and medical cannabis products.

(5) The Department of Food and Agriculture shall be authorized to enter into memoranda of understandings with licensing authorities for data sharing purposes, as deemed necessary by the Department of Food and Agriculture.

(6) Information received and contained in records kept by the Department of Food and Agriculture or licensing authorities for the purposes of administering this chapter are confidential and shall not be disclosed pursuant to the California Public Records Act (Chapter 3.5 (commencing with Section 6250) of Division 7 of Title 1 of the Government Code), except as necessary for authorized employees of the State of California or any city, county, or city and county to perform official duties pursuant to this chapter or a local ordinance.

(7) Upon the request of a state or local law enforcement agency, licensing authorities shall allow access to or provide information contained within the database to assist law enforcement in their duties and responsibilities pursuant to this chapter.

Business and Professions Code § 19336

(MCRSA- SB 643, Effective January 1, 2016.)

(a) Chapter 4 (commencing with Section 55121) of Part 30 of Division 2 of the Revenue and Taxation Code shall apply with respect to the bureau's collection of the fees, civil fines, and penalties imposed pursuant to this chapter.

(b) Chapter 8 (commencing with Section 55381) of Part 30 of Division 2 of the Revenue and Taxation Code shall apply with respect to the disclosure of information under this chapter.

Article 8. Licensed Transporters

Business and Professions Code § 19337

(MCRSA- SB 643, Effective January 1, 2016.)

(a) A licensee authorized to transport medical cannabis and medical cannabis products between licenses shall do so only as set forth in this chapter.

(b) Prior to transporting medical cannabis or medical cannabis products, a licensed transporter of medical cannabis or medical cannabis products shall do both of the following:

> (1) Complete an electronic shipping manifest as prescribed by the licensing authority. The shipping manifest must include the unique identifier, pursuant to Section 11362.777 of the Health and Safety Code, issued by the Department of Food and Agriculture for the original cannabis product.

> (2) Securely transmit the manifest to the bureau and the licensee that will receive the medical cannabis product. The bureau shall inform the Department of Food and Agriculture of information pertaining to commercial cannabis activity for the purpose of the track and trace program identified in Section 19335.

(c) During transportation, the licensed transporter shall maintain a physical copy of the shipping manifest and make it available upon request to agents of the Department of Consumer Affairs and law enforcement officers.

(d) The licensee receiving the shipment shall maintain each electronic shipping manifest and shall make it available upon request to the Department of Consumer Affairs and any law enforcement officers.

(e) Upon receipt of the transported shipment, the licensee receiving the shipment shall submit to the licensing agency a record verifying receipt of the shipment and the details of the shipment.

(f) Transporting, or arranging for or facilitating the transport of, medical cannabis or medical cannabis products in violation of this chapter is grounds for disciplinary action against the license.

Business and Professions Code § 19338

(MCRSA- SB 643, Effective January 1, 2016.)

(a) This chapter shall not be construed to authorize or permit a licensee to transport or cause to be transported cannabis or cannabis products outside the state, unless authorized by federal law.

(b) A local jurisdiction shall not prevent transportation of medical cannabis or medical cannabis products on public roads by a licensee transporting medical cannabis or medical cannabis products in compliance with this chapter.

Article 9. Delivery

Business and Professions Code § 19340

(MCRSA- AB 266, Effective January 1, 2016.)

(a) Deliveries, as defined in this chapter, can only be made by a dispensary and in a city, county, or city and county that does not explicitly prohibit it by local ordinance.

(b) Upon approval of the licensing authority, a licensed dispensary that delivers medical cannabis or medical cannabis products shall comply with both of the following:

(1) The city, county, or city and county in which the licensed dispensary is located, and in which each delivery is made, do not explicitly by ordinance prohibit delivery, as defined in Section 19300.5.

(2) All employees of a dispensary delivering medical cannabis or medical cannabis products shall carry a copy of the dispensary's current license authorizing those services with them during deliveries and the employee's government-issued identification, and shall present that license and identification upon request to state and local law enforcement, employees of regulatory authorities, and other state and local agencies enforcing this chapter.

(c) A county shall have the authority to impose a tax, pursuant to Article 11 (commencing with Section 19348), on each delivery transaction completed by a licensee.

(d) During delivery, the licensee shall maintain a physical copy of the delivery request and shall make it available upon request of the licensing authority and law enforcement officers. The delivery request documentation shall comply with state and federal law regarding the protection of confidential medical information.

(e) The qualified patient or primary caregiver requesting the delivery shall maintain a copy of the delivery request and shall make it available, upon request, to the licensing authority and law enforcement officers.

(f) A local jurisdiction shall not prevent carriage of medical cannabis or medical cannabis products on public roads by a licensee acting in compliance with this chapter.

Article 10. Licensed Manufacturers and Licensed Laboratories

Business and Professions Code § 19341

(MCRSA- SB 837, Effective June 27, 2016.)

The State Department of Public Health shall promulgate regulations governing the licensing of manufacturers. The State Department of Public Health shall develop standards for the manufacturing and labeling of all manufactured medical cannabis products. Licenses to be issued are as follows:

(a) "Manufacturing level 1," for manufacturing sites that produce medical cannabis products using nonvolatile solvents.

(b) "Manufacturing level 2," for manufacturing sites that produce medical cannabis products using volatile solvents. The State Department of Public Health shall limit the number of licenses of this type.

Business and Professions Code § 19342

(MCRSA- SB 837, Effective June 27, 2016.)

(a) For the purposes of testing medical cannabis or medical cannabis products, licensees shall use a testing laboratory that has adopted a standard operating procedure using methods consistent with general requirements established by the International Organization for Standardization, specifically ISO/IEC 17025, to test medical cannabis and medical cannabis products. The testing laboratory shall be accredited by a body that is a signatory to the International Laboratory Accreditation Cooperation Mutual Recognition Arrangement.

(b) An agent of a testing laboratory shall obtain samples according to a statistically valid sampling method for each lot.

(c) A testing laboratory shall analyze samples according to both of the following:

> (1) In the final form that the medical cannabis or medical cannabis products will be consumed or used, including moisture content and other attributes.

> (2) A scientifically valid methodology, as determined by the bureau.

(d) If a test result falls outside the specifications authorized by law or regulation, the testing laboratory shall follow a standard operating procedure to confirm or refute the original result.

(e) A testing laboratory shall destroy the remains of the sample of medical cannabis or medical cannabis product upon completion of the analysis.

(f) The State Department of Public Health and the Department of Pesticide Regulation shall provide assistance to the bureau in developing regulations, as requested by the bureau.

Business and Professions Code § 19343

(MCRSA- SB 837, Effective June 27, 2016.)

A testing laboratory shall not be licensed by the bureau unless the laboratory meets all of the following:

(a) A testing laboratory shall not hold a license in another license category under this chapter and shall not own or have an ownership interest in any other entity or premises licensed under a different category pursuant to this chapter.

(b) Follows the methodologies, ranges, and parameters that are contained in the scope of the accreditation for testing medical cannabis or medical cannabis products. The testing laboratory shall also comply with any other requirements specified by the bureau.

(c) Notifies the bureau within one business day after the receipt of notice of any kind that its accreditation has been denied, suspended, or revoked.

(d) Has established standard operating procedures that provide for adequate chain of custody controls for samples transferred to the testing laboratory for testing.

Business and Professions Code § 19344

(MCRSA- SB 837, Effective June 27, 2016.)

(a) A testing laboratory shall issue a certificate of analysis for each lot, with supporting data, to report both of the following:

> (1) Whether the chemical profile of the lot conforms to the specifications of the lot for compounds, including, but not limited to, all of the following, unless limited through regulation by the bureau:

>> (A) Tetrahydrocannabinol (THC).

>> (B) Tetrahydrocannabinolic Acid (THCA).

>> (C) Cannabidiol (CBD).

>> (D) Cannabidiolic Acid (CBDA).

>> (E) Terpenes required by the bureau in a regulation.

>> (F) Cannabigerol (CBG).

>> (G) Cannabinol (CBN).

>> (H) Any other compounds or contaminants required by the bureau.

> (2) That the presence of contaminants does not exceed the levels set by the bureau. In setting the levels, the bureau shall consider the American

Herbal Pharmacopoeia monograph, guidelines set by the Department of Pesticide Regulation pursuant to subdivision (b) of Section 19332, and any other relevant sources.

(A) Residual solvent or processing chemicals.

(B) Foreign material, including, but not limited to, hair, insects, or similar or related adulterant.

(C) Microbiological impurities as identified by the bureau in regulation.

(b) Residual levels of volatile organic compounds shall be below the lesser of either the specifications set by the United States Pharmacopeia (U.S.P. Chapter 467) or those set by the bureau.

Business and Professions Code § 19345

(MCRSA- SB 837, Effective June 27, 2016.)

(a) Except as provided in this chapter, a testing laboratory shall not acquire or receive medical cannabis or medical cannabis products except from a licensee in accordance with this chapter, and shall not distribute, sell, deliver, transfer, transport, or dispense medical cannabis or medical cannabis products, from the licensed premises the medical cannabis or medical cannabis products were acquired or received. All transfer or transportation shall be performed pursuant to a specified chain of custody protocol.

(b) A testing laboratory may receive and test samples of medical cannabis or medical cannabis products from a qualified patient or primary caregiver only if he or she presents his or her valid recommendation for cannabis for medical purposes from a physician. A testing laboratory shall not certify samples from a qualified patient or caregiver for resale or transfer to another party or licensee. All tests performed by a testing laboratory for a qualified patient or caregiver shall be recorded with the name of the qualified patient or caregiver and the amount of medical cannabis or medical cannabis product received.

(c) The bureau shall develop procedures related to all of the following:

(1) Ensuring that testing of medical cannabis and medical cannabis products occurs prior to delivery to dispensaries or any other business.

(2) Specifying how often licensees shall test medical cannabis and medi-

cal cannabis products.

(3) Requiring the destruction of harvested batches whose testing samples indicate noncompliance with health and safety standards required by state law, unless remedial measures can bring the medical cannabis or medical cannabis products into compliance with quality assurance standards as specified by state law.

(d) Cultivators and manufacturers shall pay all costs related to and associated with the testing of medical cannabis and medical cannabis products required by this chapter.

Business and Professions Code § 19347

(MCRSA- SB 837, Effective June 27, 2016.)

(a) Prior to delivery by or sale at a dispensary, medical cannabis and medical cannabis products shall be labeled and in tamper proof packaging and shall include a unique identifier, as prescribed by the Department of Food and Agriculture, for the purpose of identifying and tracking medical cannabis or medical cannabis products. Packages of medical cannabis and medical cannabis products shall meet the following requirements:

(1) Medical cannabis packages and labels shall not be made to be attractive to children.

(2) All medical cannabis and medical cannabis product labels shall include the following information, prominently displayed and in a clear and legible font:

(A) Cultivation and manufacture date and source.

(B) The statement "SCHEDULE I CONTROLLED SUBSTANCE."

(C) The statement "KEEP OUT OF REACH OF CHILDREN AND ANIMALS" in bold print.

(D) The statement "FOR MEDICAL USE ONLY."

(E) The statement "THE INTOXICATING EFFECTS OF THIS PRODUCT MAY BE DELAYED BY UP TO TWO HOURS."

(F) The statement "THIS PRODUCT MAY IMPAIR THE ABIL-

ITY TO DRIVE OR OPERATE MACHINERY. PLEASE USE EXTREME CAUTION."

(G) For packages containing only dried flower, the net weight of medical cannabis in the package.

(H) A warning if nuts or other known allergens are used in the manufacturing of the medical cannabis products.

(I) List of ingredients and pharmacologically active ingredients, including, but not limited to, tetrahydrocannabinol (THC), cannabidiol (CBD), and other cannabinoid content, the THC, CBD, and other cannabinoid amount in milligrams per serving, servings per package, and the THC, CBD, and other cannabinoid amount in milligrams for the package total.

(J) Clear indication, in bold type, that the product contains medical cannabis.

(K) Any other requirement set by the bureau or the State Department of Public Health.

(L) Information associated with the unique identifier issued by the Department of Food and Agriculture pursuant to Section 11362.777 of the Health and Safety Code.

(M) All manufactured and edible medical cannabis products shall be sold only in special packaging constructed to be child-resistant unless otherwise exempted by regulation.

(b) Only generic food names may be used to describe edible medical cannabis products.

Business and Professions Code § 19347.1

(MCRSA- SB 837, Effective June 27, 2016.)

(a) The State Department of Public Health may issue a citation, which may contain an order of abatement and an order to pay an administrative fine assessed by the department where the licensee is in violation of this chapter or any regulation adopted pursuant to it.

(1) Citations shall be in writing and shall describe with particularity the nature of the violation, including specific reference to the provision of

law determined to have been violated.

(2) Whenever appropriate, the citation shall contain an order of abatement fixing a reasonable time for abatement of the violation.

(3) In no event shall the administrative fine assessed by the State Department of Public Health exceed five thousand dollars ($5,000) for each violation, unless a different fine amount is expressly provided by this chapter. In assessing a fine, the licensing authority shall give due consideration to the appropriateness of the amount of the fine with respect to factors such as the gravity of the violation, the good faith of the licensee, and the history of previous violations.

(4) A citation issued or a fine assessed pursuant to this section shall notify the licensee that if the licensee desires a hearing to contest the finding of a violation, that hearing shall be requested by written notice to the State Department of Public Health within 30 days of the date of issuance of the citation or fine. If a hearing is not requested pursuant to this section, payment of any fine shall not constitute an admission of the violation charged. Hearings shall be held pursuant to Chapter 5 (commencing with Section 11500) of Part 1 of Division 3 of Title 2 of the Government Code.

(5) Failure of a licensee to pay a fine within 30 days of the date of assessment of the fine, unless assessment of the fine or the citation is being appealed, may result in further legal action being taken by the State Department of Public Health. If a licensee does not contest a citation or pay the fine, the full amount of the fine shall be added to the fee for renewal of the license. A license shall not be renewed without payment of the renewal fee, including the amount of the fine.

(6) A citation may be issued without the assessment of an administrative fine.

(7) The State Department of Public Health may limit the assessment of administrative fines to only particular violations of the chapter and establish any other requirement for implementation of the citation system by regulation.

(b) Notwithstanding any other law, if a fine is paid to satisfy an assessment based on the finding of a violation, payment of the fine shall be represented as satisfactory resolution of the matter for purposes of public disclosure.

Business and Professions Code § 19347.2

(MCRSA- SB 837, Effective June 27, 2016.)

The State Department of Public Health may, in addition to the administrative citation system authorized by Section 19347.1, also establish by regulation a similar system for the issuance of an administrative citation to an unlicensed person who is acting in the capacity of a licensee under the jurisdiction of the State Department of Public Health as pertains to this chapter. The administrative citation system authorized by this section shall meet the requirements of Section 19347.1 and shall not be applied to an unlicensed person who is otherwise exempt from the licensing provisions of this chapter. The establishment of an administrative citation system for unlicensed activity does not preclude the use of other enforcement statutes for unlicensed activities at the discretion of the State Department of Public Health.

Business and Professions Code § 19347.3

(MCRSA- SB 837, Effective June 27, 2016.)

In determining whether to exercise its discretion when enforcing this chapter, the State Department of Public Health may consider whether the public interest will be adequately served in the circumstances by a suitable written notice or warning. The State Department of Public Health may also require licensees to provide it with a written plan of correction and correct a violation within a timeframe the State Department of Public Health deems necessary under the circumstances.

Business and Professions Code § 19347.4

(MCRSA- SB 837, Effective June 27, 2016.)

The State Department of Public Health may notify the public regarding any medical cannabis product when the State Department of Public Health deems it necessary for the protection of the health and safety of the consumer or for his or her protection from fraud.

Business and Professions Code § 19347.5

(MCRSA- SB 837, Effective June 27, 2016.)

(a) A medical cannabis product is misbranded if it is any of the following:

(1) Manufactured, packed, or held in this state in a manufacturing site not duly licensed as provided in this chapter.

(2) Its labeling is false or misleading in any particular.

(3) Its labeling or packaging does not conform to the requirements of Section 19347 or any other labeling or packaging requirement established pursuant to this chapter.

(b) It is unlawful for any person to manufacture, sell, deliver, hold, or offer for sale a medical cannabis product that is misbranded.

(c) It is unlawful for any person to misbrand a medical cannabis product.

(d) It is unlawful for any person to receive in commerce a medical cannabis product that is misbranded or to deliver or offer for delivery any such medical cannabis product.

Business and Professions Code § 19347.6

(MCRSA- SB 837, Effective June 27, 2016.)

(a) A medical cannabis product is adulterated if it is any of the following:

(1) It has been produced, prepared, packed, or held under insanitary conditions in which it may have become contaminated with filth or in which it may have been rendered injurious.

(2) It consists in whole or in part of any filthy, putrid, or decomposed substance.

(3) It bears or contains any poisonous or deleterious substance that may render it injurious to users under the conditions of use suggested in the labeling or under conditions as are customary or usual.

(4) It bears or contains a substance that is restricted or limited under this chapter or regulations promulgated pursuant to this chapter and the level of substance in the product exceeds the limits specified pursuant to this chapter or in regulation.

(5) Its concentrations differ from, or its purity or quality is below, that which it is represented to possess.

(6) The methods, facilities, or controls used for its manufacture, packing, or holding do not conform to or are not operated or administered

in conformity with practices established by regulations adopted under this chapter to ensure that the medical cannabis product meets the requirements of this chapter as to safety and has the concentrations it purports to have and meets the quality and purity characteristics that it purports or is represented to possess.

(7) Its container is composed, in whole or in part, of any poisonous or deleterious substance that may render the contents injurious to health.

(8) It is an edible cannabis product and any substance has been mixed or packed with it after testing by a testing laboratory so as to reduce its quality or concentration or if any substance has been substituted, wholly or in part, for the edible cannabis product.

(b) It is unlawful for a person to manufacture, sell, deliver, hold, or offer for sale a medical cannabis product that is adulterated.

(c) It is unlawful for any person to adulterate a medical cannabis product.

(d) It is unlawful for any person to receive in commerce a medical cannabis product that is adulterated or to deliver or proffer for delivery any such medical cannabis product.

Business and Professions Code § 19347.7

(MCRSA- SB 837, Effective June 27, 2016.)

(a) When the State Department of Public Health has evidence that a medical cannabis product is adulterated or misbranded, the department shall notify the manufacturer.

(b) The State Department of Public Health may order a manufacturer to immediately cease distribution of a medical cannabis product and recall the product if the department determines both of the following:

(1) The manufacture, distribution, or sale of the medical cannabis product creates or poses an immediate and serious threat to human life or health.

(2) Other procedures available to the State Department of Public Health to remedy or prevent the occurrence of the situation would result in an unreasonable delay.

(c) The State Department of Public Health shall provide the manufacturer an opportunity for an informal proceeding on the matter, as determined by the department, within five days, on the actions required by the order and on why the product should not be recalled. Following the proceeding, the order shall be affirmed, modified, or set aside as determined appropriate by the State Department of Public Health.

(d) The State Department of Public Health's powers set forth in this section expressly include the power to order movement, segregation, isolation, or destruction of medical cannabis products, as well as the power to hold those products in place.

(e) If the State Department of Public Health determines it is necessary, it may issue the mandatory recall order and may use all appropriate measures to obtain reimbursement from the manufacturer for any and all costs associated with these orders. All funds obtained by the State Department of Public Health from these efforts shall be deposited into a fee account specific to the State Department of Public Health, to be established in the Medical Cannabis Regulation and Safety Act Fund, and will be available for use by the department upon appropriation by the Legislature.

(f) It is unlawful for any person to move or allow to be moved a medical cannabis product subject to an order issued pursuant to this section unless that person has first obtained written authorization from the State Department of Public Health.

Business and Professions Code § 19347.8

(MCRSA- SB 837, Effective June 27, 2016.)

(a) Whenever the State Department of Public Health finds or has probable cause to believe that any medical cannabis product is adulterated or misbranded within the meaning of this chapter or the sale of the medical cannabis product would be in violation of this chapter, the department shall affix to the medical cannabis product, or component thereof, a tag or other appropriate marking. The State Department of Public Health shall give notice that the medical cannabis product is, or is suspected of being, adulterated or misbranded, or the sale of which would be in violation of this chapter and has been embargoed and that no person shall remove or dispose of the medical cannabis product by sale or otherwise until permission for removal or disposal is given by the State Department of Public Health or a court.

(b) It is unlawful for any person to remove, sell, or dispose of a detained or embargoed medical cannabis product without written permission of the State Department of Public Health or a court. A violation of this subdivision is subject to a fine of not more than ten thousand dollars ($10,000).

(c) If the adulteration or misbranding can be corrected by proper labeling or additional processing of the medical cannabis product and all of the provisions of this chapter can be complied with, the claimant or owner may request the State Department of Public Health to remove the tag or other marking. If, under the supervision of the State Department of Public Health, the adulteration or misbranding has been corrected, the department may remove the tag or other marking.

(d) When the State Department of Public Health finds that a medical cannabis product that is embargoed is not adulterated, misbranded, or whose sale is not otherwise in violation of this chapter, the State Department of Public Health may remove the tag or other marking.

(e) The medical cannabis product may be destroyed by the owner pursuant to a corrective action plan approved by the State Department of Public Health and under the supervision of the department. The medical cannabis product shall be destroyed at the expense of the claimant or owner.

(f) A proceeding for condemnation of any medical cannabis product under this section shall be subject to appropriate notice to, and the opportunity for a hearing with regard to, the person affected in accordance with Section 19308.

(g) Upon a finding by the administrative law judge that the medical cannabis product is adulterated, misbranded, or whose sale is otherwise in violation of this chapter, the administrative law judge may direct the medical cannabis product to be destroyed at the expense of the claimant or owner. The administrative law judge may also direct a claimant or owner of the affected medical cannabis product to pay fees and reasonable costs, including the costs of storage and testing, incurred by the bureau or the Department of Public Health in investigating and prosecuting the action taken pursuant to this section.

(h) When, under the supervision of the State Department of Public Health, the adulteration or misbranding has been corrected by proper labeling or additional processing of the medical cannabis and medical cannabis product and when all provisions of this chapter have been complied with, and after costs, fees, and expenses have been paid, the State Department of Public

Health may release the embargo and remove the tag or other marking and the medical cannabis shall no longer be held for sale in violation of this chapter.

(i) The State Department of Public Health may condemn any medical cannabis product under provisions of this chapter. The medical cannabis product shall be destroyed at the expense of the claimant or owner.

Article 11. Taxation

Business and Professions Code § 19348

(MCRSA- SB 643, Effective January 1, 2016.)

(a) (1) A county may impose a tax on the privilege of cultivating, dispensing, producing, processing, preparing, storing, providing, donating, selling, or distributing medical cannabis or medical cannabis products by a licensee operating pursuant to this chapter.

(2) The board of supervisors shall specify in the ordinance proposing the tax the activities subject to the tax, the applicable rate or rates, the method of apportionment, if necessary, and the manner of collection of the tax. The tax may be imposed for general governmental purposes or for purposes specified in the ordinance by the board of supervisors.

(3) In addition to any other method of collection authorized by law, the board of supervisors may provide for the collection of the tax imposed pursuant to this section in the same manner, and subject to the same penalties and priority of lien, as other charges and taxes fixed and collected by the county. A tax imposed pursuant to this section is a tax and not a fee or special assessment. The board of supervisors shall specify whether the tax applies throughout the entire county or within the unincorporated area of the county.

(4) The tax authorized by this section may be imposed upon any or all of the activities set forth in paragraph (1), as specified in the ordinance, regardless of whether the activity is undertaken individually, collectively, or cooperatively, and regardless of whether the activity is for compensation or gratuitous, as determined by the board of supervisors.

(b) A tax imposed pursuant to this section shall be subject to applicable voter approval requirements imposed by law.

(c) This section is declaratory of existing law and does not limit or prohibit the levy or collection of any other fee, charge, or tax, or a license or service fee or charge upon, or related to, the activities set forth in subdivision (a) as otherwise provided by law. This section shall not be construed as a limitation upon the taxing authority of a county as provided by law.

(d) This section shall not be construed to authorize a county to impose a sales or use tax in addition to the sales and use tax imposed under an ordinance conforming to the provisions of Sections 7202 and 7203 of the Revenue and Taxation Code.

Article 13. Funding

Business and Professions Code § 19350

(MCRSA- SB 837, Effective June 27, 2016.)

Each licensing authority shall establish a scale of application, licensing, and renewal fees, based upon the cost of enforcing this chapter, as follows:

(a) Each licensing authority shall charge each licensee a licensure and renewal fee, as applicable. The licensure and renewal fee shall be calculated to cover the costs of administering this chapter. The licensure fee may vary depending upon the varying costs associated with administering the various regulatory requirements of this chapter as they relate to the nature and scope of the different licensure activities, including, but not limited to, the track and trace program required pursuant to Section 19335, but shall not exceed the reasonable regulatory costs to the licensing authority.

(b) The total fees assessed pursuant to this chapter shall be set at an amount that will fairly and proportionately generate sufficient total revenue to fully cover the total costs of administering this chapter.

(c) All license fees shall be set on a scaled basis by the licensing authority, dependent on the size of the business. License fees shall cover the costs of administering the track and trace program managed by the Department of Food and Agriculture, as identified in Article 7.5 (commencing with Section 19335).

(d) The licensing authority shall deposit all fees collected in a fee account specific to that licensing authority, to be established in the Medical Cannabis Regulation and Safety Act Fund. Moneys in the licensing authority fee accounts shall be used, upon appropriation of the Legislature, by the designated licensing authority for the administration of this chapter.

Business and Professions Code § 19351

(MCRSA- SB 837, Effective June 27, 2016.)

(a) The Medical Cannabis Regulation and Safety Act Fund is hereby established within the State Treasury. Moneys in the fund shall be available upon appropriation by the Legislature. Notwithstanding Section 16305.7 of the Government Code, the fund shall include any interest and dividends earned on the moneys in the fund.

(b) (1) Funds for the establishment and support of the regulatory activities pursuant to this chapter shall be advanced as a General Fund or special fund loan, and shall be repaid by the initial proceeds from fees collected pursuant to this chapter or any rule or regulation adopted pursuant to this chapter, by January 1, 2022. Should the initial proceeds from fees not be sufficient to repay the loan, moneys from the Medical Cannabis Fines and Penalties Account shall be made available to the bureau, by appropriation of the Legislature, to repay the loan.

(2) Funds advanced pursuant to this subdivision shall be appropriated to the bureau, which shall distribute the moneys to the appropriate licensing authorities, as necessary to implement the provisions of this chapter.

(3) The Director of Finance may provide an initial operating loan from the General Fund to the Medical Cannabis Regulation and Safety Act Fund that does not exceed ten million dollars ($10,000,000).

(c) Except as otherwise provided, all moneys collected pursuant to this chapter as a result of fines or penalties imposed under this chapter shall be deposited directly into the Medical Cannabis Fines and Penalties Account, which is hereby established within the fund, and shall be available, upon appropriation by the Legislature to the bureau, for the purposes of funding the enforcement grant program pursuant to subdivision (d).

(d) (1) The bureau shall establish a grant program to allocate moneys from the Medical Cannabis Fines and Penalties Account to state and local entities for the following purposes:

(A) To assist with medical cannabis regulation and the enforcement of this chapter and other state and local laws applicable to cannabis activities.

(B) For allocation to state and local agencies and law enforcement to remedy the environmental impacts of cannabis cultivation. .

(2) The costs of the grant program under this subdivision shall, upon appropriation by the Legislature, be paid for with moneys in the Medical Cannabis Fines and Penalties Account.

(3) The grant program established by this subdivision shall only be implemented after the loan specified in this section is repaid.

Business and Professions Code § 19352

(MCRSA- AB 243, Effective January 1, 2016.)

The sum of ten million dollars ($10,000,000) is hereby appropriated from the Medical Marijuana Regulation and Safety Act Fund to the Department of Consumer Affairs to begin the activities of the Bureau of Medical Marijuana Regulation. Funds appropriated pursuant to this section shall not include moneys received from fines or penalties.

Article 14. Reporting

Business and Professions Code § 19353

**(MCRSA- AB 266, Effective January 1, 2016- January 1, 2017 when Amended by AB 2679.)

Beginning on March 1, 2023, and on or before March 1 of each following year, each licensing authority shall prepare and submit to the Legislature an annual report on the authority's activities and post the report on the authority's Internet Web site. The report shall include, but not be limited to, the following information for the previous fiscal year:

(a) The amount of funds allocated and spent by the licensing authority for medical cannabis licensing, enforcement, and administration.

(b) The number of state licenses issued, renewed, denied, suspended, and revoked, by state license category.

(c) The average time for processing state license applications, by state license category.

(d) The number and type of enforcement activities conducted by the licensing authorities and by local law enforcement agencies in conjunction with the licensing authorities or the bureau.

(e) The number, type, and amount of penalties, fines, and other disciplinary actions taken by the licensing authorities.

Business and Professions Code § 19353

**(MCRSA- Amended by AB 2679, Effective January 1, 2017.)

Beginning on March 1, 2023, and on or before March 1 of each year thereafter, each licensing authority shall prepare and submit to the Legislature an annual report on the authority's activities, in compliance with Section 9795 of the Government Code, and post the report on the authority's Internet Web site. The report shall include, but not be limited to, the following information for the previous fiscal year:

(a) The amount of funds allocated and spent by the licensing authority for medical cannabis licensing, enforcement, and administration.

(b) The number of state licenses issued, renewed, denied, suspended, and revoked, by state license category.

(c) The average time for processing state license applications, by state license category.

(d) The number of appeals from the denial of state licenses or other disciplinary actions taken by the licensing authority and the average time spent on these appeals.

(e) The number of complaints submitted by citizens or representatives of cities or counties regarding licensees, provided as both a comprehensive statewide number and by geographical region.

(f) The number and type of enforcement activities conducted by the licensing authorities and by local law enforcement agencies in conjunction with the licensing authorities or the bureau.

(g) The number, type, and amount of penalties, fines, and other disciplinary actions taken by the licensing authorities.

Business and Professions Code § 19354

(MCRSA- AB 266, Effective January 1, 2016.)

The bureau shall contract with the California Marijuana Research Program, known as the Center for Medicinal Cannabis Research, authorized pursuant to Section 11362.9 of the Health and Safety Code, to develop a study that identifies the impact that cannabis has on motor skills.

Article 15. Privacy

Business and Professions Code § 19355

(MCRSA- AB 266, Effective January 1, 2016.)

(a) Information identifying the names of patients, their medical conditions, or the names of their primary caregivers received and contained in records kept by the office or licensing authorities for the purposes of administering this chapter are confidential and shall not be disclosed pursuant to the California Public Records Act (Chapter 3.5 (commencing with Section 6250) of Division 7 of Title 1 of the Government Code), except as necessary for authorized employees of the State of California or any city, county, or city and county to perform official duties pursuant to this chapter, or a local ordinance.

(b) Information identifying the names of patients, their medical conditions, or the names of their primary caregivers received and contained in records kept by the bureau for the purposes of administering this chapter shall be maintained in accordance with Chapter 1 (commencing with Section 123100) of Part 1 of Division 106 of the Health and Safety Code, Part 2.6 (commencing with Section 56) of Division 1 of the Civil Code, and other state and federal laws relating to confidential patient information.

(c) Nothing in this section precludes the following:

(1) Employees of the bureau or any licensing authorities notifying state or local agencies about information submitted to the agency that the employee suspects is falsified or fraudulent.

(2) Notifications from the bureau or any licensing authorities to state or local agencies about apparent violations of this chapter or applicable local ordinance.

(3) Verification of requests by state or local agencies to confirm licenses and certificates issued by the regulatory authorities or other state agency.

(4) Provision of information requested pursuant to a court order or subpoena issued by a court or an administrative agency or local governing body authorized by law to issue subpoenas.

(d) Information shall not be disclosed by any state or local agency beyond what is necessary to achieve the goals of a specific investigation, notification, or the parameters of a specific court order or subpoena.

Article 17. Penalties and Violations

Business and Professions Code § 19360

(MCRSA- SB 837, Effective June 27, 2016.)

(a) A person engaging in commercial cannabis activity without a license and associated unique identifiers required by this chapter shall be subject to civil penalties of up to twice the amount of the license fee for each violation, and the department, state or local authority, or court may order the destruction of medical cannabis associated with that violation. A violator shall be responsible for the cost of the destruction of medical cannabis associated with his or her violation, in addition to any amount covered by a bond required as a condition of licensure. Each day of operation shall constitute a separate violation of this section. All civil penalties imposed and collected pursuant to this section by a licensing authority shall be deposited into the Medical Cannabis Fines and Penalties Account established pursuant to Section 19351.

(b) If an action for civil penalties is brought against a licensee pursuant to this chapter by the Attorney General on behalf of the people, the penalty collected shall be deposited into the Medical Cannabis Fines and Penalties Account. If the action is brought by a district attorney or county counsel, the penalty collected shall be paid to the treasurer of the county in which the judgment was entered. If the action is brought by a city attorney or city prosecutor, the penalty collected shall be paid to the treasurer of the city or city and county in which the judgment was entered. If the action is brought by a city attorney and is adjudicated in a superior court located in the unincorporated area or another city in the same county, the penalty shall be paid one-half to the treasurer of the city in which the complaining attorney has jurisdiction and one-half to the treasurer of the county in which the judgment is entered.

(c) Notwithstanding subdivision (a), criminal penalties shall continue to apply to an unlicensed person or entity engaging in cannabis activity in violation of this chapter, including, but not limited to, those individuals covered under Section 11362.7 of the Health and Safety Code.

Part B: Adult Use of Marijuana Act

Chapter 1. General Provisions and Definitions

Business and Professions Code § 26000

(AUMA, Effective November 9, 2016.)

(a) The purpose and intent of this division is to establish a comprehensive system to control and regulate the cultivation, distribution, transport, storage, manufacturing, processing, and sale of nonmedical marijuana and marijuana products for adults 21 years of age and over.

(b) In the furtherance of subdivision (a), this division expands the power and duties of the existing state agencies responsible for controlling and regulating the medical cannabis industry under Chapter 3.5 of Division 8 to include the power and duty to control and regulate the commercial nonmedical marijuana industry.

(c) The Legislature may, by majority vote, enact laws to implement this division, provided such laws are consistent with the purposes and intent of the Control, Regulate and Tax Adult Use of Marijuana Act.

Business and Professions Code § 26001

(AUMA, Effective November 9, 2016.)

For purposes of this division, the following definitions shall apply:

(a) "Applicant" means the following:

> (1) The owner or owners of a proposed licensee. "Owner" means all persons having (A) an aggregate ownership interest (other than a security interest, lien, or encumbrance) of 20 percent or more in the licensee and (B) the power to direct or cause to be directed, the management or control of the licensee.

> (2) If the applicant is a publicly traded company, "owner" includes the chief executive officer and any member of the board of directors and

any person or entity with an aggregate ownership interest in the company of 20 percent or more. If the applicant is a nonprofit entity, "owner" means both the chief executive officer and any member of the board of directors.

(b) "Bureau" means the Bureau of Marijuana Control within the Department of Consumer Affairs.

(c) "Child resistant" means designed or constructed to be significantly difficult for children under five years of age to open, and not difficult for normal adults to use properly.

(d) "Commercial marijuana activity" includes the cultivation, possession, manufacture, distribution, processing, storing, laboratory testing, labeling, transportation, distribution, delivery or sale of marijuana and marijuana products as provided for in this division.

(e) "Cultivation" means any activity involving the planting, growing, harvesting, drying, curing, grading, or trimming of marijuana.

(f) "Customer" means a natural person 21 years of age or over.

(g) "Day care center" shall have the same meaning as in Section 1596.76 of the Health and Safety Code.

(h) "Delivery" means the commercial transfer of marijuana or marijuana products to a customer. "Delivery" also includes the use by a retailer of any technology platform owned and controlled by the retailer, or independently licensed under this division, that enables customers to arrange for or facilitate the commercial transfer by a licensed retailer of marijuana or marijuana products.

(i) "Director" means the Director of the Department of Consumer Affairs.

(j) "Distribution" means the procurement, sale, and transport of marijuana and marijuana products between entities licensed pursuant to this division.

(k) "Fund" means the Marijuana Control Fund established pursuant to Section 26210.

(l) "Kind" means applicable type or designation regarding a particular marijuana variant or marijuana product type, including, but not limited to, strain name or other grower trademark, or growing area designation.

(m) "License" means a state license issued under this division.

(n) "Licensee " means any person or entity holding a license under this division.

(o) "Licensing authority" means the state agency responsible for the issuance, renewal, or reinstatement of the license, or the state agency authorized to take disciplinary action against the licensee.

(p) "Local jurisdiction" means a city, county, or city and county.

(q) "Manufacture" means to compound, blend, extract, infuse, or otherwise make or prepare a marijuana product.

(r) "Manufacturer" means a person that conducts the production, preparation, propagation, or compounding of marijuana or marijuana products either directly or indirectly or by extraction methods, or independently by means of chemical synthesis, or by a combination of extraction and chemical synthesis at a fixed location that packages or repackages marijuana or marijuana products or labels or re-labels its container, that holds a state license pursuant to this division.

(s) "Marijuana" has the same meaning as in Section 11018 of the Health and Safety Code, except that it does not include marijuana that is cultivated, processed, transported, distributed, or sold for medical purposes under Chapter 3.5 of Division 8.

(t) "Marijuana accessories" has the same meaning as in Section 11018.2 of the Health and Safety Code.

(u) "Marijuana products" has the same meaning as in Section 11018.1 of the Health and Safety Code, except that it does not include marijuana products manufactured, processed, transported, distributed, or sold for medical purposes under Chapter 3.5 of Division 8.

(v) "Nursery" means a licensee that produces only clones, immature plants, seeds, and other agricultural products used specifically for the planting, propagation, and cultivation of marijuana.

(w) "Operation" means any act for which licensure is required under the provisions of this division, or any commercial transfer of marijuana or 1narijuana products.

(x) "Package" means any container or receptacle used for holding marijuana or marijuana products.

(y) "Person" includes any individual, firm, co-partnership, joint venture, association, corporation, limited liability company, estate, trust, business trust, receiver, syndicate, or any other group or combination acting as a unit, and the plural as well as the singular.

(z) "Purchaser" means the customer who is engaged in a transaction with a licensee for purposes of obtaining marijuana or marijuana products.

(aa) "Sell, " "sale, " and "to sell" include any transaction whereby, for any consideration, title to marijuana is transferred from one person to another, and includes the delivery of marijuana or marijuana products pursuant to an order placed for the purchase of the same and soliciting or receiving an order for the same, but does not include the return of marijuana or marijuana products by a licensee to the licensee from whom such marijuana or marijuana product was purchased.

(bb) "Testing service" means a laboratory, facility, or entity in the state, that offers or performs tests of marijuana or marijuana products, including the equipment provided by such laboratory, facility, or entity, and that is both of the following:

(1) Accredited by an accrediting body that is independent from all other persons involved in commercial marijuana activity in the state.

(2) Registered with the Department of Public Health.

(cc) "Unique identifier" means an alphanumeric code or designation used for reference to a specific plant on a licensed premises.

(dd) "Unreasonably impracticable" means that the measures necessary to comply with the regulations require such a high investment of risk, money, time, or any other resource or asset, that the operation of a marijuana establishment is not worthy of being carried out in practice by a reasonably prudent business person.

(ee) "Youth center" shall have the same meaning as in Section 11353.1 of the Health and Safety Code.

Chapter 2. Administration

Business and Professions Code § 26010

(AUMA, Effective November 9, 2016.)

(a) The Bureau of Medical Marijuana Regulation established in Section 19302 in Chapter 3.5 of Division 8 is hereby renamed the Bureau of Marijuana Control. The director shall administer and enforce the provisions of this division in addition to the provisions of Chapter 3.5 of Division 8. The director shall have the same power and authority as provided by subdivisions (b) and (c) of Section 19302.1 for purposes of this division.

(b) The bureau and the director shall succeed to and are vested with all the duties, powers, purposes, responsibilities, and jurisdiction vested in the Bureau of Medical Marijuana Regulation under Chapter 3.5 of Division 8.

(c) In addition to the powers, duties, purposes, responsibilities, and jurisdiction referenced in subdivision (b), the bureau shall heretofore have the power, duty, purpose, responsibility, and jurisdiction to regulate commercial marijuana activity as provided in this division.

(d) Upon the effective date of this section, whenever "Bureau of Medical Marijuana Regulation" appears in any statute, regulation, or contract, or in any other code, it shall be construed to refer to the bureau.

Business and Professions Code § 26011

(AUMA, Effective November 9, 2016.)

Neither the chief of the bureau nor any member of the Marijuana Control Appeals Panel established under Section 26040 shall have nor do any of the following:

(a) Receive any commission or profit whatsoever, directly or indirectly, from any person applying for or receiving any license or permit under this division or Chapter 3.5 of Division 8.

(b) Engage or have any interest in the sale or any insurance covering a licensee's business or premises.

(c) Engage or have any interest in the sale of equipment for use upon the premises of a licensee engaged in commercial marijuana activity.

(d) Knowingly solicit any licensee for the purchase of tickets for benefits or contributions for benefits.

(e) Knowingly request any licensee to donate or receive money, or any other thing of value, for the benefit of any person whatsoever.

Business and Professions Code § 26012

(AUMA, Effective November 9, 2016.)

(a) It being a matter of statewide concern, except as otherwise authorized in this division:

> (1) The Department of Consumer Affairs shall have the exclusive authority to create, issue, renew, discipline, suspend, or revoke licenses for the transportation, storage unrelated to manufacturing activities, distribution, and sale of marijuana within the state.

> (2) The Department of Food and Agriculture shall administer the provisions of this division related to and associated with the cultivation of marijuana. The Department of Food and Agriculture shall have the authority to create, issue, and suspend or revoke cultivation licenses for violations of this division.

> (3) The Department of Public Health shall administer the provisions of this division related to and associated with the manufacturing and testing of marijuana. The Department of Public Health shall have the authority to create, issue, and suspend or revoke manufacturing and testing licenses for violations of this division.

(b) The licensing authorities and the bureau shall have the authority to collect fees in connection with activities they regulate concerning marijuana. The bureau may create licenses in addition to those identified in this division that the bureau deems necessary to effectuate its duties under this division.

(c) Licensing authorities shall begin issuing licenses under this division by January 1, 2018.

Business and Professions Code § 26013

(AUMA, Effective November 9, 2016.)

(a) Licensing authorities shall make and prescribe reasonable rules and regulations as may be necessary to implement, administer and enforce their respective duties under this division in accordance with Chapter 3.5 (commencing with Section 11340) of Part 1 of Division 3 of Title 2 of the Government Code. Such rules and regulations shall be consistent with the purposes and intent of the Control, Regulate and Tax Adult Use of Marijuana Act.

(b) Licensing authorities may prescribe, adopt, and enforce any emergency regulations as necessary to implement, administer and enforce their respective duties under this division. Any emergency regulation prescribed, adopted or enforced pursuant to this section shall be adopted in accordance with Chapter 3.5 (commencing with Section 11340) of Part 1 of Division 3 of Title 2 of the Government Code, and, for purposes of that chapter, including Section 11349.6 of the Government Code, the adoption of the regulation is an emergency and shall be considered by the Office of Administrative Law as necessary for the immediate preservation of the public peace, health and safety, and general welfare.

(c) Regulations issued under this division shall be necessary to achieve the purposes of this division, based on best available evidence, and shall mandate only commercially feasible procedures, technology; or other requirements, and shall not unreasonably restrain or inhibit the development of alternative procedures or technology to achieve the same substantive requirements, nor shall such regulations make compliance unreasonably impracticable.

Business and Professions Code § 26014

(AUMA, Effective November 9, 2016.)

(a) The bureau shall convene an advisory committee to advise the bureau and licensing authorities on the development of standards and regulations pursuant to this division, including best practices and guidelines that protect public health and safety while ensuring a regulated environment for commercial marijuana activity that does not impose such unreasonably impracticable barriers so as to perpetuate, rather than reduce and eliminate, the illicit market for marijuana.

(b) The advisory committee members shall include, but not be limited to, representatives of the marijuana industry, representatives of labor organizations, appropriate state and local agencies, public health experts, and other subject matter experts, including representatives from the Department of Alcoholic Beverage Control, with expertise in regulating commercial activity for adult-use intoxicating substances. The advisory committee members shall be determined by the director.

(c) Commencing on January 1, 2019, the advisory committee shall publish an annual public report describing its activities including, but not limited to, the recommendations the advisory committee made to the bureau and licensing authorities during the immediately preceding calendar year and whether those recommendations were implemented by the bureau or licensing authorities.

Business and Professions Code § 26015

(AUMA, Effective November 9, 2016.)

A licensing authority may make or cause to be made such investigation as it deems necessary to carry out its duties under this division.

Business and Professions Code § 26016

(AUMA, Effective November 9, 2016.)

For any hearing held pursuant to this division, except a hearing held under Chapter 4, a licensing authority may delegate the power to hear and decide to an administrative law judge. Any hearing before an administrative law judge shall be pursuant to the procedures, rules, and limitations prescribed in Chapter 5 (commencing with Section 11500) of Part 1 of Division 3 of Title 2 of the Government Code.

Business and Professions Code § 26017

(AUMA, Effective November 9, 2016.)

In any hearing before a licensing authority pursuant to this division, the licensing authority may pay any person appearing as a witness at the hearing at the request of the licensing authority pursuant to a subpoena, his or her actual, necessary, and reasonable travel, food, and lodging expenses, not to exceed the amount authorized for state employees.

Business and Professions Code § 26018

(AUMA, Effective November 9, 2016.)

A licensing authority may on its own motion at any time before a penalty assessment is placed into effect, and without any further proceedings, review the penalty, but such review shall be limited to its reduction.

Chapter 3. Enforcement

Business and Professions Code § 26030

(AUMA, Effective November 9, 2016.)

Grounds for disciplinary action include:

(a) Failure to comply with the provisions of this division or any rule or regulation adopted pursuant to this division.

(b) Conduct that constitutes grounds for denial of licensure pursuant to Chapter 3 (commencing with Section 490) of Division 1.5.

(c) Any other grounds contained in regulations adopted by a licensing authority pursuant to this division.

(d) Failure to comply with any state law including, but not limited to, the payment of taxes as required under the Revenue and Taxation Code, except as provided for in this division or other California law.

(e) Knowing violations of any state or local law, ordinance, or regulation conferring worker protections or legal rights on the employees of a licensee.

(f) Failure to comply with the requirement of a local ordinance regulating commercial marijuana activity.

(g) The intentional and knowing sale of marijuana or marijuana products by a licensee to a person under the legal age to purchase or possess.

Business and Professions Code § 26031

(AUMA, Effective November 9, 2016.)

Each licensing authority may suspend or revoke licenses, after proper notice and hearing to the licensee, if the licensee is found to have committed any of the acts or omissions constituting grounds for disciplinary action. The disciplinary proceedings under this chapter shall be conducted in accordance with Chapter 5 (commencing with Section 11500) of Part 1 of Division 3 of Title

2 of the Government Code, and the director of each licensing authority shall have all the powers granted therein.

Business and Professions Code § 26032

(AUMA, Effective November 9, 2016.)

Each licensing authority may take disciplinary action against a licensee for any violation of this division when the violation was committed by the licensee's agent or employee while acting on behalf of the licensee or engaged in commercial marijuana activity.

Business and Professions Code § 26033

(AUMA, Effective November 9, 2016.)

Upon suspension or revocation of a license, the licensing authority shall inform the bureau. The bureau shall then inform all other licensing authorities.

Business and Professions Code § 26034

(AUMA, Effective November 9, 2016.)

Accusations against licensees under this division shall be filed within the same time limits as specified in Section 19314 or as otherwise provided by law.

Business and Professions Code § 26035

(AUMA, Effective November 9, 2016.)

The director shall designate the persons employed by the Department of Consumer Affairs for purposes of the administration and enforcement of this division. The director shall ensure that a sufficient number of employees are qualified peace officers for purposes of enforcing this division.

Business and Professions Code § 26036

(AUMA, Effective November 9, 2016.)

Nothing in this division shall be interpreted to supersede or limit state agencies from exercising their existing enforcement authority, including, but not limited to, under the Fish and Game Code, the Food and Agricultural Code, the Government Code, the Health and Safety Code, the Public Resources Code, the Water Code, or the application of those laws.

Business and Professions Code § 26037

(AUMA, Effective November 9, 2016.)

(a) The actions of a licensee, its employees, and its agents that are:

(1) permitted under a license issued under this division and any applicable local ordinances; and

(2) conducted in accordance with the requirements of this division and regulations adopted pursuant to this division, are not unlawful under state law and shall not be an offense subject to arrest, prosecution, or other sanction under state law, or be subject to a civil fine or be a basis for seizure or forfeiture of assets under state law.

(b) The actions of a person who, in good faith, allows his or her property to be used by a licensee, its employees, and its agents, as permitted pursuant to a state license and any applicable local ordinances, are not unlawful under state law and shall not be an offense subject to arrest, prosecution, or other sanction under state law, or be subject to a civil fine or be a basis for seizure or forfeiture of assets under state law.

Business and Professions Code § 26038

(AUMA, Effective November 9, 2016.)

(a) A person engaging in commercial marijuana activity without a license required by this division shall be subject to civil penalties of up to three times the amount of the license fee for each violation, and the court may order the destruction of marijuana associated with that violation in accordance with Section 11479 of the Health and Safety Code. Each day of operation shall constitute a separate violation of this section. All civil penalties imposed and collected pursuant to this section by a licensing authority shall be deposited into the General Fund except as provided in subdivision (b).

(b) If an action for civil penalties is brought against a licensee pursuant to this division by the Attorney General on behalf of the people, the penalty collected shall be deposited into the General Fund. If the action is brought by a district attorney or county counsel, the penalty shall first be used to reimburse the district attorney or county counsel for the costs of bringing the action for civil penalties, with the remainder, if any, to be deposited into the General Fund. If the action is brought by a city attorney or city prosecutor, the penalty collected shall first be used to reimburse the city attorney or city prosecutor for the costs of bringing the action for civil penalties, with the remainder, if any, to be deposited into the General Fund.

(c) Notwithstanding subdivision (a), criminal penalties shall continue to apply to an unlicensed person engaging in commercial marijuana activity in violation of this division.

Chapter 4. Appeals

Business and Professions Code § 26040

(AUMA, Effective November 9, 2016.)

(a) There is established in state government a Marijuana Control Appeals Panel which shall consist of three members appointed by the Governor and subject to confirmation by a majority vote of all of the members elected to the Senate. Each member, at the time of his or her initial appointment, shall be a resident of a different county from the one in which either of the other members resides. Members of the panel shall receive an annual salary as provided for by Chapter 6 (commencing with Section 11550) of Part 1 of Division 3 of Title 2 of the Government Code.

(b) The members of the panel may be removed from office by the Governor, and the Legislature shall have the power, by a majority vote of all members elected to each house, to remove any member from office for dereliction of duty, corruption or incompetency.

(c) A concurrent resolution for the removal of any member of the panel may be introduced in the Legislature only if five Members of the Senate, or ten Members of the Assembly, join as authors.

Business and Professions Code § 26041

(AUMA, Effective November 9, 2016.)

All personnel of the panel shall be appointed, employed, directed, and controlled by the panel consistent with state civil service requirements. The director shall furnish the equipment, supplies, and housing necessary for the authorized activities of the panel and shall perform such other mechanics of administration as the panel and the director may agree upon.

Business and Professions Code § 26042

(AUMA, Effective November 9, 2016.)

The panel shall adopt procedures for appeals similar to the procedures used in Articles 3 and 4 in Chapter 1.5 in Division 9 of the Business and Professions Code. Such procedures shall be adopted in accordance with the Administrative Procedure Act (Government Code, Title 2, Division 3, section 11340 et seq.).

Business and Professions Code § 26043

(AUMA, Effective November 9, 2016.)

(a) When any person aggrieved thereby appeals from a decision of the bureau or any licensing authority ordering any penalty assessment, issuing, denying, transferring, conditioning, suspending or revoking any license provided for under this division, the panel shall review the decision subject to such limitations as may be imposed by the Legislature. In such cases, the panel shall not receive evidence in addition to that considered by the bureau or the licensing authority.

(b) Review by the panel of a decision of the bureau or a licensing authority shall be limited to the following questions:

(1) Whether the bureau or any licensing authority has proceeded without or in excess of its jurisdiction.

(2) Whether the bureau or any licensing authority has proceeded in the manner required by law.

(3) Whether the decision is supported by the findings.

(4) Whether the findings are supported by substantial evidence in the light of the whole record.

Business and Professions Code § 26044

(AUMA, Effective November 9, 2016.)

(a) In appeals where the panel finds that there is relevant evidence which, in the exercise of reasonable diligence, could not have been produced or which was improperly excluded at the hearing before the bureau or licensing authority, it may enter an order remanding the matter to the bureau or licensing authority for reconsideration in the light of such evidence.

(b) Except as provided in subdivision (a), in all appeals, the panel shall enter an order either affirming or reversing the decision of the bureau or licensing authority. When the order reverses the decision of the bureau or licensing authority, the board may direct the reconsideration of the matter in the light of its order and may direct the bureau or licensing authority to take such further action as is specially enjoined upon it by law, but the order shall not limit or control in any way the discretion vested by law in the bureau or licensing authority.

Business and Professions Code § 26045

(AUMA, Effective November 9, 2016.)

Orders of the panel shall be subject to judicial review under Section 1094.5 of the Code of Civil Procedure upon petition by the bureau or licensing authority or any party aggrieved by such order.

Chapter 5. Licensing

Business and Professions Code § 26050

(AUMA, Effective November 9, 2016.)

(a) The license classification pursuant to this division shall, at a minimum, be as follows:

(1) Type I = Cultivation; Specialty outdoor; Small.

(2) Type IA = Cultivation; Specialty indoor; Small.

(3) Type IB = Cultivation; Specialty mixed-light; Small.

(4) Type 2 = Cultivation; Outdoor; Small.

(5) Type 2A = Cultivation; Indoor; Small.

(6) Type 2B = Cultivation; Mixed-light; Small.

(7) Type 3 = Cultivation; Outdoor; Medium.

(8) Type 3A = Cultivation; Indoor; Medium.

(9) Type 3B = Cultivation; Mixed-light; Medium.

(10) Type 4 = Cultivation; Nursery.

(11) Type 5 = Cultivation; Outdoor; Large.

(12) Type 5A =Cultivation; Indoor; Large.

(13) Type 5B = Cultivation; Mixed-light; Large.

(14) Type 6 = Manufacturer 1.

(15) Type 7 = Manufacturer 2.

(16) Type 8 = Testing.

(17) Type 10 = Retailer.

(18) Type 11 = Distributor.

(19) Type 12 =Microbusiness.

(b) All licenses issued under this division shall bear a clear designation indicating that the license is for commercial marijuana activity as distinct from commercial medical cannabis activity licensed under Chapter 3.5 of Division 8. Examples of such a designation include, but are not limited to, "Type 1-Nonmedical, "or "Type 1 NM."

(c) A license issued pursuant to this division shall be valid for 12 months from the date of issuance. The license may be renewed annually.

(d) Each licensing authority shall establish procedures for the issuance and renewal of licenses.

(e) Notwithstanding subdivision (c), a licensing authority may issue a temporary license for a period of less than 12 months. This subdivision shall cease to be operable on January 1, 2019.

Business and Professions Code § 26051

(AUMA, Effective November 9, 2016.)

(a) In determining whether to grant, deny, or renew a license authorized under this division, a licensing authority shall consider factors reasonably related to the determination, including, but not limited to, whether it is reasonably foreseeable that issuance, denial, or renewal of the license could:

(1) allow unreasonable restrains on competition by creation or maintenance of unlawful monopoly power;

(2) perpetuate the presence of an illegal market for marijuana or marijuana products in the state or out of the state;

(3) encourage underage use or adult abuse of marijuana or marijuana products, or illegal diversion of marijuana or marijuana products out of the state;

(4) result in an excessive concentration of licensees in a given city, county, or both;

(5) present an unreasonable risk of minors being exposed to marijuana or marijuana products; or

(6) result in violations of any environmental protection laws.

(b) A licensing authority may deny a license or renewal of a license based upon the considerations in subdivision (a).

(c) For purposes of this section, "excessive concentration" means when the premises for a retail license, microbusiness license, or a license issued under Section 26070.5 is located in an area where either of the following conditions exist:

(1) The ratio of a licensee to population in the census tract or census division in which the applicant premises are located exceeds the ratio of licensees to population in the county in which the applicant premises are located, unless denial of the application would unduly limit the development of the legal market so as to perpetuate the illegal market for marijuana or marijuana products.

(2) The ratio of retail licenses, microbusiness licenses, or licenses under Section 26070.5 to population in the census tract, division or jurisdic-

tion exceeds that allowable by local ordinance adopted under Section 26200.

Business and Professions Code § 26052

(AUMA, Effective November 9, 2016.)

(a) No licensee shall perform any of the following acts, or permit any such acts to be performed by any employee, agent, or contractor of such licensee:

(1) Make any contract in restraint of trade in violation of Section 16600;

(2) Form a trust or other prohibited organization in restraint of trade in violation of Section 16720;

(3) Make a sale or contract for the sale of marijuana or marijuana products, or to fix a price charged therefor, or discount from, or rebate upon, such price, on the condition, agreement or understanding that the consumer or purchaser thereof shall not use or deal in the goods, merchandise, machinery, supplies, commodities, or services of a competitor or competitors of such seller, where the effect of such sale, contract, condition, agreement or understanding may be to substantially lessen competition or tend to create a monopoly in any line of trade or commerce;

(4) Sell any marijuana or marijuana products at less than cost for the purpose of injuring competitors, destroying competition, or misleading or deceiving purchasers or prospective purchasers;

(5) Discriminate between different sections, communities, or cities or portions thereof, or between different locations in such sections, communities, cities or portions thereof in this state, by selling or furnishing marijuana or marijuana products at a lower price in one section, community, or city or 'any portion thereof, or in one location in such section, community, or city or any portion thereof, than in another, for the purpose of injuring competitors or destroying competition; or

(6) Sell any marijuana or marijuana products at less than the cost thereof to such vendor, or to give away any article or product for the purpose of injuring competitors or destroying competition.

(b) Any person who, either as director, officer or agent of any firm or corporation, or as agent of any person, violates the provisions of this chapter, assists or aids, directly or indirectly, in such violation is responsible therefor equally with the person, firm or corporation for which such person acts.

(c) A licensing authority may enforce this section by appropriate regulation.

(d) Any person or trade association may bring an action to enjoin and restrain any violation of this section for the recovery of damages.

Business and Professions Code § 26053

(AUMA, Effective November 9, 2016.)

(a) The bureau and licensing authorities may issue licenses under this division to persons or entities that hold licenses under Chapter 3.5 of Division 8.

(b) Notwithstanding subdivision (a), a person or entity that holds a state testing license under this division or Chapter 3.5 of Division 8 is prohibited from licensure for any other activity, except testing, as authorized under this division.

(c) Except as provided in subdivision (b), a person or entity may apply for and be issued more than one license under this division.

Business and Professions Code § 26054

(AUMA, Effective November 9, 2016.)

(a) A licensee shall not also be licensed as a retailer of alcoholic beverages under Division 9 or of tobacco products.

(b) No licensee under this division shall be located within a 600-foot radius of a school providing instruction in kindergarten or any grades 1 through 12, day care center, or youth center that is in existence at the time the license is issued, unless a licensing authority or a local jurisdiction specifies a different radius. The distance specified in this section shall be measured in the same manner as provided in paragraph (c) of Section 11362.768 of the Health and Safety Code unless otherwise provided by law.

(c) It shall be lawful under state and local law, and shall not be a violation of state or local law, for a business engaged in the manufacture of marijuana accessories to possess, transport, purchase or otherwise obtain small amounts of marijuana or marijuana products as necessary to conduct research and development related to such marijuana accessories, provided such marijuana and marijuana products are obtained from a person or entity licensed under this division or Chapter 3.5 of Division 8 permitted to provide or deliver such marijuana or marijuana products.

Business and Professions Code § 26054.1

(AUMA, Effective November 9, 2016.)

(a) No licensing authority shall issue or renew a license to any person that cannot demonstrate continuous California residency from or before January 1, 2015. In the case of an applicant or licensee that is an entity, the entity shall not be considered a resident if any person controlling the entity cannot demonstrate continuous California residency from and before January 1, 2015.

(b) Subdivision (a) shall cease to be operable on December 31, 2019 unless reenacted prior thereto by the Legislature.

Business and Professions Code § 26054.2

(AUMA, Effective November 9, 2016.)

(a) A licensing authority shall give priority in issuing licenses under this division to applicants that can demonstrate to the authority's satisfaction that the applicant operated in compliance with the Compassionate Use Act and its implementing laws before September 1, 2016, or currently operates in compliance with Chapter 3.5 of Division 8.

(b) The bureau shall request that local jurisdictions identify for the bureau potential applicants for licensure based on the applicants' prior operation in the local jurisdiction in compliance with state law, including the Compassionate Use Act and its implementing laws, and any applicable local laws. The bureau shall make the requested information available to licensing authorities.

(c) In addition to or in lieu of the information described in subdivision (b), an applicant may furnish other evidence to demonstrate operation in compliance with the Compassionate Use Act or Chapter 3.5 of Division 8. The bureau and licensing authorities may accept such evidence to demonstrate eligibility for the priority provided for in subdivision (a).

(d) This section shall cease to be operable on December 31, 2019 unless otherwise provided by law.

Business and Professions Code § 26055

(AUMA, Effective November 9, 2016.)

(a) Licensing authorities may issue state licenses only to qualified applicants.

(b) Revocation of a state license issued under this division shall terminate the ability of the licensee to operate within California until the licensing authority reinstates or reissues the state license.

(c) Separate licenses shall be issued for each of the premises of any licensee having more than one location, except as otherwise authorized by law or regulation.

(d) After issuance or transfer of a license, no licensee shall change or alter the premises in a manner which materially or substantially alters the premises, the usage of the premises, or the mode or character of business operation conducted from the premises, from the plan contained in the diagram on file with the application, unless and until prior written assent of the licensing authority or bureau has been obtained. For purposes of this section, material or substantial physical changes of the premises, or in the usage of the premises, shall include, but not be limited to, a substantial increase or decrease in the total area of the licensed premises previously diagrammed, or any other physical modification resulting in substantial change in the mode or character of business operation.

(e) Licensing authorities shall not approve an application for a state license under this division if approval of the state license will violate the provisions of any local ordinance or regulation adopted in accordance with Section 26200.

Business and Professions Code § 26056

(AUMA, Effective November 9, 2016.)

An applicant for any type of state license issued pursuant to this division shall comply with the same requirements as set forth in Section 19322 of Chapter 3.5 of Division 8 unless otherwise provided by law, including electronic submission of finger print images, and any other requirements imposed by law or a licensing authority, except as follows:

(a) not with standing paragraph (2) of subdivision (a) of Section 19322 of Chapter 3.5 of Division 8, an applicant need not provide documentation that the applicant has obtained a license, permit or other authorization to operate from the local jurisdiction in which the applicant seeks to operate;

(b) an application for a license under this division shall include evidence that the proposed location meets the restriction in subdivision (b) of Section 26054; and

(c) for applicants seeking licensure to cultivate, distribute, or manufacture nonmedical marijuana or marijuana products, the application shall also include a detailed description of the applicant's operating procedures for all of the following, as required by the licensing authority:

(1) Cultivation.

(2) Extraction and infusion methods.

(3) The transportation process.

(4) The inventory process.

(5) Quality control procedures.

(6) The source or sources of water the applicant will use for the licensed activities, including a certification that the applicant may use that water legally under state law.

(d) The applicant shall provide a complete detailed diagram of the proposed premises wherein the license privileges will be exercised, with sufficient particularity to enable ready determination of the bounds of the premises, showing all boundaries, dimensions, entrances and exits, interior partitions, walls, rooms, and common or shared entryways, and include a brief statement or description of the principal activity to be conducted therein, and, for licenses permitting cultivation, measurements of the planned canopy including aggregate square footage and individual square footage of separate cultivation areas, if any.

Business and Professions Code § 26056.5

(AUMA, Effective November 9, 2016.)

The bureau shall devise protocols that each licensing authority shall implement to ensure compliance with state laws and regulations related to environmental impacts, natural resource protection, water quality, water supply, hazardous materials, and pesticide use in accordance with regulations, including but not limited to, the California Environmental Quality Act (Public Resources Code, Section 21000, et seq.), the California Endangered Species Act (Fish and Game Code, Section 2800 et. seq.), lake or streambed alteration agreements (Fish and Game Code, Section 1600 et. seq.), the Clean Water Act, the Porter-Cologne Water Quality Control Act, timber production zones, wastewater discharge requirements, and any permit or right necessary to divert water.

Business and Professions Code § 26057

(AUMA, Effective November 9, 2016.)

(a) The licensing authority shall deny an application if either the applicant, or the premises for which a state license is applied, do not qualify for licensure under this division.

(b) The licensing authority may deny the application for licensure or renewal of a state license if any of the following conditions apply:

(1) Failure to comply with the provisions of this division, any rule or regulation adopted pursuant to this division, or any requirement imposed to protect natural resources, including, but not limited to, protections for in stream flow and water quality.

(2) Conduct that constitutes grounds for denial of licensure under Chapter 2 of Division 1.5, except as otherwise specified in this section and Section 26059.

(3) Failure to provide information required by the licensing authority.

(4) The applicant or licensee has been convicted of an offense that is substantially related to the qualifications, functions, or duties of the business or profession for which the application is made, except that if the licensing authority determines that the applicant or licensee is otherwise suitable to be issued a license, and granting the license would not compromise public safety, the licensing authority shall conduct a thorough review of the nature of the crime, conviction, circumstances, and evidence of rehabilitation of the applicant, and shall evaluate the suitability of the applicant or licensee to be issued a license based on the evidence found through the review. In determining which offenses are substantially related to the qualifications, functions, or duties of the business or profession for which the application is made, the licensing

authority shall include, but not be limited to, the following:

(A) A violent felony conviction, as specified in subdivision (c) of Section 667.5 of the Penal Code.

(B) A serious felony conviction, as specified in subdivision (c) of Section 1192.7 of the Penal Code.

(C) A felony conviction involving fraud, deceit, or embezzlement.

(D) A felony conviction for hiring, employing, or using a minor in transporting, carrying, selling, giving away, preparing for sale, or peddling, any controlled substance to a minor; or selling, offering to sell, furnishing, offering to furnish, administering, or giving any controlled substance to a minor.

(E) A felony conviction for drug trafficking with enhancements pursuant to Sections 11370.4 or 11379.8.

(5) Except as provided in subparagraphs (D) and (E) of paragraph (4) and notwithstanding Chapter 2 of Division 1. 5, a prior conviction, where the sentence, including any term of probation, incarceration, or supervised release, is completed, for possession of, possession for sale, sale, manufacture, transportation, or cultivation of a controlled substance is not considered substantially related, and shall not be the sole ground for denial of a license. Conviction for any controlled substance felony subsequent to licensure shall be grounds for revocation of a license or denial of the renewal of a license.

(6) The applicant, or any of its officers, directors, or owners, has been subject to fines or penalties for cultivation or production of a controlled substance on public or private lands pursuant to Sections 12025 or 12025.1 of the Fish and Game Code.

(7) The applicant, or any of its officers, directors, or owners, has been sanctioned by a licensing authority or a city, county, or city and county for unauthorized commercial marijuana activities or commercial medical cannabis activities, has had a license revoked under this division or Chapter 3.5 of Division 8 in the three years immediately preceding the date the application is filed with the licensing authority, or has been sanctioned under Sections 12025 or 12025.1 of the Fish and Game Code.

(8) Failure to obtain and maintain a valid seller's permit required pur-

suant to Part 1 (commencing with Section 6001) of Division 2 of the Revenue and Taxation Code.

(9) Any other condition specified in law.

Business and Professions Code § 26058

(AUMA, Effective November 9, 2016.)

Upon the denial of any application for a license, the licensing authority shall notify the applicant in writing.

Business and Professions Code § 26059

(AUMA, Effective November 9, 2016.)

An applicant shall not be denied a state license if the denial is based solely on any of the following:

(a) A conviction or act that is substantially related to the qualifications, functions, or duties of the business or profession for which the application is made for which the applicant or licensee has obtained a certificate of rehabilitation pursuant to Chapter 3.5 (commencing with Section 4852.0l) of Title 6 of Part 3 of the Penal Code.

(b) A conviction that was subsequently dismissed pursuant to Sections 1203.4, l203.4a, or 1203.41 of the Penal Code or any other provision allowing for dismissal of a conviction.

Chapter 6. Licensed Cultivation Sites

Business and Professions Code § 26060

(AUMA, Effective November 9, 2016.)

(a) Regulations issued by the Department of Food and Agriculture governing the licensing of indoor, outdoor, and mixed-light cultivation sites shall apply to licensed cultivators under this division.

(b) Standards developed by the Department of Pesticide Regulation, in consultation with the Department of Food and Agriculture, for the use of pesticides in cultivation, and maximum tolerances for pesticides and other foreign object residue in harvested cannabis shall apply to licensed cultivators under this division.

(c) The Department of Food and Agriculture shall include conditions in each license requested by the Department of Fish and Wildlife and the State Water Resources Control Board to ensure that individual and cumulative effects of water diversion and discharge associated with cultivation do not affect the in stream flows needed for fish spawning, migration, and rearing, and the flows needed to maintain natural flow variability, and to otherwise protect fish, wildlife, fish and wildlife habitat, and water quality.

(d) The regulations promulgated by the Department of Food and Agriculture under this division shall, at a minimum, address in relation to commercial marijuana activity, the same matters described in subdivision (e) of Section 19332 of Chapter 3.5 of Division 8.

(e) The Department of Pesticide Regulation, in consultation with the State Water Resources Control Board, shall promulgate regulations that require that the application of pesticides or other pest control in connection with the indoor, outdoor, or mixed light cultivation of marijuana meets standards equivalent to Division 6 (commencing with Section 11401) of the Food and Agricultural Code and its implementing regulations.

Business and Professions Code § 26061

(AUMA, Effective November 9, 2016.)

(a) The state cultivator license types to be issued by the Department of Food and Agriculture under this division shall include Type 1, Type 1A, Type 1B, Type 2, Type 2A, Type 2B, Type 3, Type 3A, Type 3B, Type 4, and Type 5, Type 5A, and Type 5B unless otherwise provided by law.

(b) Except as otherwise provided by law, Type 1, Type 1A, Type 1B, Type 2, Type 2A, Type 2B, Type 3, Type 3A, Type 3B and Type 4 licenses shall provide for the cultivation of marijuana in the same amount as the equivalent license type for cultivation of medical cannabis as specified in subdivision (g) of Section 19332 of Chapter 3.5 of Division 8.

(c) Except as otherwise provided by law:

(1) Type 5, or "outdoor," means for outdoor cultivation using no artificial lighting greater than one acre, inclusive, of total canopy size on one premises.

(2) Type 5A, or "indoor," means for indoor cultivation using exclusively artificial lighting greater than 22,000 square feet, inclusive, of total canopy size on one premises.

(3) Type 5B, or "mixed-light," means for cultivation using a combination of natural and supplemental artificial lighting at a maximum threshold to be determined by the licensing authority, greater than 22,000 square feet, inclusive, of total canopy size on one premises.

(d) No Type 5, Type 5A, or Type 5B cultivation licenses may be issued before January 1, 2023.

(e) Commencing on January 1, 2023, a Type 5, Type 5A, or Type 5B licensee may apply for and hold a Type 6 or Type 7 license and apply for and hold Type 10 license. A Type 5, Type 5A, or Type 5B licensee shall not be eligible to apply for or hold a Type 8, Type 11, or Type 12 license.

Business and Professions Code § 26062

(AUMA, Effective November 9, 2016.)

The Department of Food and Agriculture, in conjunction with the bureau, shall establish a certified organic designation and organic certification program for marijuana and marijuana products in the same manner as provided in Section 19332.5 of Chapter 3.5 of Division 8.

Business and Professions Code § 26063

(AUMA, Effective November 9, 2016.)

(a) The bureau shall establish standards for recognition of a particular appellation of origin applicable to marijuana grown or cultivated in a certain geographical area in California.

(b) Marijuana shall not be marketed, labeled, or sold as grown in a California county when the marijuana was not grown in that county.

(c) The name of a California county shall not be used in the labeling, marketing, or packaging of marijuana products unless the marijuana contained in the product was grown in that county.

Business and Professions Code § 26064

(AUMA, Effective November 9, 2016.)

Each licensed cultivator shall ensure that the licensed premises do not pose an unreasonable risk of fire or combustion. Each cultivator shall ensure that all lighting, wiring, electrical and mechanical devices, or other relevant property is carefully maintained to avoid unreasonable or dangerous risk to the property or others.

Business and Professions Code § 26065

(AUMA, Effective November 9, 2016.)

An employee engaged in the cultivation of marijuana under this division shall be subject to Wage Order No. 4-2001 of the Industrial Welfare Commission.

Business and Professions Code § 26066

(AUMA, Effective November 9, 2016.)

Indoor and outdoor marijuana cultivation by persons and entities licensed under this division shall be conducted in accordance with state and local laws related to land conversion, grading, electricity usage, water usage, water quality, woodland and riparian habitat protection, agricultural discharges, and similar matters. State agencies, including, but not limited to, the Board of Forestry and Fire Protection, the Department of Fish and Wildlife, the State Water Resources Control Board, the California regional water quality control boards, and traditional state law enforcement agencies, shall address environmental impacts of marijuana cultivation and shall coordinate when appropriate with cities and counties and their law enforcement agencies in enforcement efforts.

Business and Professions Code § 26067

(AUMA, Effective November 9, 2016.)

(a) The Department of Food and Agriculture shall establish a Marijuana Cultivation Program to be administered by the secretary. The secretary shall administer this section as it pertains to the cultivation of marijuana. For purposes of this division, marijuana is an agricultural product.

(b) A person or entity shall not cultivate marijuana without first obtaining a state license issued by the department pursuant to this section.

(c)(1) The department, in consultation with, but not limited to, the bureau, the State Water Resources Control Board, and the Department of Fish and Wildlife, shall implement a unique identification program for marijuana. In implementing the program, the department shall consider issues including, but not limited to, water use and environmental impacts. In implementing the program, the department shall ensure that:

(A) Individual and cumulative effects of water diversion and discharge associated with cultivation do not affect the in stream flows needed for fish spawning, migration, and rearing, and the flows needed to maintain natural flow variability. If a watershed cannot support additional cultivation, no new plant identifiers will be issued for that watershed.

(B) Cultivation will not negatively impact springs, riparian wetlands and aquatic habitats.

(c)(2) The department shall establish a program for the identification of permitted marijuana plants at a cultivation site during the cultivation period. A unique identifier shall be issued for each marijuana plant. The department shall ensure that unique identifiers are issued as quickly as possible to ensure the implementation of this division. The unique identifier shall be attached at the base of each plant or as otherwise required by law or regulation.

(A) Unique identifiers will only be issued to those persons appropriately licensed by this section.

(B) Information associated with the assigned unique identifier and licensee shall be included in the trace and track program specified in Section 26170.

(C) The department may charge a fee to cover the reasonable costs of issuing the unique identifier and monitoring, tracking, and inspecting each marijuana plant.

(D) The department may promulgate regulations to implement this section.

(c)(3) The department shall take adequate steps to establish protections against fraudulent unique identifiers and limit illegal diversion of unique identifiers to unlicensed persons.

(d) Unique identifiers and associated identifying information administered by local jurisdictions shall adhere to the requirements set by the department and be the equivalent to those administered by the department.

(e)(1) This section does not apply to the cultivation of marijuana in accordance with Section 11362.1 of the Health and Safety Code or the Compassionate Use Act.

(e)(2) Subdivision (b) of this section does not apply to persons or entities licensed under either paragraph (3) of subdivision (a) of Section 26070 or subdivision (b) of Section 26070.5.

(f) "Department" for purposes of this section means the Department of Food and Agriculture.

Chapter 7. Retailers and Distributors

Business and Professions Code § 26070

(AUMA, Effective November 9, 2016.)

(a) State licenses to be issued by the Department of Consumer Affairs are as follows:

(1) "Retailer," for the retail sale and delivery of marijuana or marijuana products to customers.

(2) "Distributor," for the distribution of marijuana and marijuana products. A distributor licensee shall be bonded and insured at a minimum level established by the licensing authority.

(3) "Microbusiness," for the cultivation of marijuana on an area less than 10,000 square feet and to act as a licensed distributor, Level 1 manufacturer, and retailer under this division, provided such licensee complies with all requirements imposed by this division on licensed cultivators, distributors, Level 1 manufacturers, and retailers to the extent the licensee engages in such activities. Microbusiness licenses that authorize cultivation of marijuana shall include conditions requested by the Department of Fish and Wildlife and the State Water Resources Control Board to ensure that individual and cumulative effects of water diversion and discharge associated with cultivation do not affect the in stream flows needed for fish spawning, migration, and rearing, and

the flow needed to maintain flow variability, and otherwise protect fish, wildlife, fish and wildlife habitat, and water quality.

(b) The bureau shall establish minimum security and transportation safety requirements for the commercial distribution and delivery of marijuana and marijuana products. The transportation safety standards established by the bureau shall include, but not be limited to, minimum standards governing the types of vehicles in which marijuana and marijuana products may be distributed and delivered and minimum qualifications for persons eligible to operate such vehicles.

(c) Licensed retailers and microbusinesses, and licensed nonprofits under Section 26070.5, shall implement security measures reasonably designed to prevent unauthorized entrance into areas containing marijuana or marijuana products and theft of marijuana or marijuana products from the premises. These security measures shall include, but not be limited to, all of the following:

(1) Prohibiting individuals from remaining on the licensee's premises if they are not engaging in activity expressly related to the operations of the dispensary.

(2) Establishing limited access areas accessible only to authorized personnel.

(3) Other than limited amounts of marijuana used for display purposes, samples, or immediate sale, storing all finished marijuana and marijuana products in a secured and locked room, safe, or vault, and in a manner reasonably designed to prevent diversion, theft, and loss.

Business and Professions Code § 26070.5

(AUMA, Effective November 9, 2016.)

(a) The bureau shall, by January 1, 2018, investigate the feasibility of creating one or more classifications of nonprofit licenses under this section. The feasibility determination shall be made in consultation with the relevant licensing agencies and representatives of local jurisdictions which issue temporary licenses pursuant to subdivision (b). The bureau shall consider factors including, but not limited to, the following:

(1) Should nonprofit licensees be exempted from any or all state taxes, licensing fees and regulatory provisions applicable to other licenses in

this division?

(2) Should funding incentives be created to encourage others licensed under this division to provide professional services at reduced or no cost to nonprofit licensees?

(3) Should nonprofit licenses be limited to, or prioritize those, entities previously operating on a not-for-profit basis primarily providing whole-plant marijuana and marijuana products and a diversity of marijuana strains and seed stock to low income persons?

(b) Any local jurisdiction may issue temporary local licenses to nonprofit entities primarily providing whole-plant marijuana and marijuana products and a diversity of marijuana strains and seed stock to low income persons so long as the local jurisdiction:

(1) confirms the license applicant's status as a nonprofit entity registered with the California Attorney General's Registry of Charitable Trusts and that the applicant is in good standing with all state requirements governing nonprofit entities;

(2) licenses and regulates any such entity to protect public health and safety, and so as to require compliance with all environmental requirements in this division;

(3) provides notice to the bureau of any such local licenses issued, including the name and location of any such licensed entity and all local regulations governing the licensed entity's operation, and;

(4) certifies to the bureau that any such licensed entity will not generate annual gross revenues in excess of two million dollars ($2,000,000).

(c) Temporary local licenses authorized under subdivision (b) shall expire after twelve months unless renewed by the local jurisdiction.

(d) The bureau may impose reasonable additional requirements on the local licenses authorized under subdivision (b).

(e)(1) No new temporary local licenses shall be issued pursuant to this section after the date the bureau determines that creation of nonprofit licenses under this division is not feasible, or if the bureau determines such licenses are feasible, after the date a licensing agency commences issuing state nonprofit licenses.

(e)(2) If the bureau determines such licenses are feasible, no temporary license issued under subdivision (b) shall be renewed or extended after the date on which a licensing agency commences issuing state nonprofit licenses.

(e)(3) If the bureau determines that creation of nonprofit licenses under this division is not feasible, the bureau shall provide notice of this determination to all local jurisdictions that have issued temporary licenses under subdivision (b). The bureau may, in its discretion, permit any such local jurisdiction to renew or extend on an annual basis any temporary license previously issued under subdivision (b).

Chapter 8. Distribution and Transport

Business and Professions Code § 26080

(AUMA, Effective November 9, 2016.)

(a) This division shall not be construed to authorize or permit a licensee to transport or distribute, or cause to be transported or distributed, marijuana or marijuana products outside the state, unless authorized by federal law.

(b) A local jurisdiction shall not prevent transportation of marijuana or marijuana products on public roads by a licensee transporting marijuana or marijuana products in compliance with this division.

Chapter 9. Delivery

Business and Professions Code § 26090

(AUMA, Effective November 9, 2016.)

(a) Deliveries, as defined in this division, may only be made by a licensed retailer or microbusiness, or a licensed nonprofit under Section 26070.5.

(b) A customer requesting delivery shall maintain a physical or electronic copy of the delivery request and shall make it available upon request by the licensing authority and law enforcement officers.

(c) A local jurisdiction shall not prevent delivery of marijuana or marijuana products on public roads by a licensee acting in compliance with this division and local law as adopted under Section 26200.

Chapter 10. Manufacturers and Testing Laboratories

Business and Professions Code § 26100

(AUMA, Effective November 9, 2016.)

The Department of Public Health shall promulgate regulations governing the licensing of marijuana manufacturers and testing laboratories. Licenses to be issued are as follows:

(a) "Manufacturing Level 1," for sites that manufacture marijuana products using nonvolatile solvents, or no solvents.

(b) "Manufacturing Level 2," for sites that manufacture marijuana products using volatile solvents.

(c) "Testing," for testing of marijuana and marijuana products. Testing licensees shall have their facilities or devices licensed according to regulations set forth by the Department. A testing licensee shall not hold a license in another license category of this division and shall not own or have ownership interest in a non-testing facility licensed pursuant to this division.

(d) For purposes of this section, "volatile solvents" shall have the same meaning as in subdivision (d) of Section 11362.2 of the Health and Safety Code unless otherwise provided by law or regulation.

Business and Professions Code § 26101

(AUMA, Effective November 9, 2016.)

(a) Except as otherwise provided by law, no marijuana or marijuana products may be sold pursuant to a license provided for under this division unless a representative sample of such marijuana or marijuana product has been tested by a certified testing service to determine:

(1) Whether the chemical profile of the sample conforms to the labeled content of compounds, including, but not limited to, all of the following:

(A) Tetrahydrocannabinol (THC).

(B) Tetrahydrocannabinolic Acid (THCA).

(C) Cannabidiol (CBD).

(D) Cannabidiolic Acid (CBDA).

(E) The terpenes described in the most current version of the cannabis inflorescence monograph published by the American Herbal Pharmacopoeia.

(F) Cannabigerol (CBG).

(G) Cannabinol (CBN).

(2) That the presence of contaminants does not exceed the levels in the most current version of the American Herbal Pharmacopoeia monograph. For purposes of this paragraph, contaminants includes, but is not limited to, all of the following:

(A) Residual solvent or processing chemicals, including explosive gases, such as Butane, propane, 02 or H2, and poisons, toxins, or carcinogens, such as Methanol, Iso-propyl Alcohol, Methylene Chloride, Acetone, Benzene, Toluene, and Tri-chloro-ethylene.

(B) Foreign material, including, but not limited to, hair, insects, or similar or related adulterant.

(C) Microbiological impurity, including total aerobic microbial count, total yeast mold count, P. aeruginosa, aspergillus spp., s. aureus, aflatoxin Bl, B2, GI, or G2, or ochratoxin A.

(b) Residual levels of volatile organic compounds shall satisfy standards of the cannabis inflorescence monograph set by the United States Pharmacopeia (U.S.P. Chapter 467).

(c) The testing required by paragraph (a) shall be performed in a manner consistent with general requirements for the competence of testing and calibrations activities, including sampling, using standard methods established by the International Organization for Standardization, specifically ISOIIEC 17020 and ISOIIEC 17025 to test marijuana and marijuana products that are approved by an accrediting body that is a signatory to the International Laboratory Accreditation Cooperation Mutual Recognition Agreement.

(d) Any pre-sale inspection, testing transfer, or transportation of marijuana products pursuant to this section shall conform to a specified chain of custody protocol and any other requirements imposed under this division.

Business and Professions Code § 26102

(AUMA, Effective November 9, 2016.)

A licensed testing service shall not handle, test, or analyze marijuana or marijuana products unless the licensed testing laboratory meets the requirements of Section 19343 in Chapter 3.5 of Division 8 or unless otherwise provided by law.

Business and Professions Code § 26103

(AUMA, Effective November 9, 2016.)

A licensed testing service shall issue a certificate of analysis for each lot, with supporting data, to report the same information required in Section 19344 in Chapter 3.5 of Division 8 or unless otherwise provided by law.

Business and Professions Code § 26104

(AUMA, Effective November 9, 2016.)

(a) A licensed testing service shall, in performing activities concerning marijuana and marijuana products, comply with the requirements and restrictions set forth in applicable law and regulations.

(b) The Department of Public Health shall develop procedures to:

(1) ensure that testing of marijuana and marijuana products occurs prior to distribution to retailers, microbusinesses, or nonprofits licensed under Section 26070.5;

(2) specify how often licensees shall test marijuana and marijuana products, and that the cost of testing marijuana shall be borne by the licensed cultivators and the cost of testing marijuana products shall be borne by the licensed manufacturer, and that the costs of testing marijuana and marijuana products shall be borne a nonprofit licensed under Section 26070.5; and

(3) require destruction of harvested batches whose testing samples indicate noncompliance with health and safety standards promulgated by the Department of Public Health, unless remedial measures can bring the marijuana or marijuana products into compliance with quality assurance standards as promulgated by the Department of Public Health.

Business and Professions Code § 26105

(AUMA, Effective November 9, 2016.)

Manufacturing Level 2 licensees shall enact sufficient methods or procedures to capture or otherwise limit risk of explosion, combustion, or any other unreasonably dangerous risk to public safety created by volatile solvents. The Department of Public Health shall establish minimum standards concerning such methods and procedures for Level 2 licensees.

Business and Professions Code § 26106

(AUMA, Effective November 9, 2016.)

Standards for the production and labeling of all marijuana products developed by the Department of Public Health shall apply to licensed manufacturers and microbusinesses, and nonprofits licensed under Section 26070.5 unless otherwise specified by the Department of Public Health.

Chapter 11. Quality Assurance, Inspection, and Testing

Business and Professions Code § 26110

(AUMA, Effective November 9, 2016.)

(a) All marijuana and marijuana products shall be subject to quality assurance, inspection, and testing.

(b) All marijuana and marijuana products shall undergo quality assurance, inspection, and testing in the same manner as provided in Section 19326 in Chapter 3.5 of Division 8 except as otherwise provided in this division or by law.

Chapter 12. Packaging and Labeling

Business and Professions Code § 26120

(AUMA, Effective November 9, 2016.)

(a) Prior to delivery or sale at a retailer, marijuana and marijuana products shall be labeled and placed in a resealable, child resistant package.

(b) Packages and labels shall not be made to be attractive to children.

(c) All marijuana and marijuana product labels and inserts shall include the following information prominently displayed in a clear and legible fashion in accordance with the requirements, including font size, prescribed by the bureau or the Department of Public Health:

(1) Manufacture date and source.

(2) The following statements, in bold print:

(A) For marijuana: "GOVERNMENT WARNING: THIS PACKAGE CONTAINS MARIJUANA, A SCHEDULE 1 CONTROLLED SUBSTANCE. KEEP OUT OF REACH OF CHILDREN AND ANIMALS. MARIJUANA MAY ONLY BE POSSESSED OR CONSUMED BY PERSONS 21 YEARS OF AGE OR OLDER UNLESS THE PERSON IS A QUALIFIED PATIENT. MARIJUANA USE WHILE PREGNANT OR BREASTFEEDING MAY BE HARMFUL. CONSUMPTION OF MARIJUANA IMPAIRS YOUR ABILITY TO DRIVE AND OPERATE MACHINERY. PLEASE USE EXTREME CAUTION."

(B) For marijuana products: "GOVERNMENT WARNING: THIS PRODUCT CONTAINS MARIJUANA, A SCHEDULE 1 CONTROLLED SUBSTANCE. KEEP OUT OF REACH OF CHILDREN AND ANIMALS. MARIJUANA PRODUCTS MAY ONLY BE POSSESSED OR CONSUMED BY PERSONS 21 YEARS OF AGE OR OLDER UNLESS THE PERSON IS A QUALIFIED PATIENT. THE INTOXICATING EFFECTS OF MARIJUANA PRODUCTS MAY BE DELAYED UP TO TWO HOURS. MARIJUANA USE WHILE PREGNANT OR BREASTFEEDING MAY BE HARMFUL. CONSUMPTION OF MARIJUANA PRODUCTS IMPAIRS YOUR ABILITY TO DRIVE

AND OPERATE MACHINERY. PLEASE USE EXTREME CAU-
TION"

(3) For packages containing only dried flower, the net weight of marijuana in the package.

(4) Identification of the source and date of cultivation, the type of marijuana or marijuana product and the date of manufacturing and packaging.

(5) The appellation of origin, if any.

(6) List of pharmacologically active ingredients, including, but not
limited to, tetrahydrocannabinol (THC), cannabidiol (CBD), and other
cannabinoid content, the THC and other cannabinoid amount in milligrams per serving, servings per package, and the THC and other cannabinoid amount in milligrams for the package total, and the potency
of the marijuana or marijuana product by reference to the amount of
tetrahydrocannabinol and cannabidiol in each serving.

(7) For marijuana products, a list of all ingredients and disclosure of
nutritional information in the same manner as the federal nutritional
labeling requirements in 21 C.F.R. section 101.9.

(8) A list of any solvents, nonorganic pesticides, herbicides, and fertilizers that were used in the cultivation, production, and manufacture of
such marijuana or marijuana product.

(9) A warning if nuts or other known allergens are used.

(10) Information associated with the unique identifier issued by the
Department of Food and Agriculture.

(11) Any other requirement set by the bureau or the Department of
Public Health.

(d) Only generic food names may be used to describe the ingredients in edible
marijuana products.

(e) In the event the bureau determines that marijuana is no longer a schedule I
controlled substance under federal law, the label prescribed in subdivision (c)
shall no longer require a statement that marijuana is a schedule I controlled
substance.

Chapter 13. Marijuana Products

Business and Professions Code § 26130

(AUMA, Effective November 9, 2016.)

(a) Marijuana products shall be:

(1) Not designed to be appealing to children or easily confused with commercially sold candy or foods that do not contain marijuana.

(2) Produced and sold with a standardized dosage of cannabinoids not to exceed ten (10) milligrams tetrahydrocannabinol per serving.

(3) Delineated or scored into standardized serving sizes if the marijuana product contains more than one serving and is an edible marijuana product in solid form.

(4) Homogenized to ensure uniform disbursement of cannabinoids throughout the product.

(5) Manufactured and sold under sanitation standards established by the Department of Public Health, in consultation with the bureau, for preparation, storage, handling and sale of food products.

(6) Provided to customers with sufficient information to enable the informed consumption of such product, including the potential effects of the marijuana product and directions as to how to consume the marijuana product, as necessary.

(b) Marijuana, including concentrated cannabis, included in a marijuana product manufactured in compliance with law is not considered an adulterant under state law.

Chapter 14. Protection of Minors

Business and Professions Code § 26140

(AUMA, Effective November 9, 2016.)

(a) No licensee shall:

(1) Sell marijuana or marijuana products to persons under 21 years of age.

(2) Allow any person under 21 years of age on its premises.

(3) Employ or retain persons under 21 years of age.

(4) Sell or transfer marijuana or marijuana products unless the person to whom the marijuana or marijuana product is to be sold first presents documentation which reasonably appears to be a valid government-issued identification card showing that the person is 21 years of age or older.

(b) Persons under 21 years of age may be used by peace officers in the enforcement of this division and to apprehend licensees, or employees or agents of licensees, or other persons who sell or furnish marijuana to minors. Notwithstanding any provision of law, any person under 21 years of age who purchases or attempts to purchase any marijuana while under the direction of a peace officer is immune from prosecution for that purchase or attempt to purchase marijuana. Guidelines with respect to the use of persons under 21 years of age as decoys shall be adopted and published by the bureau in accordance with the rule making portion of the Administrative Procedure Act (Chapter 3.5 (commencing with Section 11340) of Part 1 of Division 3 of Title 2 of the Government Code).

(c) Notwithstanding subdivision (a), a licensee that is also a dispensary licensed under Chapter 3.5 of Division 8 may:

(1) Allow on the premises any person 18 years of age or older who possesses a valid identification card under Section 11362. 71 of the Health and Safety Code and a valid government-issued identification card;

(2) Sell marijuana, marijuana products, and marijuana accessories to a person 18 years of age or older who possesses a valid identification card under Section 11362.71 of the Health and Safety Code and a valid government-issued identification card.

Chapter 15. Advertising and Marketing Restrictions

Business and Professions Code § 26150

(AUMA, Effective November 9, 2016.)

For purposes of this chapter:

(a) "Advertise" means the publication or dissemination of an advertisement.

(b) "Advertisement" includes any written or verbal statement, illustration, or depiction which is calculated to induce sales of marijuana or marijuana products, including any written, printed, graphic, or other material, billboard, sign, or other outdoor display, public transit card, other periodical literature, publication, or in a radio or television broadcast, or in any other media; except that such term shall not include:

(1) Any label affixed to any marijuana or marijuana products, or any individual covering, carton, or other wrapper of such container that constitutes a part of the labeling under provisions of this division.

(2) Any editorial or other reading material (e.g., news release) in any periodical or publication or newspaper for the publication of which no money or valuable consideration is paid or promised, directly or indirectly, by any licensee, and which is not written by or at the direction of the licensee.

(c) "Advertising sign" is any sign, poster, display, billboard, or any other stationary or permanently-affixed advertisement promoting the sale of marijuana or marijuana products which are not cultivated, manufactured, distributed, or sold on the same lot.

(d) "Health-related statement" means any statement related to health, and includes statements of a curative or therapeutic nature that, expressly or by implication, suggest a relationship between the consumption of marijuana or marijuana products and health benefits, or effects on health.

(e) "Market" or "Marketing" means any act or process of promoting or selling marijuana or marijuana products, including but not limited to, sponsorship of sporting events, point of sale advertising, development of products specifically designed to appeal to certain demographics, etc.

Business and Professions Code § 26151

(AUMA, Effective November 9, 2016.)

(a) All advertisements and marketing shall accurately and legibly identify the licensee responsible for its content.

(b) Any advertising or marketing placed in broadcast, cable, radio, print and digital communications shall only be displayed where at least 71.6 percent of the audience is reasonably expected to be 21 years of age or older, as determined by reliable, up-to-date audience composition data.

(c) Any advertising or marketing involving direct, individualized communication or dialogue controlled by the licensee shall utilize a method of age affirmation to verify that the recipient is 21 years of age or older prior to engaging in such communication or dialogue controlled by the licensee. For purposes of this section, such method of age affirmation may include user confirmation, birth date disclosure, or other similar registration method.

(d) All advertising shall be truthful and appropriately substantiated.

Business and Professions Code § 26152

(AUMA, Effective November 9, 2016.)

No licensee shall:

(a) Advertise or market in a manner that is false or untrue in any material particular, or that, irrespective of falsity, directly, or by ambiguity, omission, or inference, or by the addition of irrelevant, scientific or technical matter tends to create a misleading impression;

(b) Publish or disseminate advertising or marketing containing any statement concerning a brand or product that is inconsistent with any statement on the labeling thereof;

(c) Publish or disseminate advertising or marketing containing any statement, design, device, or representation which tends to create the impression that the marijuana originated in a particular place or region, unless the label of the advertised product bears an appellation of origin, and such appellation of origin appears in the advertisement;

(d) Advertise or market on a billboard or similar advertising device located on an Interstate Highway or State Highway which crosses the border of any other state;

(e) Advertise or market marijuana or marijuana products in a manner intended to encourage persons under the age of 21 years to consume marijuana or marijuana products;

(f) Publish or disseminate advertising or marketing containing symbols, language, music, gestures, cartoon characters or other content elements known to appeal primarily to persons below the legal age of consumption; or

(g) Advertise or market marijuana or marijuana products on an advertising sign within 1,000 feet of a day care center, school providing instruction in kindergarten or any grades 1 through 12, playground, or youth center.

Business and Professions Code § 26153

(AUMA, Effective November 9, 2016.)

No licensee shall give away any amount of marijuana or marijuana products, or any marijuana accessories, as part of a business promotion or other commercial activity.

Business and Professions Code § 26154

(AUMA, Effective November 9, 2016.)

No licensee shall publish or disseminate advertising or marketing containing any health-related statement that is untrue in any particular manner or tends to create a misleading impression as to the effects on health of marijuana consumption.

Business and Professions Code § 26155

(AUMA, Effective November 9, 2016.)

(a) The provisions of subsection (g) of section 26152 shall not apply to the placement of advertising signs inside a licensed premises and which are not visible by normal unaided vision from a public place, provided that such advertising signs do not advertise marijuana or marijuana products in a manner intended to encourage persons under the age of 21years to consume marijuana or marijuana products.

(b) This chapter does not apply to any noncommercial speech.

Chapter 16. Records

Business and Professions Code § 26160

(AUMA, Effective November 9, 2016.)

(a) A licensee shall keep accurate records of commercial marijuana activity.

(b) All records related to commercial marijuana activity as defined by the licensing authorities shall be maintained for a minimum of seven years.

(c) The bureau may examine the books and records of a licensee and inspect the premises of a licensee as the licensing authority, or a state or local agency, deems necessary to perform its duties under this division. All inspections shall be conducted during standard business hours of the licensed facility or at any other reasonable time.

(d) Licensees shall keep records identified by the licensing authorities on the premises of the location licensed. The licensing authorities may make any examination of the records of any licensee. Licensees shall also provide and deliver copies of documents to the licensing agency upon request.

(e) A licensee, or its agent or employee, that refuses, impedes, obstructs, or interferes with an inspection of the premises or records of the licensee pursuant to this section, has engaged in a violation of this division.

(f) If a licensee, or an agent or employee of a licensee, fails to maintain or provide the records required pursuant to this section, the licensee shall be subject to a citation and fine of up to thirty thousand dollars ($30,000) per individual violation.

Business and Professions Code § 26161

(AUMA, Effective November 9, 2016.)

(a) Every sale or transport of marijuana or marijuana products from one licensee to another licensee must be recorded on a sales invoice or receipt. Sales invoices and receipts may be maintained electronically and must be filed in such manner as to be readily accessible for examination by employees of the bureau or Board of Equalization and shall not be commingled with invoices covering other commodities.

(b) Each sales invoice required by subdivision (a) shall include the name and address of the seller and shall include the following information:

(1) Name and address of the purchaser.

(2) Date of sale and invoice number.

(3) Kind, quantity, size, and capacity of packages of marijuana or marijuana products sold.

(4) The cost to the purchaser, together with any discount applied to the price as shown on the invoice.

(5) The place from which transport of the marijuana or marijuana product was made unless transport was made from the premises of the licensee.

(6) Any other information specified by the bureau or the licensing authority.

Chapter 17. Track and Trace System

Business and Professions Code § 26170

(AUMA, Effective November 9, 2016.)

(a) The Department of Food and Agriculture, in consultation with the bureau and the State Board of Equalization, shall expand the track and trace program provided for under Article 7.5 to include the reporting of the movement of marijuana and marijuana products throughout the distribution chain and provide, at a minimum, the same level of information for marijuana and marijuana products as required to be reported for medical cannabis and medical cannabis products, and in addition, the amount of the cultivation tax due pursuant to Part 14.5 of the Revenue and Taxation Code. The expanded track and trace program shall include an electronic seed to sale software tracking system with data points for the different stages of commercial activity including, but not limited to, cultivation, harvest, processing, distribution, inventory, and sale.

(b) The Department, in consultation with the bureau, shall ensure that licensees under this division are allowed to use third-party applications, programs and information technology systems to comply with the requirements of the expanded track and trace program described in subdivision (a) to report the movement of marijuana and marijuana products throughout the distribution chain and communicate such information to licensing agencies as required by law.

(c) Any software, database or other information technology system utilized by the Department to implement the expanded track and trace program shall support interoperability with third-party cannabis business software applications and allow all licensee-facing system activities to be performed through a secure application programming interface (API) or comparable technology which is well documented, bi-directional, and accessible to any third-party application that has been validated and has appropriate credentials. The API or comparable technology shall have version control and provide adequate notice of updates to third-party applications. The system should provide a test environment for third-party applications to access that mirrors the production environment.

Chapter 18. License Fees

Business and Professions Code § 26180

(AUMA, Effective November 9, 2016.)

Each licensing authority shall establish a scale of application, licensing, and renewal fees, based upon the cost of enforcing this division, as follows:

(a) Each licensing authority shall charge each licensee a licensure and renewal fee, as applicable. The licensure and renewal fee shall be calculated to cover the costs of administering this division. The licensure fee may vary depending upon the varying costs associated with administering the various regulatory requirements of this division as they relate to the nature and scope of the different licensure activities, including, but not limited to, the track and trace program required pursuant to Section 26170, but shall not exceed the reasonable regulatory costs to the licensing authority.

(b) The total fees assessed pursuant to this division shall be set at an amount that will fairly and proportionately generate sufficient total revenue to fully cover the total costs of administering this division.

(c) All license fees shall be set on a scaled basis by the licensing authority, dependent on the size of the business.

(d) The licensing authority shall deposit all fees collected in a fee account specific to that licensing authority, to be established in the Marijuana Control Fund. Moneys in the licensing authority fee accounts shall be used, upon appropriation by the Legislature, by the designated licensing authority for the administration of this division.

Business and Professions Code § 26181

(AUMA, Effective November 9, 2016.)

The State Water Resources Control Board, the Department of Fish and Wildlife, and other agencies may establish fees to cover the costs of their marijuana regulatory programs.

Chapter 19. Annual Reports; Performance Audit

Business and Professions Code § 26190

(AUMA, Effective November 9, 2016.)

Beginning on March 1, 2020, and on or before March 1 of each year thereafter, each licensing authority shall prepare and submit to the Legislature an annual report on the authority's activities concerning commercial marijuana activities and post the report on the authority's website. The report shall include, but not be limited to, the same type of information specified in Section 19353, and a detailed list of the petitions for regulatory relief or rulemaking changes received by the office from licensees requesting modifications of the enforcement of rules under this division.

Business and Professions Code § 26191

(AUMA, Effective November 9, 2016.)

(a) Commencing January 1, 2019, and by January 1 of each year thereafter, the Bureau of State Audits shall conduct a performance audit of the bureau's activities under this division, and shall report its findings to the bureau and the Legislature by July 1 of that same year. The report shall include, but not be limited to, the following:

(1) The actual costs of the program.

(2) The overall effectiveness of enforcement programs.

(3) Any report submitted pursuant to this section shall be submitted in compliance with Section 9795 of the Government Code.

(b) The Legislature shall provide sufficient funds to the Bureau of State Audits to conduct the annual audit required by this section.

Chapter 20. Local Control

Business and Professions Code § 26200

(AUMA, Effective November 9, 2016.)

(a) Nothing in this division shall be interpreted to supersede or limit the authority of a local jurisdiction to adopt and enforce local ordinances to regulate businesses licensed under this division, including, but not limited to, local zoning and land use requirements, business license requirements, and requirements related to reducing exposure to second hand smoke, or to completely prohibit the establishment or operation of one or more types of businesses licensed under this division within the local jurisdiction.

(b) Nothing in this division shall be interpreted to require a licensing authority to undertake local law enforcement responsibilities, enforce local zoning requirements, or enforce local licensing requirements.

(c) A local jurisdiction shall notify the bureau upon revocation of any local license, permit, or authorization for a licensee to engage in commercial marijuana activity within the local jurisdiction. Within ten (10) days of notification, the bureau shall inform the relevant licensing authorities. Within ten (10) days of being so informed by the bureau, the relevant licensing authorities shall commence proceedings under Chapter 3 o f this Division to determine whether a license issued to the licensee should be suspended or revoked.

(d) Notwithstanding paragraph (1) of subdivision (a) of Section 11362.3 of the Health and Safety Code, a local jurisdiction may allow for the smoking, vaporizing, and ingesting of marijuana or marijuana products on the premises of a retailer or microbusiness licensed under this division if:

(1) Access to the area where marijuana consumption is allowed is restricted to persons 21 years of age and older;

(2) Marijuana consumption is not visible from any public place or non-age restricted area; and

(3) Sale or consumption of alcohol or tobacco is not allowed on the premises.

Business and Professions Code § 26201

(AUMA, Effective November 9, 2016.)

Any standards, requirements, and regulations regarding health and safety, environmental protection, testing, security, food safety, and worker protections established by the state shall be the minimum standards for all licensees under this division statewide. A local jurisdiction may establish additional standards, requirements, and regulations.

Business and Professions Code § 26202

(AUMA, Effective November 9, 2016.)

(a) A local jurisdiction may enforce this division and the regulations promulgated by the bureau or any licensing authority if delegated the power to do so by the bureau or a licensing authority.

(b) The bureau or any licensing authority shall implement the delegation of enforcement authority in subdivision (a) through a memorandum of understanding between the bureau or licensing authority and the local jurisdiction to which enforcement authority is to be delegated.

Chapter 21. Funding

Business and Professions Code § 26210

(AUMA, Effective November 9, 2016.)

(a) The Medical Marijuana Regulation and Safety Act Fund established in Section 19351 of Chapter 3. 5 of Division 8 is hereby renamed the Marijuana Control Fund.

(b) Upon the effective date of this section, whenever "Medical Marijuana Regulation and Safety Act Fund" appears in any statute, regulation, or contract, or in any other code, it shall be construed to refer to the Marijuana Control Fund.

Business and Professions Code § 26211

(AUMA, Effective November 9, 2016.)

(a) Funds for the initial establishment and support of the regulatory activities under this division, including the public information program described in subdivision (c), and for the activities of the Board of Equalization under Part 14.5 of Division 2 of the Revenue and Taxation Code until July 1, 2017, or until the 2017 Budget Act is enacted, whichever occurs later, shall be advanced from the General Fund and shall be repaid by the initial proceeds from fees collected pursuant to this division, any rule or regulation adopted pursuant to this division, or revenues collected from the tax imposed by Sections 34011 and 34012 of the Revenue and Taxation Code, by January 1, 2025.

(1) Funds advanced pursuant to this subdivision shall be appropriated to the bureau, which shall distribute the moneys to the appropriate licensing authorities, as necessary to implement the provisions of this division, and to the Board of Equalization, as necessary, to implement the provisions of Part 14.5 of Division 2 of the Revenue and Taxation Code.

(2) Within 45 days of this section becoming operative:

(A) The Director of Finance shall determine an amount of the initial advance from the General Fund to the Marijuana Control Fund that does not exceed thirty million dollars ($30,000,000); and

(B) There shall be advanced a sum of five million dollars ($5,000,000) from the General Fund to the Department of Health Care Services to provide for the public information program described in subdivision (c).

(b) Notwithstanding subdivision (a), the Legislature shall provide sufficient funds to the Marijuana Control Fund to support the activities of the bureau, state licensing authorities under this division, and the Board of Equalization to support its activities under Part 14.5 of Division 2 of the Revenue and Taxation Code. It is anticipated that this funding will be provided annually beginning on July 1, 2017.

(c) The Department of Health Care Services shall establish and implement a public information program no later than September 1, 2017. This public information program shall, at a minimum, describe the provisions of the Control, Regulate, and Tax Adult Use of Marijuana Act of 2016, the scientific basis for restricting access of marijuana and marijuana products to persons under the age of 21 years, describe the penalties for providing access to marijuana and marijuana products to persons under the age of 21 years, provide information regarding the dangers of driving a motor vehicle, boat, vessel, aircraft, or other vehicle used for transportation while impaired from marijuana use, the potential harms of using marijuana while pregnant or breastfeeding, and the potential harms of overusing marijuana or marijuana products.

II. Fish and Game Code Sections

Fish and Game Code § 1602

(MCRSA- SB 837, Effective June 27, 2016.)

(a) An entity shall not substantially divert or obstruct the natural flow of, or substantially change or use any material from the bed, channel, or bank of, any river, stream, or lake, or deposit or dispose of debris, waste, or other material containing crumbled, flaked, or ground pavement where it may pass into any river, stream, or lake, unless all of the following occur:

> (1) The department receives written notification regarding the activity in the manner prescribed by the department. The notification shall include, but is not limited to, all of the following:
>
> > (A) A detailed description of the project's location and a map.
> >
> > (B) The name, if any, of the river, stream, or lake affected.
> >
> > (C) A detailed project description, including, but not limited to, construction plans and drawings, if applicable.
> >
> > (D) A copy of any document prepared pursuant to Division 13 (commencing with Section 21000) of the Public Resources Code.
> >
> > (E) A copy of any other applicable local, state, or federal permit or agreement already issued.
> >
> > (F) Any other information required by the department.
>
> (2) The department determines the notification is complete in accordance with Chapter 4.5 (commencing with Section 65920) of Division 1 of Title 7 of the Government Code, irrespective of whether the activity constitutes a development project for the purposes of that chapter.
>
> (3) The entity pays the applicable fees, pursuant to Section 1609.
>
> (4) One of the following occurs:
>
> > (A) (i) The department informs the entity, in writing, that the activity will not substantially adversely affect an existing fish or wildlife resource, and that the entity may commence the activity without an agreement, if the entity conducts the activity as de-

scribed in the notification, including any measures in the notification that are intended to protect fish and wildlife resources.

(ii) Each region of the department shall log the notifications of activities where no agreement is required. The log shall list the date the notification was received by the department, a brief description of the proposed activity, and the location of the activity. Each item shall remain on the log for one year. Upon written request by any person, a regional office shall send the log to that person monthly for one year. A request made pursuant to this clause may be renewed annually.

(B) The department determines that the activity may substantially adversely affect an existing fish or wildlife resource and issues a final agreement to the entity that includes reasonable measures necessary to protect the resource, and the entity conducts the activity in accordance with the agreement.

(C) A panel of arbitrators issues a final agreement to the entity in accordance with subdivision (b) of Section 1603, and the entity conducts the activity in accordance with the agreement.

(D) The department does not issue a draft agreement to the entity within 60 days from the date notification is complete, and the entity conducts the activity as described in the notification, including any measures in the notification that are intended to protect fish and wildlife resources.

(b) (1) If an activity involves the routine maintenance and operation of water supply, drainage, flood control, or waste treatment and disposal facilities, notice to and agreement with the department shall not be required after the initial notification and agreement, unless the department determines either of the following:

(A) The work described in the agreement has substantially changed.

(B) Conditions affecting fish and wildlife resources have substantially changed, and those resources are adversely affected by the activity conducted under the agreement.

(2) This subdivision applies only if notice to, and agreement with, the department was attained prior to January 1, 1977, and the department

has been provided a copy of the agreement or other proof of the existence of the agreement that satisfies the department, if requested.

(c) Notwithstanding subdivision (a), the department is not required to determine whether the notification is complete or otherwise process the notification until the department has received the applicable fees.

(d) (1) Notwithstanding subdivision (a), an entity shall not be required to obtain an agreement with the department pursuant to this chapter for activities authorized by a license or renewed license for cannabis cultivation issued by the Department of Food and Agriculture for the term of the license or renewed license if all of the following occur:

(A) The entity submits all of the following to the department:

(i) The written notification described in paragraph (1) of subdivision (a).

(ii) A copy of the license or renewed license for cannabis cultivation issued by the Department of Food and Agriculture that includes the requirements specified in subdivisions (d), (e), and (f) of Section 19332.2 of the Business and Professions Code.

(iii) The fee specified in paragraph (3) of subdivision (a).

(B) The department determines in its sole discretion that compliance with the requirements specified in subdivisions (d), (e), and (f) of Section 19332.2 of the Business and Professions Code that are included in the license will adequately protect existing fish and wildlife resources that may be substantially adversely affected by the cultivation without the need for additional measures that the department would include in a draft streambed alteration agreement in accordance with Section 1603.

(C) The department notifies the entity in writing that the exemption applies to the cultivation authorized by the license or renewed license.

(2) The department shall notify the entity in writing whether the exemption in paragraph (1) applies to the cultivation authorized by the license or renewed license within 60 days from the date that the notification is complete and the fee has been paid.

(3) If an entity receives an exemption pursuant to this subdivision and

fails to comply with any of the requirements described in subdivision (d), (e), or (f) of Section 19332.2 of the Business and Professions Code that are included in the license, the failure shall constitute a violation under this section, and the department shall notify the Department of Food and Agriculture of any enforcement action taken.

(e) It is unlawful for any entity to violate this chapter.

Fish and Game Code § 1617

(MCRSA- SB 837, Effective June 27, 2016.)

(a) The department may adopt regulations establishing the requirements and procedure for the issuance of a general agreement in a geographic area for a category or categories of activities related to cannabis cultivation.

(b) A general agreement adopted by the department subsequent to adoption of regulations under this section shall be in lieu of an individual agreement described in subparagraph (B) of paragraph (4) of subdivision (a) of Section 1602.

(c) Subparagraph (D) of paragraph (4) of subdivision (a) of Section 1602 and all other time periods to process agreements specified in this chapter do not apply to the issuance of a general agreement adopted by the department pursuant to this section.

(d) The department general agreement issued by the department pursuant to this section is a final agreement and is not subject to Section 1603 or 1604.

(e) The department shall charge a fee for a general agreement adopted by the department under this section in accordance with Section 1609.

(f) Regulations adopted pursuant to this section, and any amendment thereto, shall not be subject to Division 13 (commencing with Section 21000) of the Public Resources Code.

Fish and Game Code § 2080

(Amended by Statute, Effective January 1, 1995.)

No person shall import into this state, export out of this state, or take, possess, purchase, or sell within this state, any species, or any part or product thereof, that the commission determines to be an endangered species or a threatened species, or attempt any of those acts, except as otherwise provided in this chapter, the Native Plant Protection Act (Chapter 10 (commencing with Section 1900) of this code), or the California Desert Native Plants Act (Division 23 (commencing with Section 80001) of the Food and Agricultural Code).

Fish and Game Code § 3513

(Amended by Statute, Effective 1977.)

It is unlawful to take or possess any migratory nongame bird as designated in the Migratory Bird Treaty Act or any part of such migratory nongame bird except as provided by rules and regulations adopted by the Secretary of the Interior under provisions of the Migratory Treaty Act.

Fish and Game Code § 5650

(Amended by Statute, Effective January 1, 2008.)

(a) Except as provided in subdivision (b), it is unlawful to deposit in, permit to pass into, or place where it can pass into the waters of this state any of the following:

(1) Any petroleum, acid, coal or oil tar, lampblack, aniline, asphalt, bitumen, or residuary product of petroleum, or carbonaceous material or substance.

(2) Any refuse, liquid or solid, from any refinery, gas house, tannery, distillery, chemical works, mill, or factory of any kind.

(3) Any sawdust, shavings, slabs, or edgings.

(4) Any factory refuse, lime, or slag.

(5) Any cocculus indicus.

(6) Any substance or material deleterious to fish, plant life, mammals, or bird life.

(b) This section does not apply to a discharge or a release that is expressly authorized pursuant to, and in compliance with, the terms and conditions of a waste discharge requirement pursuant to Section 13263 of the Water Code or a waiver issued pursuant to subdivision (a) of Section 13269 of the Water

Code issued by the State Water Resources Control Board or a regional water quality control board after a public hearing, or that is expressly authorized pursuant to, and in compliance with, the terms and conditions of a federal permit for which the State Water Resources Control Board or a regional water quality control board has, after a public hearing, issued a water quality certification pursuant to Section 13160 of the Water Code. This section does not confer additional authority on the State Water Resources Control Board, a regional water quality control board, or any other entity.

(c) It shall be an affirmative defense to a violation of this section if the defendant proves, by a preponderance of the evidence, all of the following:

(1) The defendant complied with all applicable state and federal laws and regulations requiring that the discharge or release be reported to a government agency.

(2) The substance or material did not enter the waters of the state or a storm drain that discharges into the waters of the state.

(3) The defendant took reasonable and appropriate measures to effectively mitigate the discharge or release in a timely manner.

(d) The affirmative defense in subdivision (c) does not apply and may not be raised in an action for civil penalties or injunctive relief pursuant to Section 5650.1.

(e) The affirmative defense in subdivision (c) does not apply and may not be raised by any defendant who has on two prior occasions in the preceding five years, in any combination within the same county in which the case is prosecuted, either pleaded nolo contendere, been convicted of a violation of this section, or suffered a judgment for a violation of this section or Section 5650.1. This subdivision shall apply only to cases filed on or after January 1, 1997.

(f) The affirmative defense in subdivision (c) does not apply and may not be raised by the defendant in any case in which a district attorney, city attorney, or Attorney General alleges, and the court finds, that the defendant acted willfully.

Fish and Game Code § 5652

(Amended by Statute, Effective January 1, 2008.)

(a) It is unlawful to deposit, permit to pass into, or place where it can pass into the waters of the state, or to abandon, dispose of, or throw away, within 150 feet of the high water mark of the waters of the state, any cans, bottles, garbage, motor vehicle or parts thereof, rubbish, litter, refuse, waste, debris, or the viscera or carcass of any dead mammal, or the carcass of any dead bird.

(b) The abandonment of any motor vehicle in any manner that violates this section shall constitute a rebuttable presumption affecting the burden of producing evidence that the last registered owner of record, not having complied with Section 5900 of the Vehicle Code, is responsible for that abandonment and is thereby liable for the cost of removal and disposition of the vehicle. This section prohibits the placement of a vehicle body on privately owned property along a streambank by the property owner or tenant for the purpose of preventing erosion of the streambank.

(c) This section does not apply to a refuse disposal site that is authorized by the appropriate local agency having jurisdiction or to the depositing of those materials in a container from which the materials are routinely removed to a legal point of disposal.

(d) This section shall be enforced by all law enforcement officers of this state.

Fish and Game Code § 12025.2

(MCRSA- SB-837, Effective June 27, 2016.)

The director or his or her designee may issue a complaint to any person or entity in accordance with Section 1055 of the Water Code alleging a violation for which liability may be imposed under Section 1052 or 1847 of the Water Code that harms fish and wildlife resources. The complaint is subject to the substantive and procedural requirements set forth in Section 1055 of the Water Code, and the department shall be designated a party to any proceeding before the State Water Resources Control Board regarding a complaint filed pursuant to this section.

Fish and Game Code § 12029

(MCRSA- SB 837, Effective June 27, 2016.)

(a) The Legislature finds and declares all of the following:

(1) The environmental impacts associated with cannabis cultivation have increased, and unlawful water diversions for cannabis irrigation have a detrimental effect on fish and wildlife and their habitat, which are held in trust by the state for the benefit of the people of the state.

(2) The remediation of existing cannabis cultivation sites is often complex and the permitting of these sites requires greater department staff time and personnel expenditures. The potential for cannabis cultivation sites to significantly impact the state's fish and wildlife resources requires immediate action on the part of the department's lake and streambed alteration permitting staff.

(b) In order to address unlawful water diversions and other violations of the Fish and Game Code associated with cannabis cultivation, the department shall establish the watershed enforcement program to facilitate the investigation, enforcement, and prosecution of these offenses.

(c) The department, in coordination with the State Water Resources Control Board and the Department of Food and Agriculture, shall establish a permanent multiagency task force to address the environmental impacts of cannabis cultivation. The multiagency task force, to the extent feasible and subject to available resources, shall expand its enforcement efforts on a statewide level to ensure the reduction of adverse impacts of cannabis cultivation on fish and wildlife and their habitats throughout the state.

(d) In order to facilitate the remediation and permitting of cannabis cultivation sites, the department may adopt regulations to enhance the fees on any entity subject to Section 1602 for cannabis cultivation sites that require remediation. The fee schedule established pursuant to this subdivision shall not exceed the fee limits in Section 1609.

III. Food and Agricultural Code Sections

Food and Agricultural Code § 37104

(MCRSA- SB 837, Effective June 27, 2016.)

Notwithstanding Section 19300.5 of the Business and Professions Code, butter purchased from a licensed milk products plant or retail location that is subsequently infused or mixed with medical cannabis at the premises or location that is not subject to licensing as a milk product plant is exempt from the provisions of this division.

Food and Agricultural Code § 52452

(MCRSA- SB 837, Effective June 27, 2016.)

(a) Except as otherwise provided in Section 52454, each container of agricultural seed that is for sale or sold within this state for sowing purposes shall bear upon it or have attached to it in a conspicuous place a plainly written or printed label or tag in the English language that includes all of the following information:

(1) The commonly accepted name of the kind, kind and variety, or kind and type of each agricultural seed component in excess of 5 percent of the whole, and the percentage by weight of each. If the aggregate of agricultural seed components, each present in an amount not exceeding 5 percent of the whole, exceeds 10 percent of the whole, each component in excess of 1 percent of the whole shall be named together with the percentage by weight of each. If more than one component is required to be named, the names of all components shall be shown in letters of the same type and size.

(2) The lot number or other lot identification.

(3) The percentage by weight of all weed seeds.

(4) The name and approximate number of each kind of restricted noxious weed seed per pound.

(5) The percentage by weight of any agricultural seed except that which is required to be named on the label.

(6) The percentage by weight of inert matter. If a percentage by weight is required to be shown by any provision of this section, that percentage shall be exclusive of any substance that is added to the seed as a coating and shown on the label as such.

(7) For each agricultural seed in excess of 5 percent of the whole, stated in accordance with paragraph (1), the percentage of germination exclusive of hard seed, the percentage of hard seed, if present, and the calendar month and year the test was completed to determine the percentages. Following the statement of those percentages, the additional statement "total germination and hard seed" may be stated.

(8) The name and address of the person who labeled the seed or of the person who sells the seed within this state.

(b) Subdivision (a) does not apply in the following instances:

(1) The sale is an occasional sale of seed grain by the producer of the seed grain to his or her neighbor for use by the purchaser within the county of production.

(2) Any cannabis seed, as defined in subdivision (f) of Section 19300.5 of the Business and Professions Code, sold or offered for sale in the state.

(c) All determinations of noxious weed seeds are subject to tolerances and methods of determination prescribed in the regulations that are adopted pursuant to this chapter.

(d) For purposes of this section, "neighbor" means a person who lives in close proximity, not to exceed three miles, to another.

Food and Agricultural Code § 81000

(AUMA, Effective November 9, 2016.)

For purposes of this division, the following terms have the following meanings:

(a) "Board" means the Industrial Hemp Advisory Board.

(b) "Commissioner" means the county agricultural commissioner.

(c) "Established agricultural research institution" means any institution that is either:

> (1) a public or private institution or organization that maintains land or facilities for agricultural research, including colleges, universities, agricultural research centers, and conservation research centers; or

> (2) an institution of higher education (as defined in Section 1001 of the Higher Education Act of 1965 (20 USC. 1001)) that grows, cultivates or manufactures industrial hemp for purposes of research conducted under an agricultural pilot program or other agricultural or academic research.

(d) "Industrial hemp" has the same meaning as the term is defined in Section 11018.5 of the Health and Safety Code.

(e) "Secretary" means the Secretary of Food and Agriculture.

(f) "Seed breeder" means an individual or public or private institution or organization that is registered with the commissioner to develop seed cultivars intended for sale or research.

(g) "Seed cultivar" means a variety of industrial hemp.

(h) "Seed development plan" means a strategy devised by a seed breeder, or applicant seed breeder, detailing his or her plam1ed approach to growing and developing a new seed cultivar for industrial hemp.

Food and Agricultural Code § 81006

(AUMA, Effective November 9, 2016.)

(a)(1) Except when grown by an established agricultural research institution or a registered seed breeder, industrial hemp shall be grown only as a densely planted fiber or oilseed crop, or both, in acreages of not less than one-tenth of an acre at the same time.

(a)(2) Registered seed breeders, for purposes of seed production, shall only grow industrial hemp as a densely planted crop in acreages of not less than one-tenth of an acre at the same time.

(a)(3) Registered seed breeders, for purposes of developing a new California seed cultivar, shall grow industrial hemp as densely as possible in dedicated acreage of not less than one-tenth of an acre and in accordance with the seed development plan. The entire area of the dedicated acreage is not required to be used for the cultivation of the particular seed cultivar.

(b) Ornamental and clandestine cultivation of industrial hemp is prohibited. All plots shall have adequate signage indicating they are industrial hemp.

(c) Pruning and tending of individual industrial hemp plants is prohibited, except when grown by an established agricultural research institution or when the action is necessary to perform the tetrahydrocannabinol (THC) testing described in this section.

(d) Culling of industrial hemp is prohibited, except when grown by an established agricultural research institution, when the action is necessary to perform the THC testing described in this section, or for purposes of seed production and development by a registered seed breeder.

(e) Industrial hemp shall include products imported under the Harmonized Tariff Schedule of the United States (2013) of the United States International Trade Commission, including, but not limited to, hemp seed, per subheading 1207.99.03, hemp oil, per subheading 1515.90.80, oilcake, per subheading 2306.90.01, true hemp, per heading 5302, true hemp yam, per subheading 5308.20.00, and woven fabrics of true hemp fibers, per subheading 5311.00.40.

(f) Except when industrial hemp is grown by an established agricultural research institution, a registrant that grows industrial hemp under this section shall, before the harvest of each crop and as provided below, obtain a laboratory test report indicating the THC levels of a random sampling of the dried flowering tops of the industrial hemp grown.

(1) Sampling shall occur as soon as practicable when the THC content of the leaves surrounding the seeds is at its peak and shall commence as the seeds begin to mature, when the first seeds of approximately 50 percent of the plants are resistant to compression.

(2) The entire fruit-bearing part of the plant including the seeds shall be used as a sample. The sample cut shall be made directly underneath the inflorescence found in the top one-third of the plant.

(3) The sample collected for THC testing shall be accompanied by the following documentation:

(A) The registrant's proof of registration.

(B) Seed certification documentation for the seed cultivar used.

(C) The THC testing report for each certified seed cultivar used.

(4) The laboratory test report shall be issued by a laboratory registered with the federal Drug Enforcement Administration, shall state the percentage content of THC, shall indicate the date and location of samples taken, and shall state the Global Positioning System coordinates and total acreage of the crop. If the laboratory test report indicates a percentage content of THC that is equal to or less than three-tenths of 1 percent, the words "PASSED AS CALIFORNIA INDUSTRIAL HEMP" shall appear at or near the top of the laboratory test report. If the laboratory test report indicates a percentage content of THC that is greater than three-tenths of 1 percent, the words "FAILED AS CALIFORNIA INDUSTRIAL HEMP" shall appear at or near the top of the laboratory test report.

(5) If the laboratory test report indicates a percentage content of THC that is equal to or less than three-tenths of 1 percent, the laboratory shall provide the person who requested the testing not less than 10 original copies signed by an employee authorized by the laboratory and shall retain one or more original copies of the laboratory test report for a minimum of two years from its date of sampling.

(6) If the laboratory test report indicates a percentage content of THC that is greater than three-tenths of 1 percent and does not exceed 1 percent, the registrant that grows industrial hemp shall submit additional samples for testing of the industrial hemp grown.

(7) A registrant that grows industrial hemp shall destroy the industrial hemp grown upon receipt of a first laboratory test report indicating a percentage content of THC that exceeds 1 percent or a second laboratory test report pursuant to paragraph (6) indicating a percentage content of THC that exceeds three-tenths of 1 percent but is less than 1 percent. If the percentage content of THC exceeds 1 percent, the destruction shall take place within 48 hours after receipt of the laboratory test report. If the percentage content of THC in the second laboratory test report exceeds three-tenths of 1 percent but is less than 1 percent, the destruction shall take place as soon as practicable, but no later than 45 days after receipt of the second test report.

(8) A registrant that intends to grow industrial hemp and who complies with this section shall not be prosecuted for the cultivation or possession of marijuana as a result of a laboratory test report that indicates a percentage content of THC that is greater than three-tenths of 1 percent but does not exceed 1 percent.

(9) Established agricultural research institutions shall be permitted to cultivate or possess industrial hemp with a laboratory test report that indicates a percentage content of THC that is greater than three-tenths of 1 percent if that cultivation or possession contributes to the development of types of industrial hemp that will comply with the three-tenths of 1 percent THC limit established in this division.

(10) Except for an established agricultural research institution, a registrant that grows industrial hemp shall retain an original signed copy of the laboratory test report for two years from its date of sampling, make an original signed copy of the laboratory test report available to the department, the commissioner, or law enforcement officials or their designees upon request, and shall provide an original copy of the laboratory test report to each person purchasing, transporting, or otherwise obtaining from the registrant that grows industrial hemp the fiber, oil, cake, or seed, or any component of the seed, of the plant.

(g) If, in the Attorney General's opinion issued pursuant to Section 8 of the act that added this division, it is determined that the provisions of this section are not sufficient to comply with federal law, the department, in consultation with the board, shall establish procedures for this section that meet the requirements of federal law.

Food and Agricultural Code § 81008

(AUMA, Effective November 9, 2016.)

(a) Not later than January 1, 2019, the Attorney General shall report to the Assembly and Senate Committees on Agriculture and the Assembly and Senate Committees on Public Safety the reported incidents, if any, of the following:

(1) A field of industrial hemp being used to disguise marijuana cultivation.

(2) Claims in a court hearing by persons other than those exempted in

subdivision (f) of Section 81006 that marijuana is industrial hemp.

(b) A report submitted pursuant to subdivision (a) shall be submitted in compliance with Section 9795 of the Government Code.

(c) Pursuant to Section 10231.5 of the Government Code, this section is repealed on January 1, 2023, or four years after the date that the report is due, whichever is later.

Food and Agricultural Code § 81010

(AUMA, Effective November 9, 2016.)

(a) This division, and Section 221 of the Food and Agricultural Code, shall become operative on January 1, 2017.

(b) The possession, use, purchase, sale, production, manufacture, packaging, labeling, transporting, storage, distribution, use, and transfer of industrial hemp shall be regulated in accordance with this division. The Bureau of Marijuana Control has authority to regulate and control plants and products that fit within the definition of industrial hemp but that are produced, processed, manufactured, tested, delivered, or otherwise handled pursuant to a license issued under Division 10 of the Business and Professions Code.

IV. Government Code Sections

Government Code § 9147.7

(MCRSA- AB 266, Effective January 1, 2016.)

(a) For the purpose of this section, "eligible agency" means any agency, authority, board, bureau, commission, conservancy, council, department, division, or office of state government, however denominated, excluding an agency that is constitutionally created or an agency related to postsecondary education, for which a date for repeal has been established by statute on or after January 1, 2011.

(b) The Joint Sunset Review Committee is hereby created to identify and eliminate waste, duplication, and inefficiency in government agencies. The purpose of the committee is to conduct a comprehensive analysis over 15 years, and on a periodic basis thereafter, of every eligible agency to determine if the agency is still necessary and cost effective.

(c) Each eligible agency scheduled for repeal shall submit to the committee, on or before December 1 prior to the year it is set to be repealed, a complete agency report covering the entire period since last reviewed, including, but not limited to, the following:

(1) The purpose and necessity of the agency.

(2) A description of the agency budget, priorities, and job descriptions of employees of the agency.

(3) Any programs and projects under the direction of the agency.

(4) Measures of the success or failures of the agency and justifications for the metrics used to evaluate successes and failures.

(5) Any recommendations of the agency for changes or reorganization in order to better fulfill its purpose.

(d) The committee shall take public testimony and evaluate the eligible agency prior to the date the agency is scheduled to be repealed. An eligible agency shall be eliminated unless the Legislature enacts a law to extend, consolidate, or reorganize the eligible agency. No eligible agency shall be extended in perpetuity unless specifically exempted from the provisions of this section. The committee may recommend that the Legislature extend the statutory sunset date for no more than one year to allow the committee more time to evaluate the eligible agency.

(e) The committee shall be comprised of 10 members of the Legislature. The Senate Committee on Rules shall appoint five members of the Senate to the committee, not more than three of whom shall be members of the same political party. The Speaker of the Assembly shall appoint five members of the Assembly to the committee, not more than three of whom shall be members of the same political party. Members shall be appointed within 15 days after the commencement of the regular session. Each member of the committee who is appointed by the Senate Committee on Rules or the Speaker of the Assembly shall serve during that committee member's term of office or until that committee member no longer is a Member of the Senate or the Assembly, whichever is applicable. A vacancy on the committee shall be filled in the same manner as the original appointment. Three Assembly Members and three Senators who are members of the committee shall constitute a quorum for the conduct of committee business. Members of the committee shall receive no compensation for their work with the committee.

(f) The committee shall meet not later than 30 days after the first day of the regular session to choose a chairperson and to establish the schedule for eligible agency review provided for in the statutes governing the eligible agencies. The chairperson of the committee shall alternate every two years between a Member of the Senate and a Member of the Assembly, and the vice chairperson of the committee shall be a member of the opposite house as the chairperson.

(g) This section shall not be construed to change the existing jurisdiction of the budget or policy committees of the Legislature.

(h) This section shall not apply to the Bureau of Medical Marijuana Regulation.

Government Code § 68152

(Repealed and added by Statute, Effective January 1, 2014.)

The trial court clerk may destroy court records under Section 68153 after notice of destruction, and if there is no request and order for transfer of the records, except the comprehensive historical and sample superior court records preserved for research under the California Rules of Court, when the following times have expired after the date of final disposition of the case in the categories listed:

(a) Civil actions and proceedings, as follows:

(1) Except as otherwise specified: retain 10 years.

(2) Civil unlimited cases, limited cases, and small claims cases, including after trial de novo, if any, except as otherwise specified: retain for 10 years.

(3) Civil judgments for unlimited civil cases: retain permanently.

(4) Civil judgments for limited and small claims cases: retain for 10 years, unless judgment is renewed. If judgment is renewed, retain judgment for length of renewal pursuant to Article 2 (commencing with Section 683.110) of Chapter 3 of Division 1 of Title 9 of Part 2 of the Code of Civil Procedure.

(5) If a party in a civil case appears by a guardian ad litem: retain for 10 years after termination of the court's jurisdiction.

(6) Civil harassment, domestic violence, elder and dependent adult abuse, private postsecondary school violence, and workplace violence cases: retain for the same period of time as the duration of the restraining or other orders and any renewals thereof, then retain the restraining or other orders permanently as a judgment; 60 days after expiration of the temporary restraining or other temporary orders; retain judgments establishing paternity under Section 6323 of the Family Code permanently.

(7) Family law, except as otherwise specified: retain for 30 years.

(8) Adoption: retain permanently.

(9) Parentage: retain permanently.

(10) Change of name, gender, or name and gender: retain permanently.

(11) Probate:

(A) Decedent estates: retain permanently all orders, judgments, and decrees of the court, all inventories and appraisals, and all wills and codicils of the decedent filed in the case, including those not admitted to probate. All other records: retain for five years after final disposition of the estate proceeding.

(B) Wills and codicils transferred or delivered to the court pursuant to Section 732, 734, or 8203 of the Probate Code: retain permanently. For wills and codicils delivered to the clerk of the court under Section 8200 of the Probate Code, retain the original documents as provided in Section 26810.

(C) Substitutes for decedent estate administration:

(i) Affidavit procedures for real property of small value under Chapter 3 (commencing with Section 13100) of Part 1 of Division 8 of the Probate Code: retain permanently.

(ii) Proceedings for determining succession to property under Chapter 4 (commencing with Section 13150) of Part 1 of Division 8 of the Probate Code: retain permanently all inventories and appraisals and court orders. Other records: retain for five years after final disposition of the proceeding.

(iii) Proceedings for determination of property passing or belonging to surviving spouse under Chapter 5 (commencing with Section 13650) of Part 2 of Division 8 of the Probate Code: retain permanently all inventories and appraisals and court orders. Other records: retain for five years after final disposition of the proceeding.

(D) Conservatorships: retain permanently all court orders. Documents of trusts established under substituted judgment pursuant to Section 2580 of the Probate Code: retain as provided in clause (iii) of subparagraph (G). Other records: retain for five years after the later of either (i) the final disposition of the conservatorship proceeding, or (ii) the date of the conservatee's death, if that date is disclosed in the court's file.

(E) Guardianships: retain permanently orders terminating the guardianship, if any, and court orders settling final account and ordering distribution of the estate. Other records: retain for five years after the later of (i) the final disposition of the guardianship proceeding, or (ii) the earlier of the date of the ward's death, if that date is disclosed in the court's file, or the date the ward reaches 23 years of age.

(F) Compromise of minor's or disabled person's claim or action, and disposition of judgment for minors and disabled persons under Section 372 of the Code of Civil Procedure and Chapter 4 (commencing with Section 3600) of Part 8 of Division 4 of the Probate Code:

> (i) Retain permanently judgments in favor of minors or disabled persons, orders approving compromises of claims and actions and disposition of the proceeds of judgments, orders directing payment of expenses, costs, and fees, orders directing deposits into blocked accounts and receipts and acknowledgments of those orders, and orders for the withdrawal of funds from blocked accounts.

> (ii) Retain other records for the same retention period as for records in the underlying case. If there is no underlying case, retain for five years after the later of either (I) the date the order for payment or delivery of the final balance of the money or property is entered, or (II) the earlier of the date of the minor's death, if that date is disclosed in the court's file, or the date the minor reaches 23 years of age.

(G) Trusts:

> (i) Proceedings under Part 5 (commencing with Section 17000) of Division 9 of the Probate Code: retain permanently.

> (ii) Trusts created by substituted judgment under Section 2580 of the Probate Code: retain permanently all trust instruments and court orders. Other records: retain as long as the underlying conservatorship file is retained.

> (iii) Special needs trusts: retain permanently all trust instruments and court orders. Other records: retain until the later of either (I the retention date of "other records" in the beneficiary's conservatorship or guardianship file under subparagraph (D) or (E), if any, or (II) five years after the date of the beneficiary's death, if that date is disclosed in the court's file.

(H) All other proceedings under the Probate Code: retain as provided for civil cases.

(12) Mental health:

(A) Lanterman Developmental Disabilities Services Act: retain for 10 years.

(B) Lanterman-Petris-Short Act: retain for 20 years.

(C) Riese (capacity) hearings under Sections 5333 and 5334 of the Welfare and Institutions Code: retain for the later of either (i) 20 years after the date of the capacity determination order, or (ii) the court records retention date of the underlying involuntary treatment or commitment proceeding, if any.

(D) Petitions under Chapter 3 (commencing with Section 8100) of Division 8 of the Welfare and Institutions Code for the return of firearms to petitioners who relinquished them to law enforcement while detained in a mental health facility: retain for 10 years.

(13) Eminent domain: retain permanently.

(14) Real property other than unlawful detainer: retain permanently if the action affects title or an interest in real property.

(15) Unlawful detainer: retain for one year if judgment is only for possession of the premises; retain for 10 years if judgment is for money, or money and possession.

(b) Notwithstanding subdivision (a), any civil or small claims case in the trial court:

(1) Involuntarily dismissed by the court for delay in prosecution or failure to comply with state or local rules: retain for one year.

(2) Voluntarily dismissed by a party without entry of judgment: retain for one year.

(c) Criminal actions and proceedings, as follows:

(1) Capital felony in which the defendant is sentenced to death, and any felony resulting in a sentence of life or life without the possibility of parole: retain permanently, including records of the cases of any codefendants and any related cases, regardless of the disposition. For the purpose of this paragraph, "capital felony" means murder with special circumstances when the prosecution seeks the death penalty. Records of the cases of codefendants and related cases required to be retained

under this paragraph shall be limited to those cases that are factually linked or related to the charged offense, that are identified in the courtroom, and that are placed on the record. If a capital felony is disposed of by a sentence less than death, or imprisonment for life or life without the possibility of parole, the judgment shall be retained permanently, and the record shall be retained for 50 years or for 10 years after the official written notification of the death of the defendant. If a capital felony is disposed of by an acquittal, the record shall be retained for 10 years.

(2) Felony, except as otherwise specified, and in any felony or misdemeanor case resulting in a requirement that the defendant register as a sex offender under Section 290 of the Penal Code: retain judgment permanently. For all other documents: retain for 50 years or the maximum term of the sentence, whichever is longer. However, any record other than the judgment may be destroyed 10 years after the death of the defendant. Felony case files that do not include final sentencing or other final disposition because the case was bound over from a former municipal court to the superior court and not already consolidated with the superior court felony case file: retain for 10 years from the disposition of the superior court case.

(3) Felony reduced to a misdemeanor: retain in accordance with the retention period for the relevant misdemeanor.

(4) Felony, if the charge is dismissed, except as provided in paragraph (6): retain for three years.

(5) Misdemeanor, if the charge is dismissed, except as provided in paragraph (6): retain for one year.

(6) Dismissal under Section 1203.4 or 1203.4a of the Penal Code: retain for the same retention period as for records of the underlying case. If the records in the underlying case have been destroyed, retain for five years after dismissal.

(7) Misdemeanor, except as otherwise specified: retain for five years. For misdemeanors alleging a violation of Section 23109, 23109.5, 23152, or 23153 of the Vehicle Code: retain for 10 years.

(8) Misdemeanor alleging a marijuana violation under subdivision (c), (d), or (e) of Section 11357 of the Health and Safety Code, or subdivision (b) of Section 11360 of the Health and Safety Code: records shall

be destroyed, or redacted in accordance with subdivision (c) of Section 11361.5 of the Health and Safety Code, two years from the date of conviction, or from the date of arrest if no conviction, if the case is no longer subject to review on appeal, all applicable fines and fees have been paid, and the defendant has complied with all terms and conditions of the sentence or grant of probation. However, as provided in subdivision (a) of Section 11361.5 of the Health and Safety Code and paragraph (5) of subdivision (e) of this section, records of a misdemeanor alleging a marijuana violation under subdivision (e) of Section 11357 of the Health and Safety Code shall be retained until the offender attains 18 years of age, at which time the records shall be destroyed as provided in subdivision (c) of Section 11361.5 of the Health and Safety Code.

(9) Misdemeanor reduced to an infraction: retain in accordance with the retention period for the relevant infraction.

(10) Infraction, except as otherwise specified: retain for one year. Vehicle Code infraction: retain for three years. Infraction alleging a marijuana violation under subdivision (b) of Section 11357 of the Health and Safety Code: if records are retained past the one-year minimum retention period, the records shall be destroyed or redacted in accordance with subdivision (c) of Section 11361.5 of the Health and Safety Code two years from the date of conviction, or from the date of arrest if no conviction, if the case is no longer subject to review on appeal, all applicable fines and fees have been paid, and the defendant has complied with all terms and conditions of the sentence or grant of probation.

(11) Criminal protective order: retain until the order expires or is terminated.

(12) Arrest warrant: retain for the same retention period as for records in the underlying case. If there is no underlying case, retain for one year from the date of issue.

(13) Search warrant:

> (A) If there is no underlying case, retain for five years from the date of issue.

> (B) If there is any underlying case, retain for 10 years from the date of issue or, if the retention period for records in the underlying case is less than 10 years or if the underlying case is a capital felony described in paragraph (1) of subdivision (c), retain for the

same retention period as for records in the underlying case

(14) Probable cause declarations: retain for the same retention period as for records in the underlying case. If there is no underlying case, retain for one year from the date of declaration.

(15) Proceedings for revocation of postrelease community supervision or postrelease parole supervision: retain for five years after the period of supervision expires or is terminated.

(d) Habeas corpus:

(1) Habeas corpus in criminal and family law matters: retain for the same retention period as for records in the underlying case, whether granted or denied.

(2) Habeas corpus in mental health matters: retain all records for the same retention period as for records in the underlying case, whether granted or denied. If there is no underlying case, retain records for 20 years.

(e) Juveniles:

(1) Dependent pursuant to Section 300 of the Welfare and Institutions Code: upon reaching 28 years of age, or on written request, shall be released to the juvenile five years after jurisdiction over the person has terminated under subdivision (a) of Section 826 of the Welfare and Institutions Code. Sealed records shall be destroyed upon court order five years after the records have been sealed pursuant to subdivision (c) of Section 389 of the Welfare and Institutions Code.

(2) Ward pursuant to Section 601 of the Welfare and Institutions Code: upon reaching 21 years of age, or on written request, shall be released to the juvenile five years after jurisdiction over the person has terminated under subdivision (a) of Section 826 of the Welfare and Institutions Code. Sealed records shall be destroyed upon court order five years after the records have been sealed under subdivision (d) of Section 781 of the Welfare and Institutions Code.

(3) Ward pursuant to Section 602 of the Welfare and Institutions Code: upon reaching 38 years of age under subdivision (a) of Section 826 of the Welfare and Institutions Code. Sealed records shall be destroyed upon court order when the subject of the record reaches 38 years of age under subdivision (d) of Section 781 of the Welfare and Institutions

Code.

(4) Traffic and some nontraffic misdemeanors and infractions pursuant to Section 601 of the Welfare and Institutions Code: upon reaching 21 years of age, or five years after jurisdiction over the person has terminated under subdivision (c) of Section 826 of the Welfare and Institutions Code. Records may be microfilmed or photocopied.

(5) Marijuana misdemeanor under subdivision (e) of Section 11357 of the Health and Safety Code in accordance with procedures specified in subdivision (a) of Section 11361.5 of the Health and Safety Code: upon reaching 18 years of age, the records shall be destroyed.

(f) Court records of the appellate division of the superior court: retain for five years.

(g) Other records:

(1) Bench warrant: retain for the same retention period as for records in the underlying case. For a bench warrant issued for a misdemeanor, retain records for the same retention period as for records in the underlying misdemeanor following issuance. If there is no return on the warrant, the court may dismiss on its own motion and immediately destroy the records.

(2) Body attachment: retain for same retention period as for records in the underlying case.

(3) Bond: retain for three years after exoneration and release.

(4) Court reporter notes:

(A) Criminal and juvenile proceedings: retain notes for 10 years, except as otherwise specified. Notes reporting proceedings in capital felony cases (murder with special circumstances when the prosecution seeks the death penalty and the sentence is death), including notes reporting the preliminary hearing, shall be retained permanently, unless the Supreme Court on request of the court clerk authorizes the destruction.

(B) Civil and all other proceedings: retain notes for five years.

(5) Electronic recordings made as the official record of the oral proceedings under the California Rules of Court may be destroyed or deleted as

follows:

> (A) Any time after final disposition of the case in infraction and misdemeanor proceedings.
>
> (B) After 10 years in all other criminal proceedings.
>
> (C) After five years in all other proceedings.

(6) Electronic recordings not made as the official record of the oral proceedings under the California Rules of Court may be destroyed at any time at the discretion of the court.

(7) Fee waiver applications: retain for the same retention period as for records in the underlying case.

(8) Judgments within the jurisdiction of the superior court other than in a limited civil case, misdemeanor case, or infraction case: retain permanently.

(9) Judgments in misdemeanor cases, infraction cases, and limited civil cases: retain for the same retention period as for records in the underlying case.

(10) Juror proceedings, including sanctions: retain for one year.

(11) Minutes: retain for the same retention period as for records in the underlying case.

(12) Orders not associated with an underlying case, such as orders for the destruction of court records for telephone taps, orders to destroy drugs, and other miscellaneous court orders: retain for one year.

(13) Naturalization index: retain permanently.

(14) Index for cases alleging traffic violations: retain for the same retention period as for records in the underlying case.

(15) Index, except as otherwise specified: retain permanently.

(16) Register of actions or docket: retain for the same retention period as for records in the underlying case, but in no event less than 10 years for civil and small claims cases.

(h) Retention of the court records under this section shall be extended by order of the court on its own motion, or on application of a party or an interested member of the public for good cause shown and on those terms as are just. A fee shall not be charged for making the application.

(i) The record retention periods provided in this section, as amended effective January 1, 2014, apply to all court records in existence prior to that date as well as to records created on or after that date.

V. Health and Safety Code Sections

Health and Safety Code § 7151.36

(AB 258, Effective January 1, 2016.)

(a) A hospital, physician and surgeon, procurement organization, or other person shall not determine the ultimate recipient of an anatomical gift based solely upon a potential recipient's status as a qualified patient, as defined in Section 11362.7, or based solely upon a positive test for the use of medical marijuana by a potential recipient who is a qualified patient, as defined in Section 11362.7, except to the extent that the qualified patient's use of medical marijuana has been found by a physician and surgeon, following a case-by-case evaluation of the potential recipient, to be medically significant to the provision of the anatomical gift.

(b) Subdivision (a) shall apply to each part of the organ transplant process. The organ transplant process includes, but is not limited to, all of the following:

(1) The referral from a primary care provider to a specialist.

(2) The referral from a specialist to a transplant center.

(3) The evaluation of the patient for the transplant by the transplant center.

(4) The consideration of the patient for placement on the official waiting list.

(c) The court shall accord priority on its calendar and handle expeditiously any action brought to seek any remedy authorized by law for purposes of enforcing compliance with this section.

(d) This section shall not be deemed to require referrals or recommendations for, or the performance of, medically inappropriate organ transplants.

Health and Safety Code § 11006.5

(Added by Statute, Effective 1975.)

"Concentrated cannabis" means the separated resin, whether crude or purified, obtained from marijuana.

Health and Safety Code § 11007

(Added by Statute, Effective September 26, 1987.)

"Controlled substance," unless otherwise specified, means a drug, substance, or immediate precursor which is listed in any schedule in Section 11054, 11055, 11056, 11057, or 11058.

Health and Safety Code § 11014.5

(Added by Statute, Effective 1982.)

(a) "Drug paraphernalia" means all equipment, products and materials of any kind which are designed for use or marketed for use, in planting, propagating, cultivating, growing, harvesting, manufacturing, compounding, converting, producing, processing, preparing, testing, analyzing, packaging, repackaging, storing, containing, concealing, injecting, ingesting, inhaling, or otherwise introducing into the human body a controlled substance in violation of this division. It includes, but is not limited to:

(1) Kits designed for use or marketed for use in planting, propagating, cultivating, growing, or harvesting of any species of plant which is a controlled substance or from which a controlled substance can be derived.

(2) Kits designed for use or marketed for use in manufacturing, compounding, converting, producing, processing, or preparing controlled substances.

(3) Isomerization devices designed for use or marketed for use in increasing the potency of any species of plant which is a controlled substance.

(4) Testing equipment designed for use or marketed for use in identifying, or in analyzing the strength, effectiveness, or purity of controlled substances.

(5) Scales and balances designed for use or marketed for use in weighing or measuring controlled substances.

(6) Containers and other objects designed for use or marketed for use in storing or concealing controlled substances.

(7) Hypodermic syringes, needles, and other objects designed for use or marketed for use in parenterally injecting controlled substances into the human body.

(8) Objects designed for use or marketed for use in ingesting, inhaling, or otherwise introducing marijuana, cocaine, hashish, or hashish oil into the human body, such as:

(A) Carburetion tubes and devices.

(B) Smoking and carburetion masks.

(C) Roach clips, meaning objects used to hold burning material, such as a marijuana cigarette, that has become too small or too short to be held in the hand.

(D) Miniature cocaine spoons, and cocaine vials.

(E) Chamber pipes.

(F) Carburetor pipes.

(G) Electric pipes.

(H) Air-driven pipes.

(I) Chillums.

(J) Bongs.

(K) Ice pipes or chillers.

(b) For the purposes of this section, the phrase "marketed for use" means advertising, distributing, offering for sale, displaying for sale, or selling in a manner which promotes the use of equipment, products, or materials with controlled substances.

(c) In determining whether an object is drug paraphernalia, a court or other authority may consider, in addition to all other logically relevant factors, the following:

(1) Statements by an owner or by anyone in control of the object concerning its use.

(2) Instructions, oral or written, provided with the object concerning its use for ingesting, inhaling, or otherwise introducing a controlled substance into the human body.

(3) Descriptive materials accompanying the object which explain or depict its use.

(4) National and local advertising concerning its use.

(5) The manner in which the object is displayed for sale.

(6) Whether the owner, or anyone in control of the object, is a legitimate supplier of like or related items to the community, such as a licensed distributor or dealer of tobacco products.

(7) Expert testimony concerning its use.

(d) If any provision of this section or the application thereof to any person or circumstance is held invalid, it is the intent of the Legislature that the invalidity shall not affect other provisions or applications of the section which can be given effect without the invalid provision or application and to this end the provisions of this section are severable.

Health and Safety Code § 11018

(AUMA, Effective November 9, 2016.)

"Marijuana" means all parts of the plant Cannabis sativa L., whether growing or not; the seeds thereof; the resin extracted from any part of the plant; and every compound, manufacture, salt, derivative, mixture, or preparation of the plant, its seeds or resin. It does not include:

(a) industrial hemp, as defined in Section 11018.5; or

(b) the weight of any other ingredient combined with marijuana to prepare topical or oral administrations, food, drink, or other product.

Health and Safety Code § 11018.1

(AUMA, Effective November 9, 2016.)

"Marijuana products" means marijuana that has undergone a process whereby the plant material has been transformed into a concentrate, including, but not limited to, concentrated cannabis, or an edible or topical product containing marijuana or concentrated cannabis and other ingredients.

Health and Safety Code § 11018.2

(AUMA, Effective November 9, 2016.)

"Marijuana accessories" means any equipment, products or materials of any kind which are used, intended for use, or designed for use in planting, propagating, cultivating, growing, harvesting, manufacturing, compounding, converting, producing, processing, preparing, testing, analyzing, packaging, repackaging, storing, smoking, vaporizing, or containing marijuana, or for ingesting, inhaling, or otherwise introducing marijuana or marijuana products into the human body.

Health and Safety Code § 11018.5

(AUMA, Effective November 9, 2016.)

Industrial Hemp

(a) "Industrial hemp" means a fiber or oilseed crop, or both, that is limited to types of the plant Cannabis sativa L., having no more than three-tenths of 1 percent tetrahydrocannabinol (THC) contained in the dried flowering tops, whether growing or not; the seeds of the plant;, the resin extracted from any part of the plant; and every compound, manufacture, salt, derivative, mixture, or preparation of the plant, its seeds or resin produced therefrom.

(b) The possession, use, purchase, sale, cultivation, processing, manufacture, packaging, labeling, transporting, storage, distribution, use and transfer of industrial hemp shall not be subject to the provisions of this Division or of Division 10 of the Business and Professions Code, but instead shall be regulated by the Department of Food and Agriculture in accordance with the provisions of Division 24 of the Food and Agricultural Code, inclusive.

Health and Safety Code § 11054 (a), (d)(13), and (d)(20)

(Amended by Statute, Effective January 1, 2003.)

(a) The controlled substances listed in this section are included in Schedule I.

(d) Hallucinogenic substances. Unless specifically excepted or unless listed in another schedule, any material, compound, mixture, or preparation, which contains any quantity of the following hallucinogenic substances, or which contains any of its salts, isomers, and salts of isomers whenever the existence of those salts, isomers, and salts of isomers is possible within the specific chemical designation (for purposes of this subdivision only, the term "isomer" includes the optical, position, and geometric isomers):

> (13) Marijuana.

> (20) Tetrahydrocannabinols. Synthetic equivalents of the substances contained in the plant, or in the resinous extractives of Cannabis, sp. and/or synthetic substances, derivatives, and their isomers with similar chemical structure and pharmacological activity such as the following: delta 1 cis or trans tetrahydrocannabinol, and their optical isomers; delta 6 cis or trans tetrahydrocannabinol, and their optical isomers; delta 3,4 cis or trans tetrahydrocannabinol, and its optical isomers.

> (Since nomenclature of these substances is not internationally standardized, compounds of these structures, regardless of numerical designation of atomic positions covered).

Health and Safety Code § 11357

(AUMA, Effective November 9, 2016.)

(a) Except as authorized by law, possession of not more than 28.5 grams of marijuana, or not more than four grams of concentrated cannabis, or both, shall be punished or adjudicated as follows:

> (1) Persons under the age of 18 shall be guilty of an infraction and shall be required to:

>> (A) Upon a finding that a first offense has been committed, complete four hours of drug education or counseling and up to 10 hours of community service over a period not to exceed 60 days.

>> (B) Upon a finding that a second offense or subsequent offense has

been committed, complete six hours of drug education or counseling and up to 20 hours of community service over a period not to exceed 90 days.

(2) Persons at least 18 years of age but less than 21 years of age shall be guilty of an infraction and punishable by a fine of not more than one hundred dollars ($100).

(b) Except as authorized by law, possession of more than 28.5 grams of marijuana, or more than four grams of concentrated cannabis, shall be punished as follows:

(1) Persons under the age of 18 who possess more than 28.5 grams of marijuana or more than four grams of concentrated cannabis, or both, shall be guilty of an infraction and shall be required to:

(A) Upon a finding that a first offense has been committed, complete eight hours of drug education or counseling and up to 40 hours of community service over a period not to exceed 90 days.

(B) Upon a finding that a second or subsequent offense has been committed, complete 10 hours of drug education or counseling and up to 60 hours of community service over a period not to exceed 120 days.

(2) Persons 18 years of age or over who possess more than 28.5 grams of marijuana, or more than four grams of concentrated cannabis, or both, shall be punished by imprisonment in a county jail for a period of not more than six months or by a fine of not more than five hundred dollars ($500), or by both such fine and imprisonment.

(c) Except as authorized by law, every person 18 years of age or over who possesses not more than 28.5 grams of marijuana, or not more than four grams of concentrated cannabis, upon the grounds of, or within, any school providing instruction in kindergarten or any of grades 1 through 12 during hours the school is open for classes or school-related programs is guilty of a misdemeanor and shall be punished as follows:

(1) A fine of not more than two hundred fifty dollars ($250), upon a finding that a first offense has been committed.

(2) A fine of not more than five hundred dollars ($500), or by imprisonment in a county jail for a period of not more than 10 days, or both, upon a finding that a second or subsequent offense has been committed.

(d) Except as authorized by law, every person under the age of 18 who possesses not more than 28.5 grams of marijuana, or not more than four grams of concentrated cannabis, upon the grounds of, or within, any school providing instruction in kindergarten or any of grades 1 through 12 during hours the school is open for classes or school-related programs is guilty of an infraction and shall be punished in the same manner provided in paragraph (1) of subdivision (b) of this section.

Health and Safety Code § 11357.5

(Amended by Statute, Effective September 25, 2016.)

(a) Every person who sells, dispenses, distributes, furnishes, administers, or gives, or offers to sell, dispense, distribute, furnish, administer, or give, or possesses for sale any synthetic cannabinoid compound, or any synthetic cannabinoid derivative, to any person, is guilty of a misdemeanor, punishable by imprisonment in a county jail not to exceed six months, or by a fine not to exceed one thousand dollars ($1,000), or by both that fine and imprisonment.

(b) Every person who uses or possesses any synthetic cannabinoid compound, or any synthetic cannabinoid derivative, is guilty of a public offense, punishable as follows:

(1) A first offense is an infraction punishable by a fine not exceeding two hundred fifty dollars ($250).

(2) A second offense is an infraction punishable by a fine not exceeding two hundred fifty dollars ($250) or a misdemeanor punishable by imprisonment in a county jail not exceeding six months, a fine not exceeding five hundred dollars ($500), or by both that fine and imprisonment.

(3) A third or subsequent offense is a misdemeanor punishable by imprisonment in a county jail not exceeding six months, or by a fine not exceeding one thousand dollars ($1,000), or by both that fine and imprisonment.

(c) As used in this section, the term "synthetic cannabinoid compound" refers to any of the following substances or an analog of any of the following substances:

(1) Adamantoylindoles or adamantoylindazoles, which includes adamantyl carboxamide indoles and adamantyl carboxamide indazoles, or any compound structurally derived from 3-(1-adamantoyl)

indole, 3-(1-adamantoyl)indazole, 3-(2-adamantoyl)indole, N-(1-adamantyl)-1H-indole-3-carboxamide, or N-(1-adamantyl)-1H-indazole-3-carboxamide by substitution at the nitrogen atom of the indole or indazole ring with alkyl, haloalkyl, alkenyl, cyanoalkyl, hydroxyalkyl, cycloalkylmethyl, cycloalkylethyl, 1-(N-methyl-2-piperidinyl) methyl, 2-(4-morpholinyl)ethyl, or 1-(N-methyl-2-pyrrolidinyl)methyl, 1-(N-methyl-3-morpholinyl)methyl, or (tetrahydropyran-4-yl)methyl group, whether or not further substituted in the indole or indazole ring to any extent and whether or not substituted in the adamantyl ring to any extent, including, but not limited to, 2NE1, 5F-AKB-48, AB-001, AKB-48, AM-1248, JWH-018 adamantyl carboxamide, STS-135.

(2) Benzoylindoles, which includes any compound structurally derived from a 3-(benzoyl)indole structure with substitution at the nitrogen atom of the indole ring with alkyl, haloalkyl, cyanoalkyl, hydroxyalkyl, alkenyl, cycloalkylmethyl, cycloalkylethyl, 1-(N-methyl-2-piperidinyl) methyl, 2-(4-morpholinyl)ethyl, or 1-(N-methyl-2-pyrrolidinyl)methyl, 1-(N-methyl-3-morpholinyl)methyl, or (tetrahydropyran-4-yl)methyl group, whether or not further substituted in the indole ring to any extent and whether or not substituted in the phenyl ring to any extent, including, but not limited to, AM-630, AM-661, AM-679, AM-694, AM-1241, AM-2233, RCS-4, WIN 48,098 (Pravadoline).

(3) Cyclohexylphenols, which includes any compound structurally derived from 2-(3-hydroxycyclohexyl)phenol by substitution at the 5-position of the phenolic ring by alkyl, haloalkyl, cyanoalkyl, hydroxyalkyl, alkenyl, cycloalkylmethyl, cycloalkylethyl, 1-(N-methyl-2-piperidinyl) methyl, 2-(4-morpholinyl)ethyl, or 1-(N-methyl-2-pyrrolidinyl)methyl, 1-(N-methyl-3-morpholinyl)methyl, or tetrahydropyran-4-yl)methyl group, whether or not further substituted in the cyclohexyl ring to any extent, including, but not limited to, CP 47,497, CP 55,490, CP 55,940, CP 56,667, cannabicyclohexanol.

(4) Cyclopropanoylindoles, which includes any compound structurally derived from 3-(cyclopropylmethanoyl)indole, 3-(cyclopropylmethanone)indole, 3-(cyclobutylmethanone)indole or 3-(cyclopentylmethanone)indole by substitution at the nitrogen atom of the indole ring, whether or not further substituted in the indole ring to any extent, whether or not substituted on the cyclopropyl, cyclobutyl, or cyclopentyl rings to any extent.

(5) Naphthoylindoles, which includes any compound structurally de-

rived from 3-(1-naphthoyl)indole or 1H-indol-3-yl-(1-naphthyl)methane by substitution at the nitrogen atom of the indole ring by alkyl, haloalkyl, cyanoalkyl, hydroxyalkyl, alkenyl, cycloalkylmethyl, cycloalkylethyl, 1-(N-methyl-2-piperidinyl)methyl, 2-(4-morpholinyl)ethyl group, 1-(N-methyl-2-pyrrolidinyl)methyl, 1-(N-methyl-3-morpholinyl)methyl, or (tetrahydropyran-4-yl)methyl group, whether or not further substituted in the naphthyl ring to any extent, including, but not limited to, AM-678, AM-1220, AM-1221, AM-1235, AM-2201, AM-2232, EAM-2201, JWH-004, JWH-007, JWH-009, JWH-011, JWH-015, JWH-016, JWH-018, JWH-019, JWH-020, JWH-022, JWH-046, JWH-047, JWH-048, JWH-049, JWH-050, JWH-070, JWH-071, JWH-072, JWH-073, JWH-076, JWH-079, JWH-080, JWH-081, JWH-082, JWH-094, JWH-096, JWH-098, JWH-116, JWH-120, JWH-122, JWH-148, JWH-149, JWH-164, JWH-166, JWH-180, JWH-181, JWH-182, JWH-189, JWH-193, JWH-198, JWH-200, JWH-210, JWH-211, JWH-212, JWH-213, JWH-234, JWH-235, JWH-236, JWH-239, JWH-240, JWH-241, JWH-242, JWH-258, JWH-262, JWH-386, JWH-387, JWH-394, JWH-395, JWH-397, JWH-398, JWH-399, JWH-400, JWH-412, JWH-413, JWH-414, JWH-415, JWH-424, MAM-2201, WIN 55,212.

(6) Naphthoylnaphthalenes, which includes any compound structurally derived from naphthalene-1-yl-(naphthalene-1-yl) methanone with substitutions on either of the naphthalene rings to any extent, including, but not limited to, CB-13.

(7) Naphthoylpyrroles, which includes any compound structurally derived from 3-(1-naphthoyl)pyrrole by substitution at the nitrogen atom of the pyrrole ring by alkyl, haloalkyl, cyanoalkyl, hydroxyalkyl, alkenyl, cycloalkylmethyl, cycloalkylethyl, 1-(N-methyl-2-piperidinyl) methyl, 2-(4-morpholinyl)ethyl, or 1-N-methyl-2-pyrrolidinyl)methyl, 1-(N-methyl-3-morpholinyl)methyl, or (tetrahydropyran-4-yl)methyl group, whether or not further substituted in the pyrrole ring to any extent and whether or not substituted in the naphthyl ring to any extent, including, but not limited to, JWH-030, JWH-031, JWH-145, JWH-146, JWH-147, JWH-150, JWH-156, JWH-243, JWH-244, JWH-245, JWH-246, JWH-292, JWH-293, JWH-307, JWH-308, JWH-309, JWH-346, JWH-348, JWH-363, JWH-364, JWH-365, JWH-367, JWH-368, JWH-369, JWH-370, JWH-371, JWH-373, JWH-392.

(8) Naphthylmethylindenes, which includes any compound contain-

ing a naphthylideneindene structure or which is structurally derived from 1-(1-naphthylmethyl)indene with substitution at the 3-position of the indene ring by alkyl, haloalkyl, cyanoalkyl, hydroxyalkyl, alkenyl, cycloalkylmethyl, cycloalkylethyl, 1-(N-methyl-2-piperidinyl) methyl, 2-(4-morpholinyl)ethyl, or 1-(N-methyl-2-pyrrolidinyl)methyl, 1-(N-methyl-3-morpholinyl)methyl, or (tetrahydropyran-4-yl)methyl group, whether or not further substituted in the indene ring to any extent and whether or not substituted in the naphthyl ring to any extent, including, but not limited to, JWH-171, JWH-176, JWH-220.

(9) Naphthylmethylindoles, which includes any compound structurally derived from an H-indol-3-yl-(1-naphthyl) methane by substitution at the nitrogen atom of the indole ring by alkyl, haloalkyl, cyanoalkyl, hydroxyalkyl, alkenyl, cycloalkylmethyl, cycloalkylethyl, 1-(N-methyl-2-piperidinyl)methyl, 2-(4-morpholinyl)ethyl, or 1-(N-methyl-2-pyrrolidinyl)methyl, 1-(N-methyl-3-morpholinyl)methyl, or (tetrahydropyran-4-yl)methyl group, whether or not further substituted in the indole ring to any extent and whether or not substituted in the naphthyl ring to any extent, including, but not limited to, JWH-175, JWH-184, JWH-185, JWH-192, JWH-194, JWH-195, JWH-196, JWH-197, JWH-199.

(10) Phenylacetylindoles, which includes any compound structurally derived from 3-phenylacetylindole by substitution at the nitrogen atom of the indole ring with alkyl, haloalkyl, cyanoalkyl, hydroxyalkyl, alkenyl, cycloalkylmethyl, cycloalkylethyl, 1-(N-methyl-2-piperidinyl) methyl, 2-(4-morpholinyl)ethyl, or 1-N-methyl-2-pyrrolidinyl)methyl, 1-(N-methyl-3-morpholinyl)methyl, or (tetrahydropyran-4-yl)methyl group, whether or not further substituted in the indole ring to any extent and whether or not substituted in the phenyl ring to any extent, including, but not limited to, cannabipiperidiethanone, JWH-167, JWH-201, JWH-202, JWH-203, JWH-204, JWH-205, JWH-206, JWH-207, JWH-208, JWH-209, JWH-237, JWH-248, JWH-249, JWH-250, JWH-251, JWH-253, JWH-302, JWH-303, JWH-304, JWH-305, JWH-306, JWH-311, JWH-312, JWH-313, JWH-314, JWH-315, JWH-316, RCS-8.

(11) Quinolinylindolecarboxylates, which includes any compound structurally derived from quinolin-8-yl-1H-indole-3-carboxylate by substitution at the nitrogen atom of the indole ring with alkyl, haloalkyl, benzyl, halobenzyl, alkenyl, haloalkenyl, alkoxy, cyanoalkyl, hydroxyalkyl, cycloalkylmethyl, cycloalkylethyl, (N-methylpiperidin-2-yl)alkyl,

(4-tetrahydropyran)alkyl, or 2-(4-morpholinyl)alkyl, whether or not further substituted in the indole ring to any extent, whether or not substituted in the quinoline ring to any extent, including, but not limited to, BB-22, 5-Fluoro-PB-22, PB-22.

(12) Tetramethylcyclopropanoylindoles, which includes any compound structurally derived from 3-tetramethylcyclopropanoylindole, 3-(1-tetramethylcyclopropyl)indole, 3-(2,2,3,3-tetramethylcyclopropyl) indole or 3-(2,2,3,3-tetramethylcyclopropylcarbonyl)indole with substitution at the nitrogen atom of the indole ring by an alkyl, haloalkyl, cyanoalkyl, hydroxyalkyl, alkenyl, cycloalkylmethyl, cycloalkylethyl, 1-(N-methyl-2-piperidinyl)methyl, 2-(4-morpholinyl)ethyl, 1-(N-methyl-2-pyrrolidinyl)methyl, 1-(N-methyl-3-morpholinyl)methyl, or (tetrahydropyran-4-yl)methyl group whether or not further substituted in the indole ring to any extent and whether or not substituted in the tetramethylcyclopropanoyl ring to any extent, including, but not limited to, 5-bromo-UR-144, 5-chloro-UR-144, 5-fluoro-UR-144, A-796,260, A-834,735, AB-034, UR-144, XLR11.

(13) Tetramethylcyclopropane-thiazole carboxamides, which includes any compound structurally derived from 2,2,3,3-tetramethyl-N-(thiazol-2-ylidene)cyclopropanecarboxamide by substitution at the nitrogen atom of the thiazole ring by alkyl, haloalkyl, benzyl, halobenzyl, alkenyl, haloalkenyl, alkoxy, cyanoalkyl, hydroxyalkyl, cycloalkylmethyl, cycloalkylethyl, (N-methylpiperidin-2-yl)alkyl, (4-tetrahydropyran) alkyl, or 2-(4-morpholinyl)alkyl, whether or not further substituted in the thiazole ring to any extent, whether or not substituted in the tetramethylcyclopropyl ring to any extent, including, but not limited to, A-836,339.

(14) Unclassified synthetic cannabinoids, which includes all of the following:

(A) AM-087, (6aR,10aR)-3-(2-methyl-6-bromohex-2-yl)-6,6,9-trimethyl-6a,7,10,10a-tetrahydrobenzo[c]chromen-1-ol.

(B) AM-356, methanandamide, including (5Z,8Z,11Z,14Z)--[(1R)-2-hydroxy-1-methylethyl]icosa-5,8,11,14-tetraenamide and arachidonyl-1'-hydroxy-2'-propylamide.

(C) AM-411, (6aR,10aR)-3-(1-adamantyl)-6,6,9-trimethyl-6a,7,10,10a-tetrahydrobenzo[c]chromen-1-ol.

(D) AM-855, (4aR,12bR)-8-hexyl-2,5,5-trimethyl-1,4,4a,8,9,10,11,12b-octahydronaphtho[3,2-c]isochromen-12-ol.

(E) AM-905, (6aR,9R,10aR)-3-[(E)-hept-1-enyl]-9-(hydroxymethyl)-6,6-dimethyl-6a,7,8,9,10,10a-hexahydrobenzo[c]chromen-1-ol.

(F) AM-906, (6aR,9R,10aR)-3-[(Z)-hept-1-enyl]-9-(hydroxymethyl)-6,6-dimethyl-6a,7,8,9,10,10a-hexahydrobenzo[c]chromen-1-ol.

(G) AM-2389, (6aR,9R,10aR)-3-(1-hexyl-cyclobut-1-yl)-6a,7,8,9,10,10a-hexahydro-6,6-dimethyl-6H-dibenzo[b,d]pyran-1,9 diol.

(H) BAY 38-7271, (-)-(R)-3-(2-Hydroxymethylindanyl-4-o xy) phenyl-4,4,4-trifluorobutyl-1-sulfonate.

(I) CP 50,556-1, Levonantradol, including 9-hydroxy-6-methyl-3-[5-phenylpentan-2-yl]oxy-5,6,6a,7,8,9,10,10a-octahydrophenant hridin-1-yl]acetate; [(6S,6aR,9R, 10aR)-9-hydroxy-6-methyl-3-[(2R)-5-phenylpentan-2-yl]oxy-5,6,6a,7,8,9,10,10a-octahy-drophenanthridin-1-yl]acetate; and [9-hydroxy-6-methyl-3-[5-phenylpentan-2-yl]oxy-5,6,6a,7,8,9,10,10a-octahydrophenanthri-din-1-yl]acetate.

(J) HU-210, including (6aR,10aR)-9-(hydroxymethyl)-6,6-d imethyl-3-(2-methyloctan-2-yl)-6a,7,10,10a-tetrahydrobenzo[c] chromen-1-ol; [(6aR,10aR)-9-(hydroxymethyl)-6,6-dimethyl-3-(2-methyl octan-2-yl)-6a,7,10,10a-tetrahydrobenzo[c]chromen-1-o l and 1,1-Dimethylheptyl-11-hydroxytetrahydrocannabinol.

(K) HU-211, Dexanabinol, including (6aS, 10aS)-9-(hydroxy methyl)-6,6-dimethyl-3-(2-methyloctan-2-yl)-6a,7,10,10a-tetra-hydrobenzo[c]chromen-1-ol and (6aS, 10aS)-9-(hydroxy methyl)-6,6-dimethyl- 3-(2-methyloctan-2-yl)-6a,7,10,10a-tetrahydro-benzo[c]chromen-1-ol.

(L) HU-243, 3-dimethylheptyl-11-hydroxyhexahydrocannabinol.

(M) HU-308, [(91R,2R,5R)-2-[2,6-dimethoxy-4-(2-methyloctan-2- yl)phenyl]-7,7-dimethyl-4-bicyclo[3.1.1]hept-3-enyl]methanol.

(N) HU-331, 3-hydroxy-2-[(1R,6R)-3-methyl-6-(1-m ethylethenyl)-2-cyclohexen-1-yl]-5-pentyl-2,5-cyclohexadiene-1,4-dione.

(O) HU-336, (6aR,10aR)-6,6,9-trimethyl-3-pentyl-6a,7,10,10a-tetrahydro-1H-benzo[c]chromene-1,4(6H)-dione.

(P) JTE-907, N-(benzol[1,3]dioxol-5-ylmethyl)-7-methoxy-2-oxo-8-pentyloxy-1,2-dihydroquinoline-3-carboxamide.

(Q) JWH-051, ((6aR,10aR)-6,6-dimethyl-3-(2-methyloctan-2-yl)-6a,7,10,10a-tetrahydrobenzo[c]chromen-9-yl)methanol.

(R) JWH-057 (6aR,10aR)-3-(1,1-dimethylheptyl)-6a,7,10,10a-tetrahydro-6,6,9-trimethyl-6H-Dibenzo[b,d]pyran.

(S) JWH-133 (6aR,10aR)-3-(1,1-Dimethylbutyl)-6a,7,10,10a-tetrahydro -6,6,9-trimethyl-6H-dibenzo[b,d]pyran.

(T) JWH-359, (6aR,10aR)- 1-methoxy- 6,6,9-trimethyl- 3-[(2R)-1,1,2-trimethylbutyl]- 6a,7,10,10a-tetrahydrobenzo[c]chromene.

(U) URB-597 [3-(3-carbamoylphenyl)phenyl]-N-cyclohexylcarbamate.

(V) URB-602 [1,1'-Biphenyl]-3-yl-carbamic acid, cyclohexyl ester; OR cyclohexyl [1,1'-biphenyl]-3-ylcarbamate.

(W) URB-754 6-methyl-2-[(4-methylphenyl)amino]-4H-3,1-benzoxazin-4-one.

(X) URB-937 3'-carbamoyl-6-hydroxy-[1,1'-biphenyl]-3-yl cyclohexylcarbamate.

(Y) WIN 55,212-2, including (R)-(+)-[2,3-dihydro-5-methyl-3-(4-morpholinylmethyl)pyrrolo[1,2,3-de]-1,4-benzoxazin-6-yl]-1-napthalenylmethanone and [2,3-Dihydro-5-methyl-3-(4-morpholinylmethyl)pyrrolo[(1,2,3-de)-1,4-benzoxazin-6-yl]-1-napthalenylmethanone.

(d) The substances or analogs of substances identified in subdivision (c) may be lawfully obtained and used for bona fide research, instruction, or analysis if that possession and use does not violate federal law.

(e) As used in this section, "synthetic cannabinoid compound" does not include either of the following:

(1) Any substance for which there is an approved new drug application, as defined in Section 505 of the federal Food, Drug, and Cosmetic Act (21 U.S.C. Sec. 355) or which is generally recognized as safe and effective for use pursuant to Section 501, 502, and 503 of the federal Food, Drug, and Cosmetic Act and Title 21 of the Code of Federal Regulations.

(2) With respect to a particular person, any substance for which an exemption is in effect for investigational use for that person pursuant to Section 505 of the federal Food, Drug, and Cosmetic Act (21 U.S.C. Sec. 355), to the extent that the conduct with respect to that substance is pursuant to the exemption.

Health and Safety Code § 11358

(AUMA, Effective November 9, 2016.)

Every person who plants, cultivates, harvests, dries, or processes marijuana plants, or any part thereof, except as otherwise provided by law, shall be punished as follows:

(a) Every person under the age of 18 who plants, cultivates, harvests, dries, or processes any marijuana plants shall be punished in the same manner provided in paragraph (1) of subdivision (b) of section 11357.

(b) Every person at least 18 years of age but less than 21 years of age who plants, cultivates, harvests, dries, or processes not more than six living marijuana plants shall be guilty of an infraction and a fine of not more than one hundred dollars ($100).

(c) Every person 18 years of age or over who plants, cultivates, harvests, dries, or processes more than six living marijuana plants shall be punished by imprisonment in a county jail for a period of not more than six months or by a fine of not more than five hundred dollars ($500), or by both such fine and imprisonment.

(d) Notwithstanding subdivision (c), a person 18 years of age or over who plants, cultivates, harvests, dries, or processes more than six living marijuana plants, or any part thereof, except as otherwise provided by law, may be punished by imprisonment pursuant to subdivision (h) of Section 1170 of the Penal Code if:

(1) the person has one or more prior convictions for an offense specified

in clause (iv) of subparagraph (C) of paragraph (2) of subdivision (e) of Section 667 of the Penal Code or for an offense requiring registration pursuant to subdivision (c) of Section 290 of the Penal Code;

(2) the person has two or more prior convictions under subdivision (c); or (3) the offense resulted in any of the following:

(A) violation of Section 1052 of the Water Code relating to illegal diversion of water;

(B) violation of Section 13260, 13264, 13272, or 13387 of the Water Code relating to discharge of waste;

(C) violation of Fish and Game Code Section 5650 or Section 5652 of the Fish and Game Code relating to waters of the state;

(D) violation of Section 1602 of the Fish and Game Code relating to rivers, streams and lakes;

(E) violation of Section 374.8 of the Penal Code relating to hazardous substances or Sections 25189.5, 25189.6, or 25189.7 of the Health and Safety Code relating to hazardous waste;

(F) violation of Section 2080 of the Fish and Game Code relating to endangered and threatened species or Section 3513 of the Fish and Game Code relating to the Migratory Bird Treaty Act; or

(G) intentionally or with gross negligence causing substantial environmental harm to public lands or other public resources.

Health and Safety Code § 11359

(AUMA, Effective November 9, 2016.)

Every person who possesses for sale any marijuana, except as otherwise provided by law, shall be punished as follows:

(a) Every person under the age of 18 who possesses marijuana for sale shall be punished in the same manner provided in paragraph (1) of subdivision (b) of section 11357.

(b) Every person 18 years of age or over who possesses marijuana for sale shall be punished by imprisonment in a county jail for a period of not more than six months or by a fine of not more than five hundred dollars ($500), or by both such fine and imprisonment.

(c) Notwithstanding subdivision (b), a person 18 years of age or over who possesses marijuana for sale may be punished by imprisonment pursuant to subdivision (h) of Section 1170 of the Penal Code if:

(1) the person has one or more prior convictions for an offense specified in clause (iv) of subparagraph (C) of paragraph (2) of subdivision (e) of Section 667 of the Penal Code or for an offense requiring registration pursuant to subdivision (c) of Section 290 of the Penal Code;

(2) the person has two or more prior convictions under subdivision (b); or

(3) the offense occurred in connection with the knowing sale or attempted sale of marijuana to a person under the age of 18years.

(d) Notwithstanding subdivision (b), a person 21 years of age or over who possesses marijuana for sale may be punished by imprisonment pursuant to subdivision (h) of Section 1170 of the Penal Code if the offense involves knowingly hiring, employing, or using a person 20 years of age or younger in unlawfully cultivating, transporting, carrying, selling, offering to sell, giving away, preparing for sale, or peddling any marijuana.

Health and Safety Code § 11360

(AUMA, Effective November 9, 2016.)

(a) Except as otherwise provided by this section or as authorized by law, every person who transports, imports into this state, sells, furnishes, administers, or gives away, or offers to transport, import into this state, sell, furnish, administer, or give away, or attempts to import into this state or transport any marijuana shall be punished as follows:

(1) Persons under the age of 18 years shall be punished in the same manner as provided in paragraph (1) of subdivision (b) of section 11357.

(2) Persons 18 years of age or over shall be punished by imprisonment in a county jail for a period of not more than six months or by a fine of not more than five hundred dollars ($500), or by both such fine and imprisonment.

(3) Notwithstanding paragraph (2), a person 18 years of age or over may be punished by imprisonment pursuant to subdivision (h) of Section 1170 of the Penal Code for a period two, three, or four years if:

(A) the person has one or more prior convictions for an offense specified in clause (iv) of subparagraph (C) of paragraph (2) of subdivision (e) of Section 667 of the Penal Code or for an offense requiring registration pursuant to subdivision (c) of Section 290 of the Penal Code;

(B) the person has two or more prior convictions under paragraph (2);

(C) the offense involved the knowing sale, attempted sale, or the knowing offer to sell, furnish, administer or give away marijuana to a person under the age of 18 years; or

(D) the offense involved the import, offer to import; or attempted import into this state, or the transport for sale, offer to transport for sale, or attempted transport for sale out of this state, of more than 28.5 grams of marijuana or more than four grams of concentrated cannabis.

(b) Except as authorized by law, every person who gives away, offers to give away, transports, offers to transport, or attempts to transport not more than 28.5 grams of marijuana, other than concentrated cannabis, is guilty of an infraction and shall be punished by a fine of not more than one hundred dollars ($100). In any case in which a person is arrested for a violation of this subdivision and does not demand to be taken before a magistrate, such person shall be released by the arresting officer upon presentation of satisfactory evidence of identity and giving his or her written promise to appear in court, as provided in Section 853.6 of the Penal Code, and shall not be subjected to booking.

(c) For purposes of this section, "transport" means to transport for sale.

(d) This section does not preclude or limit prosecution for any aiding and abetting or conspiracy offenses.

Health & Safety Code § 11361

(Amended by Statute, Effective 1986.)

(a) Every person 18 years of age or over who hires, employs, or uses a minor in unlawfully transporting, carrying, selling, giving away, preparing for sale, or peddling any marijuana, who unlawfully sells, or offers to sell, any marijuana to a minor, or who furnishes, administers, or gives, or offers to furnish, administer, or give any marijuana to a minor under 14 years of age, or who induces a minor to use marijuana in violation of law shall be punished by imprisonment in the state prison for a period of three, five, or seven years.

(b) Every person 18 years of age or over who furnishes, administers, or gives, or offers to furnish, administer, or give, any marijuana to a minor 14 years of age or older shall be punished by imprisonment in the state prison for a period of three, four, or five years.

Health and Safety Code § 11361.1

(AUMA, Effective November 9, 2016.)

(a) The drug education and counseling requirements under sections 11357, 11358, 11359, and 11360 shall be:

> (1) mandatory, unless the court finds that such drug education or counseling is unnecessary for the person, or that a drug education or counseling program is unavailable;

> (2) free to participants, and the drug education provide at least four hours of group discussion or instruction based on science and evidence-based principles and practices specific to the use and abuse of marijuana and other controlled substances.

(b) For good cause, the court may grant an extension of time not to exceed 30 days for a person to complete the drug education and counseling required under sections 11357, 11358, 11359, and 11360.

Health and Safety Code § 11361.5

(Amended by Statute, Effective June 30, 1993. AUMA Amends section (a), Effective November 9, 2016.)

(a) Records of any court of this state, any public or private agency that provides services upon referral under Section 1000.2 of the Penal Code, or of any state agency pertaining to the arrest or conviction of any person for a violation of Section 11357 or subdivision (b) of Section 11360, or pertaining to the arrest or conviction of any person under the age of 18 for a violation of any provision of this article except Section 11357.5, shall not be kept beyond two years from the date of the conviction, or from the date of the arrest if there was no conviction, except with respect to a violation of subdivision (d) of Section 11357, or any other violation by a person under the age of 18 occurring upon the grounds of, or within, any school providing instruction in kindergarten or any of grades 1 through 12 during hours the school is open for classes or school-related programs, the records shall be retained until the offender attains the age of 18 years at which time the records shall be destroyed as provided in this section. Any court or agency having custody of the records, including the statewide criminal databases, shall provide for the timely destruction of the records in accordance with subdivision (c), and such records must also be purged from the statewide criminal databases. As used in this subdivision, "records pertaining to the arrest or conviction" shall include records of arrests resulting in the criminal proceeding and records relating to other offenses charged in the accusatory pleading, whether defendant was acquitted or charges were dismissed. The two-year period beyond which records shall not be kept pursuant to this subdivision shall not apply to any person who is, at the time at which this subdivision would otherwise require record destruction, incarcerated for an offense subject to this subdivision. For such persons, the two-year period shall begin to run from the date the person is released from custody. The requirements of this subdivision do not apply to records of any conviction occurring prior to January 1, 1976, or records of any arrest not followed by a conviction occurring prior to that date, or records of any arrest for an offense specified in subdivision (c) of Section 1192.7, or subdivision (c) of Section 667.5 of the Penal Code.

(b) This subdivision applies only to records of convictions and arrests not followed by conviction occurring prior to January 1, 1976, for any of the following offenses:

(1) Any violation of Section 11357 or a statutory predecessor thereof.

(2) Unlawful possession of a device, contrivance, instrument, or paraphernalia used for unlawfully smoking marijuana, in violation of Section 11364, as it existed prior to January 1, 1976, or a statutory predecessor thereof.

(3) Unlawful visitation or presence in a room or place in which marijuana is being unlawfully smoked or used, in violation of Section 11365, as it existed prior to January 1, 1976, or a statutory predecessor thereof.

(4) Unlawfully using or being under the influence of marijuana, in violation of Section 11550, as it existed prior to January 1, 1976, or a statutory predecessor thereof.

Any person subject to an arrest or conviction for those offenses may apply to the Department of Justice for destruction of records pertaining to the arrest or conviction if two or more years have elapsed since the date of the conviction, or since the date of the arrest if not followed by a conviction. The application shall be submitted upon a form supplied by the Department of Justice and shall be accompanied by a fee, which shall be established by the department in an amount which will defray the cost of administering this subdivision and costs incurred by the state under subdivision (c), but which shall not exceed thirty-seven dollars and fifty cents ($37.50). The application form may be made available at every local police or sheriff's department and from the Department of Justice and may require that information which the department determines is necessary for purposes of identification.

The department may request, but not require, the applicant to include a self-administered fingerprint upon the application. If the department is unable to sufficiently identify the applicant for purposes of this subdivision without the fingerprint or without additional fingerprints, it shall so notify the applicant and shall request the applicant to submit any fingerprints which may be required to effect identification, including a complete set if necessary, or, alternatively, to abandon the application and request a refund of all or a portion of the fee submitted with the application, as provided in this section. If the applicant fails or refuses to submit fingerprints in accordance with the department's request within a reasonable time which shall be established by the department, or if the applicant requests a refund of the fee, the department shall promptly mail a refund to the applicant at the address specified in the application or at any other address which may be specified by the applicant. However, if the department has notified the applicant that election to abandon the application will result in forfeiture of a specified amount which is a portion of the fee, the department may retain a portion of the fee which the department determines will defray the actual costs of processing the application, provided the amount of the portion retained shall not exceed ten dollars ($10).

Upon receipt of a sufficient application, the Department of Justice shall destroy records of the department, if any, pertaining to the arrest or conviction in the manner prescribed by subdivision (c) and shall notify the Federal Bureau of Investigation, the law enforcement agency which arrested the applicant, and, if the applicant was convicted, the probation department which investigated the applicant and the Department of Motor Vehicles, of the application.

(c) Destruction of records of arrest or conviction pursuant to subdivision (a) or (b) shall be accomplished by permanent obliteration of all entries or notations upon the records pertaining to the arrest or conviction, and the record shall be prepared again so that it appears that the arrest or conviction never occurred. However, where (1) the only entries upon the record pertain to the arrest or conviction and (2) the record can be destroyed without necessarily effecting the destruction of other records, then the document constituting the record shall be physically destroyed.

(d) Notwithstanding subdivision (a) or (b), written transcriptions of oral testimony in court proceedings and published judicial appellate reports are not subject to this section. Additionally, no records shall be destroyed pursuant to subdivision (a) if the defendant or a codefendant has filed a civil action against the peace officers or law enforcement jurisdiction which made the arrest or instituted the prosecution and if the agency which is the custodian of those records has received a certified copy of the complaint in the civil action, until the civil action has finally been resolved. Immediately following the final resolution of the civil action, records subject to subdivision (a) shall be destroyed pursuant to subdivision (c) if more than two years have elapsed from the date of the conviction or arrest without conviction.

Health and Safety Code § 11361.7

(Added by Statute, Effective 1976.)

(a) Any record subject to destruction or permanent obliteration pursuant to Section 11361.5, or more than two years of age, or a record of a conviction for an offense specified in subdivision (a) or (b) of Section 11361.5 which became final more than two years previously, shall not be considered to be accurate, relevant, timely, or complete for any purposes by any agency or person. The provisions of this subdivision shall be applicable for purposes of the

Privacy Act of 1974 (5 U.S.C. Section 552a) to the fullest extent permissible by law, whenever any information or record subject to destruction or permanent obliteration under Section 11361.5 was obtained by any state agency, local public agency, or any public or private agency that provides services upon referral under Section 1000.2 of the Penal Code, and is thereafter shared with or disseminated to any agency of the federal government.

(b) No public agency shall alter, amend, assess, condition, deny, limit, postpone, qualify, revoke, surcharge, or suspend any certificate, franchise, incident, interest, license, opportunity, permit, privilege, right, or title of any person because of an arrest or conviction for an offense specified in subdivision (a) or (b) of Section 11361.5, or because of the facts or events leading to such an arrest or conviction, on or after the date the records of such arrest or conviction are required to be destroyed by subdivision (a) of Section 11361.5, or two years from the date of such conviction or arrest without conviction with respect to arrests and convictions occurring prior to January 1, 1976. As used in this subdivision, "public agency" includes, but is not limited to, any state, county, city and county, city, public or constitutional corporation or entity, district, local or regional political subdivision, or any department, division, bureau, office, board, commission or other agency thereof.

(c) Any person arrested or convicted for an offense specified in subdivision (a) or (b) of Section 11361.5 may, two years from the date of such a conviction, or from the date of the arrest if there was no conviction, indicate in response to any question concerning his prior criminal record that he was not arrested or convicted for such offense.

(d) The provisions of this section shall be applicable without regard to whether destruction or obliteration of records has actually been implemented pursuant to Section 11361.5.

Health and Safety Code § 11361.8

(AUMA, Effective November 9, 2016.)

(a) A person currently serving a sentence for a conviction, whether by trial or by open or negotiated plea, who would not have been guilty of an offense or who would have been guilty of a lesser offense under the Control, Regulate and Tax Adult Use of Marijuana Act had that Act been in effect at the time of the offense may petition for a recall or dismissal of sentence before the trial court that entered the judgment of conviction in his or her case to request resentencing or dismissal in accordance with Sections 11357, 11358, 11359,

11360, 11362.1, 11362.2, 11362.3, and 11362. 4 as those sections have been amended or added by this Act.

(b) Upon receiving a petition under subdivision (a), the court shall presume the petitioner satisfies the criteria in subdivision (a) unless the party opposing the petition proves by clear and convincing evidence that the petitioner does not satisfy the criteria. If the petitioner satisfies the criteria in subdivision (a), the court shall grant the petition to recall the sentence or dismiss the sentence because it is legally invalid unless the court determines that granting the petition would pose an unreasonable risk of danger to public safety.

> (1) In exercising its discretion, the court may consider, but shall not be limited to evidence provided for in subdivision (b) of Section 1170.18 of the Penal Code.

> (2) As used in this section, "unreasonable risk of danger to public safety" has the same meaning as provided in subdivision (c) of Section 1170.18 of the Penal Code.

(c) A person who is serving a sentence and resentenced pursuant to subdivision (b) shall be given credit for any time already served and shall be subject to supervision for one year following completion of his or her time in custody or shall be subject to whatever supervision time he or she would have otherwise been subject to after release, whichever is shorter, unless the court, in its discretion, as part of its resentencing order, releases the person from supervision. Such person is subject to parole supervision under Penal Code Section 3000.08 or post-release community supervision under subdivision (a) of Section 3451 of the Penal Code by the designated agency and the jurisdiction of the court in the county in which the offender is released or resides, or in which an alleged violation of supervision has occurred, for the purpose of hearing petitions to revoke supervision and impose a term of custody.

(d) Under no circumstances may resentencing under this section result in the imposition of a term longer than the original sentence, or the reinstatement of charges dismissed pursuant to a negotiated plea agreement.

(e) A person who has completed his or her sentence for a conviction under Sections 11357, 11358, 11359, and 11360, whether by trial or open or negotiated plea, who would not have been guilty of an offense or who would have been guilty of a lesser offense under the Control, Regulate and Tax Adult Use of Marijuana Act had that Act been in effect at the time of the offense, may file an application before the trial court that entered the judgment of conviction in his or her case to have the conviction dismissed and sealed because the prior conviction is now legally invalid or redesignated as a misdemeanor or infraction in accordance with Sections 11357, 11358, 11359, 11360, 11362.1, 11362.2, 11362.3, and 11362.4 as those sections have been amended or added by this Act.

(f) The court shall presume the petitioner satisfies the criteria in subdivision (e) unless the party opposing the application proves by clear and convincing evidence that the petitioner does not satisfy the criteria in subdivision (e). Once the applicant satisfies the criteria in subdivision (e), the court shall redesignate the conviction as a misdemeanor or infraction or dismiss and seal the conviction as legally invalid as now established under the Control, Regulate and Tax Adult Use of Marijuana Act.

(g) Unless requested by the applicant, no hearing is necessary to grant or deny an application filed under subdivision (e).

(h) Any felony conviction that is recalled and resentenced under subdivision (b) or designated as a misdemeanor or infraction under subdivision (f) shall be considered a misdemeanor or infraction for all purposes. Any misdemeanor conviction that is recalled and resentenced under subdivision (b) or designated as an infraction under subdivision (f) shall be considered an infraction for all purposes.

(i) If the court that originally sentenced the petitioner is not available, the presiding judge shall designate another judge to rule on the petition or application.

(j) Nothing in this section is intended to diminish or abrogate any rights or remedies otherwise available to the petitioner or applicant.

(k) Nothing in this and related sections is intended to diminish or abrogate the finality of judgments in any case not falling within the purview of the Control, Regulate and Tax Adult Use of Marijuana Act.

(l) A resentencing hearing ordered under this act shall constitute a ''post-conviction release proceeding'' under paragraph (7) of subdivision (b) of Section 28 of Article I of the California Constitution (Marsy's Law).

(m) The provisions of this section shall apply equally to juvenile delinquency adjudications and dispositions under Section 602 of the Welfare and Institutions Code if the juvenile would not have been guilty of an offense or would have been guilty of a lesser offense under the Control, Regulate and Tax Adult Use of Marijuana Act.

(n) The Judicial Council shall promulgate and make available all necessary forms to enable the filing of the petitions and applications provided in this section.

Health and Safety Code § 11362

(Amended by Statute, Effective April 4, 2011, and Operative October 1, 2011.)

As used in this article "felony offense," and offense "punishable as a felony" refer to an offense prior to July 1, 2011, for which the law prescribes imprisonment in the state prison, or for an offense on or after July 1, 2011, imprisonment in either the state prison or pursuant to subdivision (h) of Section 1170 of the Penal Code, as either an alternative or the sole penalty, regardless of the sentence the particular defendant received.

Health and Safety Code § 11362.1

(AUMA, Effective November 9, 2016.)

(a) Subject to Sections 11362.2, 11362.3, 11362.4, and 11362.45, but notwithstanding any other provision of law, it shall be lawful under state and local law, and shall not be a violation of state or local law, for persons 21 years of age or older to:

>(1) Possess, process, transport, purchase, obtain, or give away to persons 21 years of age or older without any compensation whatsoever, not more than 28.5 grams of marijuana not in the form of concentrated cannabis;

>(2) Possess, process, transport, purchase, obtain, or give away to persons 21 years of age or older without any compensation whatsoever, not more than eight grams of marijuana in the form of concentrated cannabis, including as contained in marijuana products;

>(3) Possess, plant, cultivate, harvest, dry, or process not more than six living marijuana plants and possess the marijuana produced by the plants;

>(4) Smoke or ingest marijuana or marijuana products; and

>(5) Possess, transport, purchase, obtain, use, manufacture, or give away marijuana accessories to persons 21 years of age or older without any

compensation whatsoever.

(b) Paragraph (5) of subdivision (a) is intended to meet the requirements of subdivision (f) of Section 863 a/Title 21 of the United States Code (21 US.C. § 863(f)) by authorizing, under state law, any person in compliance with this section to manufacture, possess, or distribute marijuana accessories.

(c) Marijuana and marijuana products involved in any way with conduct deemed lawful by this section are not contraband nor subject to seizure, and no conduct deemed lawful by this section shall constitute the basis for detention, search, or arrest.

Health and Safety Code § 11362.2

(AUMA, Effective November 9, 2016.)

(a) Personal cultivation of marijuana under paragraph (3) of subdivision (a) of Section 11362.1 is subject to the following restrictions:

(1) A person shall plant, cultivate, harvest, dry, or process plants in accordance with local ordinances, if any, adopted in accordance with subdivision (b) of this section.

(2) The living plants and any marijuana produced by the plants in excess of 28.5 grams are kept within the person's private residence, or upon the grounds of that private residence (e.g., in an outdoor garden area), are in a locked space, and are not visible by normal unaided vision from a public place.

(3) Not more than six living plants may be planted, cultivated, harvested, dried, or processed within a single private residence, or upon the grounds of that private residence, at one time.

(b)(l) A city, county, or city and county may enact and enforce reasonable regulations to reasonably regulate the actions and conduct in paragraph (3) of subdivision (a) of Section 11362.1.

(2) Notwithstanding paragraph (1), no city, county, or city and county may completely prohibit persons engaging in the actions and conduct under paragraph (3) of subdivision (a) of Section 11362.1 inside a private residence, or inside an accessory structure to a private residence located upon the grounds of a private residence that is fully enclosed and secure.

(3) Notwithstanding paragraph (3) of subdivision (a) of Section 11362.1, a

city, county, or city and county may completely prohibit persons from engaging in actions and conduct under paragraph (3) of subdivision (a) of Section 11362.1 outdoors upon the grounds of a private residence.

(4) Paragraph (3) of this subdivision shall become inoperable upon a determination by the California Attorney General that nonmedical use of marijuana is lawful in the State of California under federal law, and an act taken by a city, county, or city and county under paragraph (3) shall be deemed repealed upon the date of such determination by the California Attorney General.

(5) For purposes of this section, "private residence" means a house, an apartment unit, a mobile home, or other similar dwelling.

Health and Safety Code § 11362.3

(AUMA, Effective November 9, 2016.)

(a) Nothing in Section 11362.1 shall be construed to permit any person to:

(1) Smoke or ingest marijuana or marijuana products in any public place, except in accordance with Section 26200 of the Business and Professions Code.

(2) Smoke marijuana or marijuana products in a location where smoking tobacco is prohibited.

(3) Smoke marijuana or marijuana products within 1,000 feet of a school, day care center, or youth center while children are present at such a school, day care center, or youth center, except in or upon the grounds of a private residence or in accordance with Section 26200 of the Business and Professions Code or Chapter 3.5 of Division 8 of the Business and Professions Code and only if such smoking is not detectable by others on the grounds of such a school, day care center, or youth center while children are present.

(4) Possess an open container or open package of marijuana or marijuana products while driving, operating, or riding in the passenger seat or compartment of a motor vehicle, boat, vessel, aircraft, or other vehicle used for transportation.

(5) Possess, smoke or ingest marijuana or marijuana products in or upon the grounds of a school, day care center, or youth center while children are present.

(6) Manufacture concentrated cannabis using a volatile solvent, unless done in accordance with a license under Chapter 3.5 of Division 8 or Division 10 of the Business and Professions Code.

(7) Smoke or ingest marijuana or marijuana products while driving, operating a motor vehicle, boat, vessel, aircraft, or other vehicle used for transportation.

(8) Smoke or ingest marijuana or marijuana products while riding in the passenger seat or compartment of a motor vehicle, boat, vessel, aircraft, or other vehicle used for transportation except as permitted on a motor vehicle, boat, vessel, aircraft, or other vehicle used for transportation that is operated in accordance with Section 26200 of the Business and Professions Code and while no persons under the age of 21 years are present.

(b) For purposes of this section, "day care center" has the same meaning as in Section 1596.76.

(c) For purposes of this section, "smoke" means to inhale, exhale, burn, or carry any lighted or heated device or pipe, or any other lighted or heated marijuana or marijuana product intended for inhalation, whether natural or synthetic, in any manner or in any form. "Smoke" includes the use of an electronic smoking device that creates an aerosol or vapor, in any manner or in any form, or the use of any oral smoking device for the purpose of circumventing the prohibition of smoking in a place.

(d) For purposes of this section, "volatile solvent" means volatile organic compounds, including:

(1) explosive gases, such as Butane, Propane, Xylene, Styrene, Gasoline, Kerosene, 02 or H2; and

(2) dangerous poisons, toxins, or carcinogens, such as Methanol, Iso-propyl Alcohol, Methylene Chloride, Acetone, Benzene, Toluene, and Tri-chloro-ethylene.

(e) For purposes of this section, "youth center" has the same meaning as in Section 11353.1.

(f) Nothing in this section shall be construed or interpreted to amend, repeal, affect, restrict, or preempt laws pertaining to the Compassionate Use Act of 1996.

Health and Safety Code § 11362.4

(AUMA, Effective November 9, 2016.)

(a) A person who engages in the conduct described in paragraph (1) of subdivision (a) of Section 11362.3 is guilty of an infraction punishable by no more than a one hundred dollar ($100) fine; provided, however, that persons under the age of 18 shall instead be required to complete four hours of a drug education program or counseling, and up to 10 hours of community service, over a period not to exceed 60 days once the drug education program or counseling and community service opportunity are made available to the person.

(b) A person who engages in the conduct described in paragraphs (2) through (4) of subdivision (a) of Section 11362. 3 shall be guilty of an infraction punishable by no more than a two hundred and fifty dollar ($250) fine, unless such activity is otherwise permitted by state and local law; provided, however, that persons under the age of 18 shall instead be required to complete four hours of drug education or counseling, and up to 20 hours of community service, over a period not to exceed 90 days once the drug education program or counseling and community service opportunity are made available to the person.

(c) A person who engages in the conduct described in paragraph (5) of subdivision (a) of Section 11362.3 shall be subject to the same punishment as provided under subdivisions (c) or (d) of Section 11357.

(d) A person who engages in the conduct described in paragraph (6) of subdivision (a) of Section 11362. 3 shall be subject to punishment under Section 113 79. 6.

(e) A person who violates the restrictions in subdivision (a) of Section 11362.2 is guilty of an infraction punishable by no more than a two hundred and fifty dollar ($250) fine.

(f) Notwithstanding subdivision (e), a person under the age of 18 who violates the restrictions in subdivision (a) of Section 11362.2 shall be punished under subdivision (a) of Section 11358.

(g)(1) The drug education program or counseling hours required by this section shall be mandatory unless the court makes a finding that such a program or counseling is unnecessary for the person or that a drug education program or counseling is unavailable.

(g)(2) The drug education program required by this section for persons under the age of 18 must be free to participants and provide at least four hours of group discussion or instruction based on science and evidence-based principles and practices specific to the use and abuse of marijuana and other controlled substances.

(h) Upon a finding of good cause, the court may extend the time for a person to complete the drug education or counseling, and community service required under this section.

Health and Safety Code § 11362.45

(AUMA, Effective November 9, 2016.)

Nothing in section 11362.1 shall be construed or interpreted to amend, repeal, affect, restrict, or preempt:

(a) Laws making it unlawful to drive or operate a vehicle, boat, vessel, or aircraft, while smoking, ingesting, or impaired by, marijuana or marijuana products, including, but not limited to, subdivision (e) of Section 23152 of the Vehicle Code, or the penalties prescribed for violating those laws.

(b) Laws prohibiting the sale, administering, furnishing, or giving away of marijuana, marijuana products, or marijuana accessories, or the offering to sell, administer, furnish, or give away marijuana, marijuana products, or marijuana accessories to a person younger than 21 years of age.

(c) Laws prohibiting a person younger than 21 years of age from engaging in any of the actions or conduct otherwise permitted under Section 11362.1.

(d) Laws pertaining to smoking or ingesting marijuana or marijuana products on the grounds of, or within, any facility or institution under the jurisdiction of the Department of Corrections and Rehabilitation or the Division of Juvenile Justice, or on the grounds of, or within, any other facility or institution referenced in Section 4573 of the Penal Code.

(e) Laws providing that it would constitute negligence or professional malpractice to undertake any task while impaired from smoking or ingesting marijuana or marijuana products.

(f) The rights and obligations of public and private employers to maintain a drug and alcohol free workplace or require an employer to permit or accommodate the use, consumption, possession, transfer, display, transportation, sale, or growth of marijuana in the workplace, or affect the ability of employers to have policies prohibiting the use of marijuana by employees and prospective employees, or prevent employers from complying with state or federal law.

(g) The ability of a state or local government agency to prohibit or restrict any of the actions or conduct otherwise permitted under Section 11362.1 within a building owned, leased, or occupied by the state or local government agency.

(h) The ability of an individual or private entity to prohibit or restrict any of the actions or conduct otherwise permitted under Section 11362.1 on the individual's or entity's privately owned property.

(i) Laws pertaining to the Compassionate Use Act of 1996.

Health And Safety Code § 11362.5

(Proposition 215, Effective November 5, 1996.)

SEC. 1.

(a) This section shall be known and may be cited as the Compassionate Use Act of 1996.

(b)(1) The people of the State of California hereby find and declare that the purposes of the Compassionate Use Act of 1996 are as follows:

(A) To ensure that seriously ill Californians have the right to obtain and use marijuana for medical purposes where that medical use is deemed appropriate and has been recommended by a physician who has determined that the person's health would benefit from the use of marijuana in the treatment of cancer, anorexia, AIDS, chronic pain, spasticity, glaucoma, arthritis, migraine, or any other illness for which marijuana provides relief.

(B) To ensure that patients and their primary caregivers who obtain and use marijuana for medical purposes upon the recommendation of a physician are not subject to criminal prosecution or sanction.

(C) To encourage the federal and state governments to implement a plan to provide for the safe and affordable distribution of marijuana to all patients in medical need of marijuana.

(b)(2) Nothing in this section shall be construed to supersede legislation prohibiting persons from engaging in conduct that endangers others, nor to condone the diversion of marijuana for nonmedical purposes.

(c) Notwithstanding any other provision of law, no physician in this state shall be punished, or denied any right or privilege, for having recommended marijuana to a patient for medical purposes.

(d) Section 11357, relating to the possession of marijuana, and Section 11358, relating to the cultivation of marijuana, shall not apply to a patient, or to a patient's primary caregiver, who possesses or cultivates marijuana for the personal medical purposes of the patient upon the written or oral recommendation or approval of a physician.

(e) For the purposes of this section, ''primary caregiver'' means the individual designated by the person exempted under this section who has consistently assumed responsibility for the housing, health, or safety of that person.

SEC. 2.

If any provision of this measure or the application thereof to any person or circumstance is held invalid, that invalidity shall not affect other provisions or applications of the measure that can be given effect without the invalid provision or application, and to this end the provisions of this measure are severable.

Heath and Safety Code § 11362.7

(SB 420, Effective January 1, 2004.)

For purposes of this article, the following definitions shall apply:

(a) "Attending physician" means an individual who possesses a license in good standing to practice medicine or osteopathy issued by the Medical Board of California or the Osteopathic Medical Board of California and who has taken responsibility for an aspect of the medical care, treatment, diagnosis, counseling, or referral of a patient and who has conducted a medical examination of that patient before recording in the patient's medical record the physician's assessment of whether the patient has a serious medical condition and whether the medical use of marijuana is appropriate.

(b) "Department" means the State Department of Health Services.

(c) "Person with an identification card" means an individual who is a qualified patient who has applied for and received a valid identification card pursuant to this article.

(d) "Primary caregiver" means the individual, designated by a qualified patient or by a person with an identification card, who has consistently assumed responsibility for the housing, health, or safety of that patient or person, and may include any of the following:

(1) In any case in which a qualified patient or person with an identification card receives medical care or supportive services, or both, from a clinic licensed pursuant to Chapter 1 (commencing with Section 1200) of Division 2, a health care facility licensed pursuant to Chapter 2 (commencing with Section 1250) of Division 2, a residential care facility for persons with chronic life-threatening illness licensed pursuant to Chapter 3.01 (commencing with Section 1568.01) of Division 2, a residential care facility for the elderly licensed pursuant to Chapter 3.2 (commencing with Section 1569) of Division 2, a hospice, or a home health agency licensed pursuant to Chapter 8 (commencing with Section 1725) of Division 2, the owner or operator, or no more than three employees who are designated by the owner or operator, of the clinic, facility, hospice, or home health agency, if designated as a primary caregiver by that qualified patient or person with an identification card.

(2) An individual who has been designated as a primary caregiver by more than one qualified patient or person with an identification card, if every qualified patient or person with an identification card who has designated that individual as a primary caregiver resides in the same city or county as the primary caregiver.

(3) An individual who has been designated as a primary caregiver by a qualified patient or person with an identification card who resides in a city or county other than that of the primary caregiver, if the individual has not been designated as a primary caregiver by any other qualified patient or person with an identification card.

(e) A primary caregiver shall be at least 18 years of age, unless the primary caregiver is the parent of a minor child who is a qualified patient or a person with an identification card or the primary caregiver is a person otherwise entitled to make medical decisions under state law pursuant to Sections 6922, 7002, 7050, or 7120 of the Family Code.

(f) "Qualified patient" means a person who is entitled to the protections of Section 11362.5, but who does not have an identification card issued pursuant to this article.

(g) "Identification card" means a document issued by the State Department of Health Services that document identifies a person authorized to engage in the medical use of marijuana and the person's designated primary caregiver, if any.

(h) "Serious medical condition" means all of the following medical conditions:

(1) Acquired immune deficiency syndrome (AIDS).

(2) Anorexia.

(3) Arthritis.

(4) Cachexia.

(5) Cancer.

(6) Chronic pain.

(7) Glaucoma.

(8) Migraine.

(9) Persistent muscle spasms, including, but not limited to, spasms associated with multiple sclerosis.

(10) Seizures, including, but not limited to, seizures associated with epilepsy.

(11) Severe nausea.

(12) Any other chronic or persistent medical symptom that either:

(A) Substantially limits the ability of the person to conduct one or more major life activities as defined in the Americans with Disabilities Act of 1990 (Public Law 101-336).

(B) If not alleviated, may cause serious harm to the patient's safety or physical or mental health.

(i) "Written documentation" means accurate reproductions of those portions of a patient's medical records that have been created by the attending physician, that contain the information required by paragraph (2) of subdivision (a) of Section 11362.715, and that the patient may submit to a county health department or the county's designee as part of an application for an identification card.

Health and Safety Code § 11362.71

(SB 420, Effective January 1, 2004.)

(a)(1) The department shall establish and maintain a voluntary program for the issuance of identification cards to qualified patients who satisfy the requirements of this article and voluntarily apply to the identification card program.

(2) The department shall establish and maintain a 24-hour, toll-free telephone number that will enable state and local law enforcement officers to have immediate access to information necessary to verify the validity of an identification card issued by the department, until a cost-effective Internet Web-based system can be developed for this purpose.

(b) Every county health department, or the county's designee, shall do all of the following:

(1) Provide applications upon request to individuals seeking to join the identification card program.

(2) Receive and process completed applications in accordance with Section 11362.72.

(3) Maintain records of identification card programs.

(4) Utilize protocols developed by the department pursuant to paragraph (1) of subdivision (d).

(5) Issue identification cards developed by the department to approved applicants and designated primary caregivers.

(c) The county board of supervisors may designate another health-related governmental or nongovernmental entity or organization to perform the functions described in subdivision (b), except for an entity or organization that cultivates or distributes marijuana.

(d) The department shall develop all of the following:

(1) Protocols that shall be used by a county health department or the county's designee to implement the responsibilities described in subdivision (b), including, but not limited to, protocols to confirm the accuracy of information contained in an application and to protect the confidentiality of program records.

(2) Application forms that shall be issued to requesting applicants.

(3) An identification card that identifies a person authorized to engage in the medical use of marijuana and an identification card that identifies the person's designated primary caregiver, if any. The two identification cards developed pursuant to this paragraph shall be easily distinguishable from each other.

(e) No person or designated primary caregiver in possession of a valid identification card shall be subject to arrest for possession, transportation, delivery, or cultivation of medical marijuana in an amount established pursuant to this article, unless there is reasonable cause to believe that the information contained in the card is false or falsified, the card has been obtained by means of fraud, or the person is otherwise in violation of the provisions of this article.

(f) It shall not be necessary for a person to obtain an identification card in order to claim the protections of Section 11362.5.

Health and Safety Code § 11362.712

(AUMA, Effective November 9, 2016.)

(a) Commencing on January 1, 2018, a qualified patient must possess a physician's recommendation that complies with Article 25 (commencing with Section 2525) of Chapter 5 of Division 2 of the Business and Professions Code. Failure to comply with this requirement shall not, however, affect any of the protections provided to patients or their primary caregivers by Section 11362.5.

(b) A county health department or the county's designee shall develop protocols to ensure that, commencing upon January 1, 2018, all identification cards issued pursuant to Section 11362.71 are supported by a physician's recommendation that complies with Article 25 (commencing with Section 2525) of Chapter 5 of Division 2 of the Business and Professions Code.

Health and Safety Code § 11362.713

(AUMA, Effective November 9, 2016.)

(a) Information identifying the names, addresses, or social security numbers of patients, their medical conditions, or the names of their primary caregivers, received and contained in the records of the Department of Public Health and by any county public health department are hereby deemed "medical information" within the meaning of the Confidentiality of Medical Information Act (Civil Code§ 56, et seq.) and shall not be disclosed by the Department or by any county public health department except in accordance with the restrictions on disclosure of individually identifiable information under the Confidentiality of Medical Information Act.

(b) Within 24 hours of receiving any request to disclose the name, address, or social security number of a patient, their medical condition, or the name of their primary caregiver, the Department of Public Health or any county public health agency shall contact the patient and inform the patient of the request and if the request was made in writing, a copy of the request.

(c) Notwithstanding Section 56.10 of the Civil Code, neither the Department of Public Health, nor any county public health agency, shall disclose, nor shall they be ordered by agency or court to disclose, the names, addresses, or social security numbers of patients, their medical conditions, or the names of their primary caregivers, sooner than the 10th day after which the patient whose records are sought to be disclosed has been contacted.

(d) No identification card application system or database used or maintained by the Department of Public Health or by any county department of public health or the county's designee as provided in Section 11362.71 shall contain any personal information of any qualified patient, including but not limited to, the patient's name, address, social security number, medical conditions, or the names of their primary caregivers. Such an application system or database may only contain a unique user identification number, and when that number is entered, the only information that may be provided is whether the card is valid or invalid.

Health and Safety Code § 11362.715

(SB 420, Effective January 1, 2004.)

(a) A person who seeks an identification card shall pay the fee, as provided in Section 11362.755, and provide all of the following to the county health department or the county's designee on a form developed and provided by the department:

(1) The name of the person, and proof of his or her residency within the county.

(2) Written documentation by the attending physician in the person's medical records stating that the person has been diagnosed with a serious medical condition and that the medical use of marijuana is appropriate.

(3) The name, office address, office telephone number, and California medical license number of the person's attending physician.

(4) The name and the duties of the primary caregiver.

(5) A government-issued photo identification card of the person and of the designated primary caregiver, if any. If the applicant is a person under 18 years of age, a certified copy of a birth certificate shall be deemed sufficient proof of identity.

(b) If the person applying for an identification card lacks the capacity to make medical decisions, the application may be made by the person's legal representative, including, but not limited to, any of the following:

(1) A conservator with authority to make medical decisions.

(2) An attorney-in-fact under a durable power of attorney for health care or surrogate decision maker authorized under another advanced health care directive.

(3) Any other individual authorized by statutory or decisional law to make medical decisions for the person.

(c) The legal representative described in subdivision (b) may also designate in the application an individual, including himself or herself, to serve as a primary caregiver for the person, provided that the individual meets the definition of a primary caregiver.

(d) The person or legal representative submitting the written information and documentation described in subdivision (a) shall retain a copy thereof.

Health and safety Code § 11362.72

(SB 420, Effective January 1, 2004.)

(a) Within 30 days of receipt of an application for an identification card, a county health department or the county's designee shall do all of the following:

> (1) For purposes of processing the application, verify that the information contained in the application is accurate. If the person is less than 18 years of age, the county health department or its designee shall also contact the parent with legal authority to make medical decisions, legal guardian, or other person or entity with legal authority to make medical decisions, to verify the information.

> (2) Verify with the Medical Board of California or the Osteopathic Medical Board of California that the attending physician has a license in good standing to practice medicine or osteopathy in the state.

> (3) Contact the attending physician by facsimile, telephone, or mail to confirm that the medical records submitted by the patient are a true and correct copy of those contained in the physician's office records. When contacted by a county health department or the county' s designee, the attending physician shall confirm or deny that the contents of the medical records are accurate.

> (4) Take a photograph or otherwise obtain an electronically transmissible image of the applicant and of the designated primary caregiver, if any.

> (5) Approve or deny the application. If an applicant who meets the requirements of Section 11362.715 can establish that an identification card is needed on an emergency basis, the county or its designee shall issue a temporary identification card that shall be valid for 30 days from the date of issuance. The county, or its designee, may extend the temporary identification card for no more than 30 days at a time, so long as the applicant continues to meet the requirements of this paragraph.

(b) If the county health department or the county's designee approves the application, it shall, within 24 hours, or by the end of the next working day of approving the application, electronically transmit the following information to the department:

(1) A unique user identification number of the applicant.

(2) The date of expiration of the identification card.

(3) The name and telephone number of the county health department or the county's designee that has approved the application.

(c) The county health department or the county's designee shall issue an identification card to the applicant and to his or her designated primary caregiver, if any, within five working days of approving the application.

(d) In any case involving an incomplete application, the applicant shall assume responsibility for rectifying the deficiency. The county shall have 14 days from the receipt of information from the applicant pursuant to this subdivision to approve or deny the application.

Health and Safety Code § 11362.735

(SB 420, Effective January 1, 2004.)

(a) An identification card issued by the county health department shall be serially numbered and shall contain all of the following:

(1) A unique user identification number of the cardholder.

(2) The date of expiration of the identification card.

(3) The name and telephone number of the county health department or the county's designee that has approved the application.

(4) A 24-hour, toll-free telephone number, to be maintained by the department, that will enable state and local law enforcement officers to have immediate access to information necessary to verify the validity of the card.

(5) Photo identification of the cardholder.

(b) A separate identification card shall be issued to the person's designated primary caregiver, if any, and shall include a photo identification of the caregiver.

Health and Safety Code § 11362.74

(SB 420, Effective January 1, 2004.)

(a) The county health department or the county's designee may deny an application only for any of the following reasons:

(1) The applicant did not provide the information required by Section 11362.715, and upon notice of the deficiency pursuant to subdivision (d) of Section 11362.72, did not provide the information within 30 days.

(2) The county health department or the county's designee determines that the information provided was false.

(3) The applicant does not meet the criteria set forth in this article.

(b) Any person whose application has been denied pursuant to subdivision (a) may not reapply for six months from the date of denial unless otherwise authorized by the county health department or the county's designee or by a court of competent jurisdiction.

(c) Any person whose application has been denied pursuant to subdivision (a) may appeal that decision to the department. The county health department or the county's designee shall make available a telephone number or address to which the denied applicant can direct an appeal.

Health and Safety Code § 11362.745

(SB 420, Effective January 1, 2004.)

(a) An identification card shall be valid for a period of one year.

(b) Upon annual renewal of an identification card, the county health department or its designee shall verify all new information and may verify any other information that has not changed.

(c) The county health department or the county's designee shall transmit its determination of approval or denial of a renewal to the department.

Health and Safety Code § 11362.755

(AUMA, Effective November 9, 2016.)

(a) Each county health department or the county's designee may charge a fee for all costs incurred by the county or the county's designee for administering the program pursuant to this article.

(b) In no event shall the amount of the fee charged by a county health department exceed $100 per application or renewal.

(c) Upon satisfactory proof of participation and eligibility in the Medi-Cal program, a Medi-Cal beneficiary shall receive a 50 percent reduction in the fees established pursuant to this section.

(d) Upon satisfactory proof that a qualified patient, or the legal guardian of a qualified patient under the age of 18, is a medically indigent adult who is eligible for and participates in the County Medical Services Program, the fee established pursuant to this section shall be waived.

(e) In the event the fees charged and collected by a county health department are not sufficient to pay for the administrative costs incurred in discharging the county health department's duties with respect to the mandatory identification card system, the Legislature, upon request by the county health department, shall reimburse the county health department for those reasonable administrative costs in excess of the fees charged and collected by the county health department.

Health and Safety Code § 11362.76

(SB 420, Effective January 1, 2004.)

(a) A person who possesses an identification card shall:

(1) Within seven days, notify the county health department or the county's designee of any change in the person's attending physician or designated primary caregiver, if any.

(2) Annually submit to the county health department or the county' s designee the following:

(A) Updated written documentation of the person's serious medical condition.

(B) The name and duties of the person's designated primary caregiver, if any, for the forthcoming year.

(b) If a person who possesses an identification card fails to comply with this section, the card shall be deemed expired. If an identification card expires, the identification card of any designated primary caregiver of the person shall also expire.

(c) If the designated primary caregiver has been changed, the previous primary caregiver shall return his or her identification card to the department or to the county health department or the county's designee.

(d) If the owner or operator or an employee of the owner or operator of a provider has been designated as a primary caregiver pursuant to paragraph (1) of subdivision (d) of Section 11362.7, of the qualified patient or person with an identification card, the owner or operator shall notify the county health department or the county's designee, pursuant to Section 11362.715, if a change in the designated primary caregiver has occurred.

Health and Safety Code § 11362.765

(SB 420, Effective January 1, 2004.)

(a) Subject to the requirements of this article, the individuals specified in subdivision (b) shall not be subject, on that sole basis, to criminal liability under Section 11357, 11358, 11359, 11360, 11366, 11366.5, or 11570.

However, nothing in this section shall authorize the individual to smoke or otherwise consume marijuana unless otherwise authorized by this article, nor shall anything in this section authorize any individual or group to cultivate or distribute marijuana for profit.

(b) Subdivision (a) shall apply to all of the following:

(1) A qualified patient or a person with an identification card who transports or processes marijuana for his or her own personal medical use.

(2) A designated primary caregiver who transports, processes, administers, delivers, or gives away marijuana for medical purposes, in amounts not exceeding those established in subdivision (a) of Section 11362.77, only to the qualified patient of the primary caregiver, or to the person with an identification card who has designated the individual as a pri-

mary caregiver.

(3) Any individual who provides assistance to a qualified patient or a person with an identification card, or his or her designated primary caregiver, in administering medical marijuana to the qualified patient or person or acquiring the skills necessary to cultivate or administer marijuana for medical purposes to the qualified patient or person.

(c) A primary caregiver who receives compensation for actual expenses, including reasonable compensation incurred for services provided to an eligible qualified patient or person with an identification card to enable that person to use marijuana under this article, or for payment for out-of-pocket expenses incurred in providing those services, or both, shall not, on the sole basis of that fact, be subject to prosecution or punishment under Section 11359 or 11360.

Health and Safety Code § 11362.768

(Added by Statute, Effective January 1, 2011.)

(a) This section shall apply to individuals specified in subdivision (b) of Section 11362.765.

(b) No medical marijuana cooperative, collective, dispensary, operator, establishment, or provider who possesses, cultivates, or distributes medical marijuana pursuant to this article shall be located within a 600-foot radius of a school.

(c) The distance specified in this section shall be the horizontal distance measured in a straight line from the property line of the school to the closest property line of the lot on which the medical marijuana cooperative, collective, dispensary, operator, establishment, or provider is to be located without regard to intervening structures.

(d) This section shall not apply to a medical marijuana cooperative, collective, dispensary, operator, establishment, or provider that is also a licensed residential medical or elder care facility.

(e) This section shall apply only to a medical marijuana cooperative, collective, dispensary, operator, establishment, or provider that is authorized by law to possess, cultivate, or distribute medical marijuana and that has a storefront or mobile retail outlet which ordinarily requires a local business license.

(f) Nothing in this section shall prohibit a city, county, or city and county from adopting ordinances or policies that further restrict the location or establishment of a medical marijuana cooperative, collective, dispensary, operator, establishment, or provider.

(g) Nothing in this section shall preempt local ordinances, adopted prior to January 1, 2011, that regulate the location or establishment of a medical marijuana cooperative, collective, dispensary, operator, establishment, or provider.

(h) For the purposes of this section, "school" means any public or private school providing instruction in kindergarten or grades 1 to 12, inclusive, but does not include any private school in which education is primarily conducted in private homes.

Health and Safety Code § 11362.769

(MCRSA- SB 837, Effective June 27, 2016.)

Indoor and outdoor medical cannabis cultivation shall be conducted in accordance with state and local laws. State agencies, including, but not limited to, the Department of Food and Agriculture, the State Board of Forestry and Fire Protection, the Department of Fish and Wildlife, the State Water Resources Control Board, the California regional water quality control boards, and traditional state law enforcement agencies shall address environmental impacts of medical cannabis cultivation and shall coordinate, when appropriate, with cities and counties and their law enforcement agencies in enforcement efforts.

Health and Safety Code § 11362.77

(SB 420, Effective January 1, 2004.)

(a) A qualified patient or primary caregiver may possess no more than eight ounces of dried marijuana per qualified patient. In addition, a qualified patient or primary caregiver may also maintain no more than six mature or 12 immature marijuana plants per qualified patient.

(b) If a qualified patient or primary caregiver has a doctor's recommendation that this quantity does not meet the qualified patient' s medical needs, the qualified patient or primary caregiver may possess an amount of marijuana consistent with the patient's needs.

(c) Counties and cities may retain or enact medical marijuana guidelines allowing qualified patients or primary caregivers to exceed the state limits set forth in subdivision (a).

(d) Only the dried mature processed flowers of female cannabis plant or the plant conversion shall be considered when determining allowable quantities of marijuana under this section.

(e) The Attorney General may recommend modifications to the possession or cultivation limits set forth in this section. These recommendations, if any, shall be made to the Legislature no later than December 1, 2005, and may be made only after public comment and consultation with interested organizations, including, but not limited to, patients, health care professionals, researchers, law enforcement, and local governments. Any recommended modification shall be consistent with the intent of this article and shall be based on currently available scientific research.

(f) A qualified patient or a person holding a valid identification card, or the designated primary caregiver of that qualified patient or person, may possess amounts of marijuana consistent with this article.

Health and Safety Code § 11362.775

**(MCRSA- SB 837, Effective June 27, 2016- January 1, 2017 when Amended by AB 2679.)

(a) Subject to subdivision (b), qualified patients, persons with valid identification cards, and the designated primary caregivers of qualified patients and persons with identification cards, who associate within the State of California in order collectively or cooperatively to cultivate cannabis for medical purposes, shall not solely on the basis of that fact be subject to state criminal sanctions under Section 11357, 11358, 11359, 11360, 11366, 11366.5, or 11570.

(b) This section shall remain in effect only until one year after the Bureau of Medical Cannabis Regulation posts a notice on its Internet Web site that the licensing authorities have commenced issuing licenses pursuant to the Medical Cannabis Regulation and Safety Act (Chapter 3.5 (commencing with Section 19300) of Division 8 of the Business and Professions Code).

(c) This section is repealed one year after the date upon which the notice is posted pursuant to subdivision (b).

Health and Safety Code § 11362.775

**(MCRSA- Amended by AB 2679, Effective January 1, 2017.)

(a) Subject to subdivision (d), qualified patients, persons with valid identification cards, and the designated primary caregivers of qualified patients and persons with identification cards, who associate within the State of California in order collectively or cooperatively to cultivate cannabis for medical purposes, shall not solely on the basis of that fact be subject to state criminal sanctions under Section 11357, 11358, 11359, 11360, 11366, 11366.5, or 11570.

(b) A collective or cooperative that operates pursuant to this section and manufactures medical cannabis products shall not, solely on the basis of that fact, be subject to state criminal sanctions under Section 11379.6 if the collective or cooperative abides by all of the following requirements:

(1) The collective or cooperative does either or both of the following:

(A) Utilizes only manufacturing processes that are either solventless or that employ only nonflammable, nontoxic solvents that are generally recognized as safe pursuant to the federal Food, Drug, and Cosmetic Act (21 U.S.C. Sec. 301 et seq.).

(B) Utilizes only manufacturing processes that use solvents exclusively within a closed-loop system that meets all of the following requirements:

(i) The system uses only solvents that are generally recognized as safe pursuant to the federal Food, Drug, and Cosmetic Act (21 U.S.C. Sec. 301 et seq.).

(ii) The system is designed to recapture and contain solvents during the manufacturing process, and otherwise prevent the off-gassing of solvents into the ambient atmosphere to mitigate the risks of ignition and explosion during the manufacturing process.

(iii) A licensed engineer certifies that the system was commercially manufactured, safe for its intended use, and built to codes of recognized and generally accepted good engineering practices, including, but not limited to, the American Society of Mechanical Engineers (ASME), the American National

Standards Institute (ANSI), Underwriters Laboratories (UL), the American Society for Testing and Materials (ASTM), or OSHA Nationally Recognized Testing Laboratories (NRTLs).

(iv) The system has a certification document that contains the signature and stamp of a professional engineer and the serial number of the extraction unit being certified.

(2) The collective or cooperative receives and maintains approval from the local fire official for the closed-loop system, other equipment, the extraction operation, and the facility.

(3) The collective or cooperative meets required fire, safety, and building code requirements in one or more of the following:

(A) The California Fire Code.

(B) The National Fire Protection Association (NFPA) standards.

(C) International Building Code (IBC).

(D) The International Fire Code (IFC).

(E) Other applicable standards, including complying with all applicable fire, safety, and building codes in processing, handling, and storage of solvents or gasses.

(4) The collective or cooperative is in possession of a valid seller's permit issued by the State Board of Equalization.

(5) The collective or cooperative is in possession of a valid local license, permit, or other authorization specific to the manufacturing of medical cannabis products, and in compliance with any additional conditions imposed by the city or county issuing the local license, permit, or other authorization.

(c) For purposes of this section, "manufacturing" means compounding, converting, producing, deriving, processing, or preparing, either directly or indirectly by chemical extraction or independently by means of chemical synthesis, medical cannabis products.

(d) This section shall remain in effect only until one year after the Bureau of Medical Cannabis Regulation posts a notice on its Internet Web site that the licensing authorities have commenced issuing licenses pursuant to the Medical Cannabis Regulation and Safety Act (Chapter 3.5 (commencing with Section

19300) of Division 8 of the Business and Professions Code).

(e) This section is repealed one year after the date upon which the notice is posted pursuant to subdivision (d).

Health and Safety Code § 11362.777

(MCRSA- SB 837, Effective June 27, 2016.)

(a) The Department of Food and Agriculture shall establish a Medical Cannabis Cultivation Program to be administered by the secretary and, except as specified in subdivision (c), shall administer this section as it pertains to the commercial cultivation of medical cannabis. For purposes of this section and Chapter 3.5 (commencing with Section 19300) of Division 8 of the Business and Professions Code, medical cannabis is an agricultural product.

(b) (1) A person or entity shall not cultivate medical cannabis without first obtaining both of the following:

(A) A license, permit, or other entitlement, specifically permitting cultivation pursuant to these provisions, from the city, county, or city and county in which the cultivation will occur.

(B) A state license issued by the department pursuant to this section.

(2) A person or entity shall not submit an application for a state license pursuant to this section unless that person or entity has received a license, permit, or other entitlement, specifically permitting cultivation pursuant to these provisions, from the city, county, or city and county in which the cultivation will occur.

(3) A person or entity shall not submit an application for a state license pursuant to this section if the proposed cultivation of cannabis will violate the provisions of any local ordinance or regulation, or if medical cannabis is prohibited by the city, county, or city and county in which the cultivation is proposed to occur, either expressly or otherwise under principles of permissive zoning.

(c) (1) Except as otherwise specified in this subdivision, and without limiting any other local regulation, a city, county, or city and county, through its current or future land use regulations or ordinance, may issue or deny a permit to cultivate medical cannabis pursuant to this section. A city, county, or city and county may inspect the intended cultivation site for suitability before issuing a permit. After the city, county, or city and county has approved a permit, the applicant shall apply for a state medical cannabis cultivation license from the department. A locally issued cultivation permit shall only become active upon licensing by the department and receiving final local approval. A person shall not cultivate medical cannabis before obtaining both a permit from the city, county, or city and county and a state medical cannabis cultivation license from the department.

(2) A city, county, or city and county that issues or denies conditional licenses to cultivate medical cannabis pursuant to this section shall notify the department in a manner prescribed by the secretary.

(3) A city, county, or city and county's locally issued conditional permit requirements must be at least as stringent as the department's state licensing requirements.

(d) (1) The secretary may prescribe, adopt, and enforce regulations relating to the implementation, administration, and enforcement of this part, including, but not limited to, applicant requirements, collections, reporting, refunds, and appeals.

(2) The secretary may prescribe, adopt, and enforce any emergency regulations as necessary to implement this part. Any emergency regulation prescribed, adopted, or enforced pursuant to this section shall be adopted in accordance with Chapter 3.5 (commencing with Section 11340) of Part 1 of Division 3 of Title 2 of the Government Code, and, for purposes of that chapter, including Section 11349.6 of the Government Code, the adoption of the regulation is an emergency and shall be considered by the Office of Administrative Law as necessary for the immediate preservation of the public peace, health and safety, and general welfare.

(3) The secretary may enter into a cooperative agreement with a county agricultural commissioner to carry out the provisions of this chapter, including, but not limited to, administration, investigations, inspections, licensing and assistance pertaining to the cultivation of medical cannabis. Compensation under the cooperative agreement shall be paid from assessments and fees collected and deposited pursuant to this chapter and shall provide reimbursement to the county agricultural commissioner for associated costs.

(e) (1) The department, in consultation with, but not limited to, the Bureau of Medical Cannabis Regulation, the State Water Resources Control Board, and the Department of Fish and Wildlife, shall implement a unique identification program for medical cannabis. In implementing the program, the department shall consider issues, including, but not limited to, water use and environmental impacts. In implementing the program, the department shall ensure compliance with Section 19332.2 of the Business and Professions Code.

(2) The department shall establish a program for the identification of permitted medical cannabis plants at a cultivation site during the cultivation period. The unique identifier shall be attached at the base of each plant. A unique identifier, such as, but not limited to, a zip tie, shall be issued for each medical cannabis plant.

(A) Unique identifiers will only be issued to those persons appropriately licensed by this section.

(B) Information associated with the assigned unique identifier and licensee shall be included in the trace and track program specified in Section 19335 of the Business and Professions Code.

(C) The department may charge a fee to cover the reasonable costs of issuing the unique identifier and monitoring, tracking, and inspecting each medical cannabis plant.

(D) The department may promulgate regulations to implement this section.

(3) The department shall take adequate steps to establish protections against fraudulent unique identifiers and limit illegal diversion of unique identifiers to unlicensed persons.

(f) (1) A city, county, or city and county that issues or denies licenses, permits, or other entitlements to cultivate medical cannabis pursuant to this section shall notify the department in a manner prescribed by the secretary.

(2) Unique identifiers and associated identifying information administered by a city, county, or city and county shall adhere to the requirements set by the department and be the equivalent to those administered by the department.

(g) This section does not apply to a qualified patient cultivating cannabis pursuant to Section 11362.5 if the area he or she uses to cultivate cannabis does not exceed 100 square feet and he or she cultivates cannabis for his or her personal medical use and does not sell, distribute, donate, or provide cannabis to any other person or entity. This section does not apply to a primary caregiver cultivating cannabis pursuant to Section 11362.5 if the area he or she uses to cultivate cannabis does not exceed 500 square feet and he or she cultivates cannabis exclusively for the personal medical use of no more than five specified qualified patients for whom he or she is the primary caregiver within the meaning of Section 11362.7 and does not receive remuneration for these activities, except for compensation provided in full compliance with subdivision (c) of Section 11362.765. For purposes of this section, the area used to cultivate cannabis shall be measured by the aggregate area of vegetative growth of live cannabis plants on the premises. Exemption from the requirements of this section does not limit or prevent a city, county, or city and county from exercising its police authority under Section 7 of Article XI of the California Constitution.

Health and Safety Code § 11362.78

(SB 420, Effective January 1, 2004.)

A state or local law enforcement agency or officer shall not refuse to accept an identification card issued by the department unless the state or local law enforcement agency or officer has reasonable cause to believe that the information contained in the card is false or fraudulent, or the card is being used fraudulently.

Health and Safety Code § 11362.785

(SB 420, Effective January 1, 2004.)

(a) Nothing in this article shall require any accommodation of any medical use of marijuana on the property or premises of any place of employment or during the hours of employment or on the property or premises of any jail, correctional facility, or other type of penal institution in which prisoners reside or persons under arrest are detained.

(b) Notwithstanding subdivision (a), a person shall not be prohibited or prevented from obtaining and submitting the written information and documentation necessary to apply for an identification card on the basis that the person is incarcerated in a jail, correctional facility, or other penal institution in which prisoners reside or persons under arrest are detained.

(c) Nothing in this article shall prohibit a jail, correctional facility, or other penal institution in which prisoners reside or persons under arrest are detained, from permitting a prisoner or a person under arrest who has an identification card, to use marijuana for medical purposes under circumstances that will not endanger the health or safety of other prisoners or the security of the facility.

(d) Nothing in this article shall require a governmental, private, or any other health insurance provider or health care service plan to be liable for any claim for reimbursement for the medical use of marijuana.

Health and Safety Code § 11362.79

(SB 420, Effective January 1, 2004.)

Nothing in this article shall authorize a qualified patient or person with an identification card to engage in the smoking of medical marijuana under any of the following circumstances:

(a) In any place where smoking is prohibited by law.

(b) In or within 1,000 feet of the grounds of a school, recreation center, or youth center, unless the medical use occurs within a residence.

(c) On a school bus.

(d) While in a motor vehicle that is being operated.

(e) While operating a boat.

Health and Safety Code § 11362.795

(SB 420, Effective January 1, 2004.)

(a)(1) Any criminal defendant who is eligible to use marijuana pursuant to Section 11362.5 may request that the court confirm that he or she is allowed to use medical marijuana while he or she is on probation or released on bail.

(2) The court's decision and the reasons for the decision shall be stated on the record and an entry stating those reasons shall be made in the minutes of the court.

(3) During the period of probation or release on bail, if a physician recommends that the probationer or defendant use medical marijuana, the probationer or defendant may request a modification of the conditions of probation or bail to authorize the use of medical marijuana.

(4) The court's consideration of the modification request authorized by this subdivision shall comply with the requirements of this section.

(b)(1) Any person who is to be released on parole from a jail, state prison, school, road camp, or other state or local institution of confinement and who is eligible to use medical marijuana pursuant to Section 11362.5 may request that he or she be allowed to use medical marijuana during the period he or she is released on parole. A parolee's written conditions of parole shall reflect whether or not a request for a modification of the conditions of his or her parole to use medical marijuana was made, and whether the request was granted or denied.

(2) During the period of the parole, where a physician recommends that the parolee use medical marijuana, the parolee may request a modification of the conditions of the parole to authorize the use of medical marijuana.

(3) Any parolee whose request to use medical marijuana while on parole was denied may pursue an administrative appeal of the decision. Any decision on the appeal shall be in writing and shall reflect the reasons for the decision.

(4) The administrative consideration of the modification request authorized by this subdivision shall comply with the requirements of this section.

Health and Safety Code § 11362.8

(SB 420, Effective January 1, 2004.)

No professional licensing board may impose a civil penalty or take other disciplinary action against a licensee based solely on the fact that the licensee has performed acts that are necessary or appropriate to carry out the licensee's role as a designated primary caregiver to a person who is a qualified patient or who possesses a lawful identification card issued pursuant to Section 11362.72.

However, this section shall not apply to acts performed by a physician relating to the discussion or recommendation of the medical use of marijuana to a patient. These discussions or recommendations, or both, shall be governed by Section 11362.5.

Health and Safey Code § 11362.81

(SB 420, Effective January 1, 2004.)

(a) A person specified in subdivision (b) shall be subject to the following penalties:

(1) For the first offense, imprisonment in the county jail for no more than six months or a fine not to exceed one thousand dollars ($1,000), or both.

(2) For a second or subsequent offense, imprisonment in the county jail for no more than one year, or a fine not to exceed one thousand dollars ($1,000), or both.

(b) Subdivision (a) applies to any of the following:

(1) A person who fraudulently represents a medical condition or fraudulently provides any material misinformation to a physician, county health department or the county's designee, or state or local law enforcement agency or officer, for the purpose of falsely obtaining an identification card.

(2) A person who steals or fraudulently uses any person's identification card in order to acquire, possess, cultivate, transport, use, produce, or distribute marijuana.

(3) A person who counterfeits, tampers with, or fraudulently produces an identification card.

(4) A person who breaches the confidentiality requirements of this article to information provided to, or contained in the records of, the department or of a county health department or the county's designee pertaining to an identification card program.

(c) In addition to the penalties prescribed in subdivision (a), any person described in subdivision (b) may be precluded from attempting to obtain, or obtaining or using, an identification card for a period of up to six months at the discretion of the court.

(d) In addition to the requirements of this article, the Attorney General shall develop and adopt appropriate guidelines to ensure the security and nondiversion of marijuana grown for medical use by patients qualified under the Compassionate Use Act of 1996.

Health and Safety Code § 11362.82

(SB 420, Effective January 1, 2004.)

If any section, subdivision, sentence, clause, phrase, or portion of this article is for any reason held invalid or unconstitutional by any court of competent jurisdiction, that portion shall be deemed a separate, distinct, and independent provision, and that holding shall not affect the validity of the remaining portion thereof.

Health and Safety Code § 11362.83

(SB 420, Effective January 1, 2004.)

Nothing in this article shall prevent a city or other local governing body from adopting and enforcing any of the following:

(a) Adopting local ordinances that regulate the location, operation, or establishment of a medical marijuana cooperative or collective.

(b) The civil and criminal enforcement of local ordinances described in subdivision (a).

(c) Enacting other laws consistent with this article.

Health and Safety Code § 11362.84

(AUMA, Effective November 9, 2016.)

The status and conduct of a qualified patient who acts in accordance with the Compassionate Use Act shall not, by itself, be used to restrict or abridge custodial or parental rights to minor children in any action or proceeding under the jurisdiction of family or juvenile court.

Health and Safety Code § 11362.85

(AUMA, Effective November 9, 2016.)

Upon a determination by the California Attorney General that the federal schedule of controlled substances has been amended to reclassify or declassify marijuana, the Legislature may amend or repeal the provisions of the Health and Safety Code, as necessary, to conform state law to such changes in federal law.

Health and Safety Code § 11362.9

**(SB 420, Effective January 1, 2004- January 1, 2017 when Amended by AB 2679.)

(a)(1) It is the intent of the Legislature that the state commission objective scientific research by the premier research institute of the world, the University of California, regarding the efficacy and safety of administering marijuana as part of medical treatment. If the Regents of the University of California, by appropriate resolution, accept this responsibility, the University of California shall create a program, to be known as the California Marijuana Research Program.

(2) The program shall develop and conduct studies intended to ascertain the general medical safety and efficacy of marijuana and, if found valuable, shall develop medical guidelines for the appropriate administration and use of marijuana.

(b) The program may immediately solicit proposals for research projects to be included in the marijuana studies. Program requirements to be used when evaluating responses to its solicitation for proposals, shall include, but not be limited to, all of the following:

(1) Proposals shall demonstrate the use of key personnel, including clinicians or scientists and support personnel, who are prepared to develop a program of research regarding marijuana's general medical efficacy and safety.

(2) Proposals shall contain procedures for outreach to patients with various medical conditions who may be suitable participants in research on marijuana.

(3) Proposals shall contain provisions for a patient registry.

(4) Proposals shall contain provisions for an information system that is designed to record information about possible study participants, investigators, and clinicians, and deposit and analyze data that accrues as part of clinical trials.

(5) Proposals shall contain protocols suitable for research on marijuana, addressing patients diagnosed with the acquired immunodeficiency syndrome (AIDS) or the human immunodeficiency virus (HIV), cancer, glaucoma, or seizures or muscle spasms associated with a chronic, debilitating condition. The proposal may also include research on other serious illnesses, provided that resources are available and medical information justifies the research.

(6) Proposals shall demonstrate the use of a specimen laboratory capa-

ble of housing plasma, urine, and other specimens necessary to study the concentration of cannabinoids in various tissues, as well as housing specimens for studies of toxic effects of marijuana.

(7) Proposals shall demonstrate the use of a laboratory capable of analyzing marijuana, provided to the program under this section, for purity and cannabinoid content and the capacity to detect contaminants.

(c) In order to ensure objectivity in evaluating proposals, the program shall use a peer review process that is modeled on the process used by the National Institutes of Health, and that guards against funding research that is biased in favor of or against particular outcomes. Peer reviewers shall be selected for their expertise in the scientific substance and methods of the proposed research, and their lack of bias or conflict of interest regarding the applicants or the topic of an approach taken in the proposed research. Peer reviewers shall judge research proposals on several criteria, foremost among which shall be both of the following:

(1) The scientific merit of the research plan, including whether the research design and experimental procedures are potentially biased for or against a particular outcome.

(2) Researchers' expertise in the scientific substance and methods of the proposed research, and their lack of bias or conflict of interest regarding the topic of, and the approach taken in, the proposed research.

(d) If the program is administered by the Regents of the University of California, any grant research proposals approved by the program shall also require review and approval by the research advisory panel.

(e) It is the intent of the Legislature that the program be established as follows:

(1) The program shall be located at one or more University of California campuses that have a core of faculty experienced in organizing multidisciplinary scientific endeavors and, in particular, strong experience in clinical trials involving psychopharmacologic agents. The campuses at which research under the auspices of the program is to take place shall accommodate the administrative offices, including the director of the program, as well as a data management unit, and facilities for storage of specimens.

(2) When awarding grants under this section, the program shall utilize

principles and parameters of the other well-tested statewide research programs administered by the University of California, modeled after programs administered by the National Institutes of Health, including peer review evaluation of the scientific merit of applications.

(3) The scientific and clinical operations of the program shall occur, partly at University of California campuses, and partly at other post-secondary institutions, that have clinicians or scientists with expertise to conduct the required studies. Criteria for selection of research locations shall include the elements listed in subdivision (b) and, additionally, shall give particular weight to the organizational plan, leadership qualities of the program director, and plans to involve investigators and patient populations from multiple sites.

(4) The funds received by the program shall be allocated to various research studies in accordance with a scientific plan developed by the Scientific Advisory Council. As the first wave of studies is completed, it is anticipated that the program will receive requests for funding of additional studies. These requests shall be reviewed by the Scientific Advisory Council.

(5) The size, scope, and number of studies funded shall be commensurate with the amount of appropriated and available program funding.

(f) All personnel involved in implementing approved proposals shall be authorized as required by Section 11604.

(g) Studies conducted pursuant to this section shall include the greatest amount of new scientific research possible on the medical uses of, and medical hazards associated with, marijuana. The program shall consult with the Research Advisory Panel analogous agencies in other states, and appropriate federal agencies in an attempt to avoid duplicative research and the wasting of research dollars.

(h) The program shall make every effort to recruit qualified patients and qualified physicians from throughout the state.

(i) The marijuana studies shall employ state-of-the-art research methodologies.

(j) The program shall ensure that all marijuana used in the studies is of the appropriate medical quality and shall be obtained from the National Institute on Drug Abuse or any other federal agency designated to supply marijuana for authorized research. If these federal agencies fail to provide a supply of adequate quality and quantity within six months of the effective date of this section, the Attorney General shall provide an adequate supply pursuant to Section 11478.

(k) The program may review, approve, or incorporate studies and research by independent groups presenting scientifically valid protocols for medical research, regardless of whether the areas of study are being researched by the committee.

(l) (1) To enhance understanding of the efficacy and adverse effects of marijuana as a pharmacological agent, the program shall conduct focused controlled clinical trials on the usefulness of marijuana in patients diagnosed with AIDS or HIV, cancer, glaucoma, or seizures or muscle spasms associated with a chronic, debilitating condition. The program may add research on other serious illnesses, provided that resources are available and medical information justifies the research. The studies shall focus on comparisons of both the efficacy and safety of methods of administering the drug to patients, including inhalational, tinctural, and oral, evaluate possible uses of marijuana as a primary or adjunctive treatment, and develop further information on optimal dosage, timing, mode of administration, and variations in the effects of different cannabinoids and varieties of marijuana.

(2) The program shall examine the safety of marijuana in patients with various medical disorders, including marijuana's interaction with other drugs, relative safety of inhalation versus oral forms, and the effects on mental function in medically ill persons.

(3) The program shall be limited to providing for objective scientific research to ascertain the efficacy and safety of marijuana as part of medical treatment, and should not be construed as encouraging or sanctioning the social or recreational use of marijuana.

(m) (1) Subject to paragraph (2), the program shall, prior to any approving proposals, seek to obtain research protocol guidelines from the National Institutes of Health and shall, if the National Institutes of Health issues research protocol guidelines, comply with those guidelines.

(2) If, after a reasonable period of time of not less than six months and not more than a year has elapsed from the date the program seeks to obtain guidelines pursuant to paragraph (1), no guidelines have been approved, the program may proceed using the research protocol guidelines it develops.

(n) In order to maximize the scope and size of the marijuana studies, the program may do any of the following:

(1) Solicit, apply for, and accept funds from foundations, private individuals, and all other funding sources that can be used to expand the scope or timeframe of the marijuana studies that are authorized under this section. The program shall not expend more than 5 percent of its General Fund allocation in efforts to obtain money from outside sources.

(2) Include within the scope of the marijuana studies other marijuana research projects that are independently funded and that meet the requirements set forth in subdivisions (a) to (c), inclusive. In no case shall the program accept any funds that are offered with any conditions other than that the funds be used to study the efficacy and safety of marijuana as part of medical treatment. Any donor shall be advised that funds given for purposes of this section will be used to study both the possible benefits and detriments of marijuana and that he or she will have no control over the use of these funds.

(o) (1) Within six months of the effective date of this section, the program shall report to the Legislature, the Governor, and the Attorney General on the progress of the marijuana studies.

(2) Thereafter, the program shall issue a report to the Legislature every six months detailing the progress of the studies. The interim reports required under this paragraph shall include, but not be limited to, data on all of the following:

(A) The names and number of diseases or conditions under study.

(B) The number of patients enrolled in each study by disease.

(C) Any scientifically valid preliminary findings.

(p) If the Regents of the University of California implement this section, the President of the University of California shall appoint a multidisciplinary Scientific Advisory Council, not to exceed 15 members, to provide policy guidance in the creation and implementation of the program. Members shall be chosen on the basis of scientific expertise. Members of the council shall serve on a voluntary basis, with reimbursement for expenses incurred in the course of their participation. The members shall be reimbursed for travel and other necessary expenses incurred in their performance of the duties of the council.

(q) No more than 10 percent of the total funds appropriated may be used for all aspects of the administration of this section.

(r) This section shall be implemented only to the extent that funding for its purposes is appropriated by the Legislature in the annual Budget Act.

Health and Safety Code § 11362.9

**(MCRSA- Amended by AB 2679, Effective January 1, 2017.)

(a) (1) It is the intent of the Legislature that the state commission objective scientific research by the premier research institute of the world, the University of California, regarding the efficacy and safety of administering marijuana as part of medical treatment. If the Regents of the University of California, by appropriate resolution, accept this responsibility, the University of California shall create a program, to be known as the California Marijuana Research Program.

(2) The program shall develop and conduct studies intended to ascertain the general medical safety and efficacy of marijuana and, if found valuable, shall develop medical guidelines for the appropriate administration and use of marijuana. The studies may include studies to ascertain the effect of marijuana on motor skills.

(b) The program may immediately solicit proposals for research projects to be included in the marijuana studies. Program requirements to be used when evaluating responses to its solicitation for proposals, shall include, but not be limited to, all of the following:

(1) Proposals shall demonstrate the use of key personnel, including clinicians or scientists and support personnel, who are prepared to develop a program of research regarding marijuana's general medical efficacy and safety.

(2) Proposals shall contain procedures for outreach to patients with various medical conditions who may be suitable participants in research on marijuana.

(3) Proposals shall contain provisions for a patient registry.

(4) Proposals shall contain provisions for an information system that is designed to record information about possible study participants, investigators, and clinicians, and deposit and analyze data that accrues

as part of clinical trials.

(5) Proposals shall contain protocols suitable for research on marijuana, addressing patients diagnosed with acquired immunodeficiency syndrome (AIDS) or human immunodeficiency virus (HIV), cancer, glaucoma, or seizures or muscle spasms associated with a chronic, debilitating condition. The proposal may also include research on other serious illnesses, provided that resources are available and medical information justifies the research.

(6) Proposals shall demonstrate the use of a specimen laboratory capable of housing plasma, urine, and other specimens necessary to study the concentration of cannabinoids in various tissues, as well as housing specimens for studies of toxic effects of marijuana.

(7) Proposals shall demonstrate the use of a laboratory capable of analyzing marijuana, provided to the program under this section, for purity and cannabinoid content and the capacity to detect contaminants.

(c) In order to ensure objectivity in evaluating proposals, the program shall use a peer review process that is modeled on the process used by the National Institutes of Health, and that guards against funding research that is biased in favor of or against particular outcomes. Peer reviewers shall be selected for their expertise in the scientific substance and methods of the proposed research, and their lack of bias or conflict of interest regarding the applicants or the topic of an approach taken in the proposed research. Peer reviewers shall judge research proposals on several criteria, foremost among which shall be both of the following:

(1) The scientific merit of the research plan, including whether the research design and experimental procedures are potentially biased for or against a particular outcome.

(2) Researchers' expertise in the scientific substance and methods of the proposed research, and their lack of bias or conflict of interest regarding the topic of, and the approach taken in, the proposed research.

(d) If the program is administered by the Regents of the University of California, any grant research proposals approved by the program shall also require review and approval by the research advisory panel.

(e) It is the intent of the Legislature that the program be established as follows:

(1) The program shall be located at one or more University of California campuses that have a core of faculty experienced in organizing multidisciplinary scientific endeavors and, in particular, strong experience in clinical trials involving psychopharmacologic agents. The campuses at which research under the auspices of the program is to take place shall accommodate the administrative offices, including the director of the program, as well as a data management unit, and facilities for storage of specimens.

(2) When awarding grants under this section, the program shall utilize principles and parameters of the other well-tested statewide research programs administered by the University of California, modeled after programs administered by the National Institutes of Health, including peer review evaluation of the scientific merit of applications.

(3) The scientific and clinical operations of the program shall occur, partly at University of California campuses, and partly at other postsecondary institutions, that have clinicians or scientists with expertise to conduct the required studies. Criteria for selection of research locations shall include the elements listed in subdivision (b) and, additionally, shall give particular weight to the organizational plan, leadership qualities of the program director, and plans to involve investigators and patient populations from multiple sites.

(4) The funds received by the program shall be allocated to various research studies in accordance with a scientific plan developed by the Scientific Advisory Council. As the first wave of studies is completed, it is anticipated that the program will receive requests for funding of additional studies. These requests shall be reviewed by the Scientific Advisory Council.

(5) The size, scope, and number of studies funded shall be commensurate with the amount of appropriated and available program funding.

(f) All personnel involved in implementing approved proposals shall be authorized as required by Section 11604.

(g) Studies conducted pursuant to this section shall include the greatest amount of new scientific research possible on the medical uses of, and medical hazards associated with, marijuana. The program shall consult with the Research Advisory Panel analogous agencies in other states, and appropriate federal agencies in an attempt to avoid duplicative research and the wasting of research dollars.

(h) The program shall make every effort to recruit qualified patients and qualified physicians from throughout the state.

(i) The marijuana studies shall employ state-of-the-art research methodologies.

(j) The program shall ensure that all marijuana used in the studies is of the appropriate medical quality and shall be obtained from the National Institute on Drug Abuse or any other federal agency designated to supply marijuana for authorized research. If these federal agencies fail to provide a supply of adequate quality and quantity within six months of the effective date of this section, the Attorney General shall provide an adequate supply pursuant to Section 11478.

(k) The program may review, approve, or incorporate studies and research by independent groups presenting scientifically valid protocols for medical research, regardless of whether the areas of study are being researched by the committee.

(l) (1) To enhance understanding of the efficacy and adverse effects of marijuana as a pharmacological agent, the program shall conduct focused controlled clinical trials on the usefulness of marijuana in patients diagnosed with AIDS or HIV, cancer, glaucoma, or seizures or muscle spasms associated with a chronic, debilitating condition. The program may add research on other serious illnesses, provided that resources are available and medical information justifies the research. The studies shall focus on comparisons of both the efficacy and safety of methods of administering the drug to patients, including inhalational, tinctural, and oral, evaluate possible uses of marijuana as a primary or adjunctive treatment, and develop further information on optimal dosage, timing, mode of administration, and variations in the effects of different cannabinoids and varieties of marijuana.

(2) The program shall examine the safety of marijuana in patients with various medical disorders, including marijuana's interaction with other drugs, relative safety of inhalation versus oral forms, and the effects on mental function in medically ill persons.

(3) The program shall be limited to providing for objective scientific research to ascertain the efficacy and safety of marijuana as part of medical treatment, and should not be construed as encouraging or sanctioning the social or recreational use of marijuana.

(m) (1) Subject to paragraph (2), the program shall, prior to any approving proposals, seek to obtain research protocol guidelines from the National Institutes of Health and shall, if the National Institutes of Health issues research protocol guidelines, comply with those guidelines.

(2) If, after a reasonable period of time of not less than six months and not more than a year has elapsed from the date the program seeks to obtain guidelines pursuant to paragraph (1), no guidelines have been approved, the program may proceed using the research protocol guidelines it develops.

(n) In order to maximize the scope and size of the marijuana studies, the program may do any of the following:

(1) Solicit, apply for, and accept funds from foundations, private individuals, and all other funding sources that can be used to expand the scope or timeframe of the marijuana studies that are authorized under this section. The program shall not expend more than 5 percent of its General Fund allocation in efforts to obtain money from outside sources.

(2) Include within the scope of the marijuana studies other marijuana research projects that are independently funded and that meet the requirements set forth in subdivisions (a) to (c), inclusive. In no case shall the program accept any funds that are offered with any conditions other than that the funds be used to study the efficacy and safety of marijuana as part of medical treatment. Any donor shall be advised that funds given for purposes of this section will be used to study both the possible benefits and detriments of marijuana and that he or she will have no control over the use of these funds.

(o) (1) Within six months of the effective date of this section, the program shall report to the Legislature, the Governor, and the Attorney General on the progress of the marijuana studies.

(2) Thereafter, the program shall issue a report to the Legislature every six months detailing the progress of the studies. The interim reports required under this paragraph shall include, but not be limited to, data on all of the following:

(A) The names and number of diseases or conditions under study.

(B) The number of patients enrolled in each study by disease.

(C) Any scientifically valid preliminary findings.

(p) If the Regents of the University of California implement this section, the President of the University of California shall appoint a multidisciplinary Scientific Advisory Council, not to exceed 15 members, to provide policy guidance in the creation and implementation of the program. Members shall be chosen on the basis of scientific expertise. Members of the council shall serve on a voluntary basis, with reimbursement for expenses incurred in the course of their participation. The members shall be reimbursed for travel and other necessary expenses incurred in their performance of the duties of the council.

(q) No more than 10 percent of the total funds appropriated may be used for all aspects of the administration of this section.

(r) This section shall be implemented only to the extent that funding for its purposes is appropriated by the Legislature in the annual Budget Act.

Health & Safety Code § 11364.5

(Amended by Statute, Effective 1984.)

(a) Except as authorized by law, no person shall maintain or operate any place of business in which drug paraphernalia is kept, displayed or offered in any manner, sold, furnished, transferred or given away unless such drug paraphernalia is completely and wholly kept, displayed or offered within a separate room or enclosure to which persons under the age of 18 years not accompanied by a parent or legal guardian are excluded. Each entrance to such a room or enclosure shall be signposted in reasonably visible and legible words to the effect that drug paraphernalia is kept, displayed or offered in such room or enclosure and that minors, unless accompanied by a parent or legal guardian, are excluded.

(b) Except as authorized by law, no owner, manager, proprietor or other person in charge of any room or enclosure, within any place of business, in which drug paraphernalia is kept, displayed or offered in any manner, sold, furnished, transferred or given away shall permit or allow any person under the age of 18 years to enter, be in, remain in or visit such room or enclosure unless such minor person is accompanied by one of his or her parents or by his or her legal guardian.

(c) Unless authorized by law, no person under the age of 18 years shall enter, be in, remain in or visit any room or enclosure in any place of business in which drug paraphernalia is kept, displayed or offered in any manner, sold, furnished, transferred or given away unless accompanied by one of his or her parents or by his or her legal guardian.

(d) As used in this section, "drug paraphernalia" means all equipment, products, and materials of any kind which are intended for use or designed for use, in planting, propagating, cultivating, growing, harvesting, manufacturing, compounding, converting, producing, processing, preparing, testing, analyzing, packaging, repackaging, storing, containing, concealing, injecting, ingesting, inhaling, or otherwise introducing into the human body a controlled substance. "Drug paraphernalia" includes, but is not limited to, all of the following:

(1) Kits intended for use or designed for use in planting, propagating, cultivating, growing or harvesting of any species of plant which is a controlled substance or from which a controlled substance can be derived.

(2) Kits intended for use or designed for use in manufacturing, compounding, converting, producing, processing, or preparing controlled substances.

(3) Isomerization devices intended for use or designed for use in increasing the potency of any species of plant which is a controlled substance.

(4) Testing equipment intended for use or designed for use in identifying, or in analyzing the strength, effectiveness or purity of controlled substances.

(5) Scales and balances intended for use or designed for use in weighing or measuring controlled substances.

(6) Diluents and adulterants, such as quinine hydrochloride, mannitol, mannite, dextrose, and lactose, intended for use or designed for use icutting controlled substances.

(7) Separation gins and sifters intended for use or designed for use in removing twigs and seeds from, or in otherwise cleaning or refining, marijuana.

(8) Blenders, bowls, containers, spoons, and mixing devices intended for use or designed for use in compounding controlled substances.

(9) Capsules, balloons, envelopes, and other containers intended for use or designed for use in packaging small quantities of controlled substances.

(10) Containers and other objects intended for use or designed for use in storing or concealing controlled substances.

(11) Hypodermic syringes, needles, and other objects intended for use or designed for use in parenterally injecting controlled substances into the human body.

(12) Objects intended for use or designed for use in ingesting, inhaling, or otherwise introducing marijuana, cocaine, hashish, or hashish oil into the human body, such as the following:

(A) Metal, wooden, acrylic, glass, stone, plastic, or ceramic pipes with or without screens, permanent screens, hashish heads, or punctured metal bowls.

(B) Water pipes.

(C) Carburetion tubes and devices.

(D) Smoking and carburetion masks.

(E) Roach clips, meaning objects used to hold burning material, such as a marijuana cigarette that has become too small or too short to be held in the hand.

(F) Miniature cocaine spoons, and cocaine vials.

(G) Chamber pipes.

(H) Carburetor pipes.

(I) Electric pipes.

(J) Air-driven pipes.

(K) Chillums.

(L) Bongs.

(M) Ice pipes or chillers.

(e) In determining whether an object is drug paraphernalia, a court or other authority may consider, in addition to all other logically relevant factors, the following:

(1) Statements by an owner or by anyone in control of the object con-

cerning its use.

(2) Prior convictions, if any, of an owner, or of anyone in control of the object, under any state or federal law relating to any controlled substance.

(3) Direct or circumstantial evidence of the intent of an owner, or of anyone in control of the object, to deliver it to persons whom he or she knows, or should reasonably know, intend to use the object to facilitate a violation of this section. The innocence of an owner, or of anyone in control of the object, as to a direct violation of this section shall not prevent a finding that the object is intended for use, or designed for use, as drug paraphernalia.

(4) Instructions, oral or written, provided with the object concerning its use.

(5) Descriptive materials, accompanying the object which explain or depict its use.

(6) National and local advertising concerning its use.

(7) The manner in which the object is displayed for sale.

(8) Whether the owner, or anyone in control of the object, is a legitimate supplier of like or related items to the community, such as a licensed distributor or dealer of tobacco products.

(9) The existence and scope of legitimate uses for the object in the community.

(10) Expert testimony concerning its use.

(f) This section shall not apply to any of the following:

(1) Any pharmacist or other authorized person who sells or furnishes drug paraphernalia described in paragraph (11) of subdivision (d) upon the prescription of a physician, dentist, podiatrist or veterinarian.

(2) Any physician, dentist, podiatrist or veterinarian who furnishes or prescribes drug paraphernalia described in paragraph (11) of subdivision (d) to his or her patients.

(3) Any manufacturer, wholesaler or retailer licensed by the California State Board of Pharmacy to sell or transfer drug paraphernalia de-

scribed in paragraph (11) of subdivision (d).

(g) Notwithstanding any other provision of law, including Section 11374, violation of this section shall not constitute a criminal offense, but operation of a business in violation of the provisions of this section shall be grounds for revocation or nonrenewal of any license, permit, or other entitlement previously issued by a city, county, or city and county for the privilege of engaging in such business and shall be grounds for denial of any future license, permit, or other entitlement authorizing the conduct of such business or any other business, if the business includes the sale of drug paraphernalia.

Health & Safety Code § 11366

(Amended by Statute, Effective 1991.)

Every person who opens or maintains any place for the purpose of unlawfully selling, giving away, or using any controlled substance which is

(1) specified in subdivision (b), (c), or (e), or paragraph (1) of subdivision (f) of Section 11054, specified in paragraph (13), (14), (15), or (20) of subdivision (d) of Section 11054, or specified in subdivision (b), (c), paragraph (1) or (2) of subdivision (d), or paragraph (3) of subdivision (e) of Section 11055, or

(2) which is a narcotic drug classified in Schedule III, IV, or V, shall be punished by imprisonment in the county jail for a period of not more than one year or the state prison.

Health & Safety Code § 11366.5

(Amended by Statute, Effective April 4, 2011, and Operative October 1, 2011.)

(a) Any person who has under his or her management or control any building, room, space, or enclosure, either as an owner, lessee, agent, employee, or mortgagee, who knowingly rents, leases, or makes available for use, with or without compensation, the building, room, space, or enclosure for the purpose of unlawfully manufacturing, storing, or distributing any controlled substance for sale or distribution shall be punished by imprisonment in the county jail for not more than one year, or pursuant to subdivision (h) of Section 1170 of the Penal Code.

(b) Any person who has under his or her management or control any building, room, space, or enclosure, either as an owner, lessee, agent, employee, or mortgagee, who knowingly allows the building, room, space, or enclosure to be fortified to suppress law enforcement entry in order to further the sale of any amount of cocaine base as specified in paragraph (1) of subdivision (f) of Section 11054, cocaine as specified in paragraph (6) of subdivision (b) of Section 11055, heroin, phencyclidine, amphetamine, methamphetamine, or lysergic acid diethylamide and who obtains excessive profits from the use of the building, room, space, or enclosure shall be punished by imprisonment pursuant to subdivision (h) of Section 1170 of the Penal Code for two, three, or four years.

(c) Any person who violates subdivision (a) after previously being convicted of a violation of subdivision (a) shall be punished by imprisonment pursuant to subdivision (h) of Section 1170 of the Penal Code for two, three, or four years.

(d) For the purposes of this section, excessive profits means the receipt of consideration of a value substantially higher than fair market value.

Health & Safety Code § 11379.6

(Amended by Statute, Effective January 1, 2016.)

(a) Except as otherwise provided by law, every person who manufactures, compounds, converts, produces, derives, processes, or prepares, either directly or indirectly by chemical extraction or independently by means of chemical synthesis, any controlled substance specified in Section 11054, 11055, 11056, 11057, or 11058 shall be punished by imprisonment pursuant to subdivision (h) of Section 1170 of the Penal Code for three, five, or seven years and by a fine not exceeding fifty thousand dollars ($50,000).

(b) Except when an enhancement pursuant to Section 11379.7 is pled and proved, the fact that a person under 16 years of age resided in a structure in which a violation of this section involving methamphetamine occurred shall be considered a factor in aggravation by the sentencing court.

(c) Except when an enhancement pursuant to Section 11379.7 is pled and proved, the fact that a violation of this section involving methamphetamine occurred within 200 feet of an occupied residence or any structure where another person was present at the time the offense was committed may be considered a factor in aggravation by the sentencing court.

(d) The fact that a violation of this section involving the use of a volatile solvent to chemically extract concentrated cannabis occurred within 300 feet of an occupied residence or any structure where another person was present at the time the offense was committed may be considered a factor in aggravation by the sentencing court.

(e) Except as otherwise provided by law, every person who offers to perform an act which is punishable under subdivision (a) shall be punished by imprisonment pursuant to subdivision (h) of Section 1170 of the Penal Code for three, four, or five years.

(f) All fines collected pursuant to subdivision (a) shall be transferred to the State Treasury for deposit in the Clandestine Drug Lab Clean-up Account, as established by Section 5 of Chapter 1295 of the Statutes of 1987. The transmission to the State Treasury shall be carried out in the same manner as fines collected for the state by the county.

Health and Safety Code § 11470

(Amended by Statute, Effective January 1, 2015.)

The following are subject to forfeiture:

(a) All controlled substances which have been manufactured, distributed, dispensed, or acquired in violation of this division.

(b) All raw materials, products, and equipment of any kind which are used, or intended for use, in manufacturing, compounding, processing, delivering, importing, or exporting any controlled substance in violation of this division.

(c) All property except real property or a boat, airplane, or any vehicle which is used, or intended for use, as a container for property described in subdivision (a) or (b).

(d) All books, records, and research products and materials, including formulas, microfilm, tapes, and data which are used, or intended for use, in violation of this division.

(e) The interest of any registered owner of a boat, airplane, or any vehicle other than an implement of husbandry, as defined in Section 36000 of the Vehicle Code, which has been used as an instrument to facilitate the manufacture of, or possession for sale or sale of 14.25 grams or more of heroin, or a substance containing 14.25 grams or more of heroin, or 14.25 grams or more of a substance containing heroin, or 28.5 grams or more of Schedule I controlled substances except marijuana, peyote, or psilocybin; 10 pounds dry weight or more of marijuana, peyote, or psilocybin; or 28.5 grams or more of cocaine, as specified in paragraph (6) of subdivision (b) of Section 11055, cocaine base as specified in paragraph (1) of subdivision (f) of Section 11054, or methamphetamine; or a substance containing 28.5 grams or more of cocaine, as specified in paragraph (6) of subdivision (b) of Section 11055, cocaine base as specified in paragraph (1) of subdivision (f) of Section 11054, or methamphetamine; or 57 grams or more of a substance containing cocaine, as specified in paragraph (6) of subdivision (b) of Section 11055, cocaine base as specified in paragraph (1) of subdivision (f) of Section 11054, or methamphetamine; or 28.5 grams or more of Schedule II controlled substances. An interest in a vehicle which may be lawfully driven on the highway with a class C, class M1, or class M2 license, as prescribed in Section 12804.9 of the Vehicle Code, shall not be forfeited under this subdivision if there is a community property interest in the vehicle by a person other than the defendant and the vehicle is the sole class C, class M1, or class M2 vehicle available to the defendant's immediate family.

(f) All moneys, negotiable instruments, securities, or other things of value furnished or intended to be furnished by any person in exchange for a controlled substance, all proceeds traceable to such an exchange, and all moneys, negotiable instruments, or securities used or intended to be used to facilitate any violation of Section 11351, 11351.5, 11352, 11355, 11359, 11360, 11378, 11378.5, 11379, 11379.5, 11379.6, 11380, 11382, or 11383 of this code, or Section 182 of the Penal Code, or a felony violation of Section 11366.8 of this code, insofar as the offense involves manufacture, sale, possession for sale, offer for sale, or offer to manufacture, or conspiracy to commit at least one of those offenses, if the exchange, violation, or other conduct which is the basis for the forfeiture occurred within five years of the seizure of the property, or the filing of a petition under this chapter, or the issuance of an order of forfeiture of the property, whichever comes first.

(g) The real property of any property owner who is convicted of violating Section 11366, 11366.5, or 11366.6 with respect to that property. However, property which is used as a family residence or for other lawful purposes, or which is owned by two or more persons, one of whom had no knowledge of its unlawful use, shall not be subject to forfeiture.

(h) (1) Subject to the requirements of Section 11488.5 and except as further limited by this subdivision to protect innocent parties who claim a property interest acquired from a defendant, all right, title, and interest in any personal property described in this section shall vest in the state upon commission of the act giving rise to forfeiture under this chapter, if the state or local governmental entity proves a violation of Section 11351, 11351.5, 11352, 11355, 11359, 11360, 11378, 11378.5, 11379, 11379.5, 11379.6, 11380, 11382, or 11383 of this code, or Section 182 of the Penal Code, or a felony violation of Section 11366.8 of this code, insofar as the offense involves the manufacture, sale, possession for sale, offer for sale, offer to manufacture, or conspiracy to commit at least one of those offenses, in accordance with the burden of proof set forth in paragraph (1) of subdivision (i) of Section 11488.4 or, in the case of cash or negotiable instruments in excess of twenty-five thousand dollars ($25,000), paragraph (4) of subdivision (i) of Section 11488.4.

(2) The operation of the special vesting rule established by this subdivision shall be limited to circumstances where its application will not defeat the claim of any person, including a bona fide purchaser or encumbrancer who, pursuant to Section 11488.5, 11488.6, or 11489, claims an interest in the property seized, notwithstanding that the interest in the property being claimed was acquired from a defendant whose property interest would otherwise have been subject to divestment pursuant to this subdivision.

Health & Safety Code § 11478

(Amended by Statute, Effective 1980.)

Marijuana may be provided by the Attorney General to the heads of research projects which have been registered by the Attorney General, and which have been approved by the research advisory panel pursuant to Section 11480.

The head of the approved research project shall personally receipt for such quantities of marijuana and shall make a record of their disposition. The receipt and record shall be retained by the Attorney General. The head of the approved research project shall also, at intervals and in the manner required by the research advisory panel, report the progress or conclusions of the research project.

Health & Safety Code § 11479

(Amended by Statute, Effective January 1, 2016.)

Notwithstanding Sections 11473 and 11473.5, at any time after seizure by a law enforcement agency of a suspected controlled substance, except in the case of growing or harvested marijuana, that amount in excess of 10 pounds in gross weight may be destroyed without a court order by the chief of the law enforcement agency or a designated subordinate. In the case of growing or harvested marijuana, that amount in excess of two pounds, or the amount of marijuana a medical marijuana patient or designated caregiver is authorized to possess by ordinance in the city or county where the marijuana was seized, whichever is greater, may be destroyed without a court order by the chief of the law enforcement agency or a designated subordinate. Destruction shall not take place pursuant to this section until all of the following requirements are satisfied:

(a) At least five random and representative samples have been taken, for evidentiary purposes, from the total amount of suspected controlled substances to be destroyed. These samples shall be in addition to the 10 pounds required above. When the suspected controlled substance consists of growing or harvested marijuana plants, at least one 2-pound sample or a sample in the amount of medical marijuana a medical marijuana patient or designated caregiver is authorized to possess by ordinance in the city or county where the marijuana was seized, whichever is greater, shall be retained. This sample may include stalks, branches, or leaves. In addition, five representative samples of leaves or buds shall be retained for evidentiary purposes from the total amount of suspected controlled substances to be destroyed.

(b) Photographs and videos have been taken that reasonably and accurately demonstrate the total amount of the suspected controlled substance to be destroyed.

(c) The gross weight of the suspected controlled substance has been determined, either by actually weighing the suspected controlled substance or by estimating that weight after dimensional measurement of the total suspected controlled substance.

(d) The chief of the law enforcement agency has determined that it is not reasonably possible to preserve the suspected controlled substance in place, or to remove the suspected controlled substance to another location. In making this determination, the difficulty of transporting and storing the suspected controlled substance to another site and the storage facilities may be taken into consideration.

Subsequent to any destruction of a suspected controlled substance pursuant to this section, an affidavit shall be filed within 30 days in the court that has jurisdiction over any pending criminal proceedings pertaining to that suspected controlled substance, reciting the applicable information required by subdivisions (a), (b), (c), and (d) together with information establishing the location of the suspected controlled substance, and specifying the date and time of the destruction. In the event that there are no criminal proceedings pending that pertain to that suspected controlled substance, the affidavit may be filed in any court within the county that would have jurisdiction over a person against whom those criminal charges might be filed.

Health and Safety Code § 11480

(Amended by Statute, Effective 1983.)

The Legislature finds that there is a need to encourage further research into the nature and effects of marijuana and hallucinogenic drugs and to coordinate research efforts on such subjects.

There is a Research Advisory Panel which consists of a representative of the State Department of Health Services, a representative of the California State Board of Pharmacy, a representative of the Attorney General, a representative of the University of California who shall be a pharmacologist, a physician, or a person holding a doctorate degree in the health sciences, a representative of a private university in this state who shall be a pharmacologist, a physician, or a person holding a doctorate degree in the health sciences, a representative of a statewide professional medical society in this state who shall be engaged in the private practice of medicine and shall be experienced in treating controlled substance dependency, a representative appointed by and serving at the pleasure of the Governor who shall have experience in drug abuse, cancer, or controlled substance research and who is either a registered nurse, licensed pursuant to Chapter 6 (commencing with Section 2700) of Division 2 of the Business and Professions Code, or other health professional. The Governor shall annually designate the private university and the professional medical society represented on the panel. Members of the panel shall be appointed by the heads of the entities to be represented, and they shall serve at the pleasure of the appointing power.

The Research Advisory Panel shall appoint two special members to the Research Advisory Panel, who shall serve at the pleasure of the Research Advisory Panel only during the period Article 6 (commencing with Section 11260) of Chapter 5 remains effective. The additional members shall be physicians and surgeons, and who are board certified in oncology, ophthalmology, or psychiatry.

The panel shall annually select a chairman from among its members.

The panel may hold hearings on, and in other ways study, research projects concerning marijuana or hallucinogenic drugs in this state. Members of the panel shall serve without compensation, but shall be reimbursed for any actual and necessary expenses incurred in connection with the performance of their duties.

The panel may approve research projects, which have been registered by the Attorney General, into the nature and effects of marijuana or hallucinogenic drugs, and shall inform the Attorney General of the head of the approved research projects which are entitled to receive quantities of marijuana pursuant to Section 11478.

The panel may withdraw approval of a research project at any time, and when approval is withdrawn shall notify the head of the research project to return any quantities of marijuana to the Attorney General.

The panel shall report annually to the Legislature and the Governor those research projects approved by the panel, the nature of each research project, and, where available, the conclusions of the research project.

Health and Safety Code § 11485

(Added by Statute, Effective October 2, 1985.)

Any peace officer of this state who, incident to a search under a search warrant issued for a violation of Section 11358 with respect to which no prosecution of a defendant results, seizes personal property suspected of being used in the planting, cultivation, harvesting, drying, processing, or transporting of marijuana, shall, if the seized personal property is not being held for evidence or destroyed as contraband, and if the owner of the property is unknown or has not claimed the property, provide notice regarding the seizure and manner of reclamation of the property to any owner or tenant of real property on which the property was seized. In addition, this notice shall be posted at the location of seizure and shall be published at least once in a newspaper of general circulation in the county in which the property was seized. If, after 90 days following the first publication of the notice, no owner appears and proves his or her ownership, the seized personal property shall be deemed to be abandoned and may be disposed of by sale to the public at public auction as set forth in Article 1 (commencing with Section 2080) of Chapter 4 of Title 6 of Part 4 of Division 3 of the Civil Code, or may be disposed of by transfer to a government agency or community service organization. Any profit from the sale or transfer of the property shall be expended for investigative services with respect to crimes involving marijuana.

Health & Safety Code § 11570

(Amended by Statute, Effective 1986.)

Every building or place used for the purpose of unlawfully selling, serving, storing, keeping, manufacturing, or giving away any controlled substance, precursor, or analog specified in this division, and every building or place wherein or upon which those acts take place, is a nuisance which shall be enjoined, abated, and prevented, and for which damages may be recovered, whether it is a public or private nuisance.

Health & Safety Code § 11590

(Amended by statute, Effective January 1, 1996.)

(a) Except as provided in subdivisions (c) and (d), any person who is convicted in the State of California of any offense defined in Section 11350, 11351, 11351.5, 11352, 11353, 11353.5, 11353.7, 11354, 11355, 11357, 11358, 11359, 11360, 11361, 11363, 11366, 11366.5, 11366.6, 11368, 11370.1, 11378, 11378.5, 11379, 11379.5, 11379.6, 11380, 11380.5, 11383, or 11550, or subdivision (a) of Section 11377, or any person who is discharged or paroled from a penal institution where he or she was confined because of the commission of any such offense, or any person who is convicted in any other state of any offense which, if committed or attempted in this state, would have been punishable as one or more of the above-mentioned offenses, shall within 30 days of his or her coming into any county or city, or city and county in which he or she resides or is temporarily domiciled for that length of time, register with the chief of police of the city in which he or she resides or the sheriff of the county if he or she resides in an unincorporated area.

For persons convicted of an offense defined in Section 11377, 11378, 11379, or 11380, this subdivision shall apply only to offenses involving controlled substances specified in paragraph (12) of subdivision (d) of Section 11054 and paragraph (2) of subdivision (d) of Section 11055, and to analogs of these substances, as defined in Section 11401. For persons convicted of an offense defined in Section 11379 or 11379.5, this subdivision shall not apply if the conviction was for transporting, offering to transport, or attempting to transport a controlled substance.

(b) Any person who is convicted in any federal court of any offense which, if committed or attempted in this state would have been punishable as one or more of the offenses enumerated in subdivision (a) shall, within 30 days of his or her coming into any county or city, or city and county, in which he or she resides or is temporarily domiciled for that length of time, register with the chief of police of the city in which he or she resides or the sheriff of the county if he or she resides in an unincorporated area.

(c) This section does not apply to a conviction of a misdemeanor under Section 11357, 11360, or 11377.

(d) The registration requirements imposed by this section for the conviction of offenses defined in Section 11353.7, 11366.5, 11366.6, 11370.1, 11377, 11378, 11378.5, 11379, 11379.5, 11379.6, 11380, 11380.5, or 11383, shall apply to any person who commits any of those offenses on and after January 1, 1990.

Health & Safety Code § 25189.5

(Amended by Statute, Effective April 4, 2011, and Operative October 1, 2011. Subd. (e) Amended on Nov. 4, 1986, by Prop. 65.)

(a) The disposal of any hazardous waste, or the causing thereof, is prohibited when the disposal is at a facility which does not have a permit from the department issued pursuant to this chapter, or at any point which is not authorized according to this chapter.

(b) Any person who is convicted of knowingly disposing or causing the disposal of any hazardous waste, or who reasonably should have known that he or she was disposing or causing the disposal of any hazardous waste, at a facility which does not have a permit from the department issued pursuant to this chapter, or at any point which is not authorized according to this chapter shall, upon conviction, be punished by imprisonment in a county jail for not more than one year or by imprisonment pursuant to subdivision (h) of Section 1170 of the Penal Code.

(c) Any person who knowingly transports or causes the transportation of hazardous waste, or who reasonably should have known that he or she was causing the transportation of any hazardous waste, to a facility which does not have a permit from the department issued pursuant to this chapter, or at any point which is not authorized according to this chapter, shall, upon conviction, be punished by imprisonment in a county jail for not more than one year or by imprisonment pursuant to subdivision (h) of Section 1170 of the Penal Code.

(d) Any person who knowingly treats or stores any hazardous waste at a facility which does not have a permit from the department issued pursuant to this chapter, or at any point which is not authorized according to this chapter, shall, upon conviction, be punished by imprisonment in a county jail for not more than one year or by imprisonment pursuant to subdivision (h) of Section 1170 of the Penal Code.

(e) The court also shall impose upon a person convicted of violating subdivision (b), (c), or (d), a fine of not less than five thousand dollars ($5,000) nor more than one hundred thousand dollars ($100,000) for each day of violation, except as further provided in this subdivision. If the act which violated subdivision (b), (c), or (d) caused great bodily injury, or caused a substantial probability that death could result, the person convicted of violating subdivision (b), (c), or (d) may be punished by imprisonment pursuant to subdivision (h) of Section 1170 of the Penal Code for one, two, or three years, in addition and consecutive to the term specified in subdivision (b), (c), or (d), and may be fined up to two hundred fifty thousand dollars ($250,000) for each day of violation.

(f) For purposes of this section, except as otherwise provided in this subdivision, "each day of violation" means each day on which a violation continues. In any case where a person has disposed or caused the disposal of any hazardous waste in violation of this section, each day that the waste remains disposed of in violation of this section and the person has knowledge thereof is a separate additional violation, unless the person has filed a report of the disposal with the department and is complying with any order concerning the disposal issued by the department, a hearing officer, or court of competent jurisdiction.

Health & Safety Code § 25189.6

(Amended by Statute, Effective April 4, 2011, and Operative October 1, 2011.)

(a) Any person who knowingly, or with reckless disregard for the risk, treats, handles, transports, disposes, or stores any hazardous waste in a manner which causes any unreasonable risk of fire, explosion, serious injury, or death is guilty of a public offense and shall, upon conviction, be punished by a fine of not less than five thousand dollars ($5,000) nor more than two hundred fifty thousand dollars ($250,000) for each day of violation, or by imprisonment in a county jail for not more than one year, or by imprisonment pursuant to subdivision (h) of Section 1170 of the Penal Code, or by both that fine and imprisonment.

(b) Any person who knowingly, at the time the person takes the actions specified in subdivision (a), places another person in imminent danger of death or serious bodily injury, is guilty of a public offense and shall, upon conviction, be punished by a fine of not less than five thousand dollars ($5,000) nor more than two hundred fifty thousand dollars ($250,000) for each day of violation, and by imprisonment pursuant to subdivision (h) of Section 1170 of the Penal Code for three, six, or nine years.

Health & Safety Code § 25189.7

(Amended by Statute, Effective April 4, 2011, and Operative October 1, 2011.)

(a) The burning or incineration of any hazardous waste, or the causing thereof, is prohibited when the burning or incineration is at a facility which does not have a permit from the department issued pursuant to this chapter, or at any point which is not authorized according to this chapter.

(b) Any person who is convicted of knowingly burning or incinerating, or causing the burning or incineration of, any hazardous waste, or who reasonably should have known that he or she was burning or incinerating, or causing the burning or incineration of, any hazardous waste, at a facility which does not have a permit from the department issued pursuant to this chapter, or at any point which is not authorized according to this chapter, shall, upon conviction, be punished by imprisonment in a county jail for not more than one year or by imprisonment pursuant to subdivision (h) of Section 1170 of the Penal Code.

(c) The court also shall impose upon a person convicted of violating subdivision (b) a fine of not less than five thousand dollars ($5,000) nor more than one hundred thousand dollars ($100,000) for each day of violation, except as otherwise provided in this subdivision. If the act which violated subdivision (b) caused great bodily injury or caused a substantial probability that death could result, the person convicted of violating subdivision (b) may be punished by imprisonment pursuant to subdivision (h) of Section 1170 of the

Penal Code for one, two, or three years, in addition and consecutive to the term specified in subdivision (b), and may be fined up to two hundred fifty thousand dollars ($250,000) for each day of violation.

VI. Labor Code Sections

Labor Code § 147.5

(MCRSA- AB 266, Effective January 1, 2016)

(a) By January 1, 2017, the Division of Occupational Safety and Health shall convene an advisory committee to evaluate whether there is a need to develop industry-specific regulations related to the activities of facilities issued a license pursuant to Chapter 3.5 (commencing with Section 19300) of Division 8 of the Business and Professions Code.

(b) By July 1, 2017, the advisory committee shall present to the board its findings and recommendations for consideration by the board. By July 1, 2017, the board shall render a decision regarding the adoption of industry-specific regulations pursuant to this section.

Labor Code § 147.6

(AUMA, Effective November 9, 2016.)

(a) By March 1, 2018, the Division of Occupational Safety and Health shall convene an advisory committee to evaluate whether there is a need to develop industry-specific regulations related to the activities of licensees under Division 10 of the Business and Professions Code, including but not limited to, whether specific requirements are needed to address exposure to second-hand marijuana smoke by employees at facilities where on-site consumption of marijuana is permitted under subdivision (d) of Section 26200 of the Business and Professions Code, and whether specific requirements are needed to address the potential risks of combustion, inhalation, armed robberies or repetitive strain injuries.

(b) By October 1, 2018, the advisory committee shall present to the board its findings and recommendations for consideration by the board. By October 1, 2018, the board shall render a decision regarding the adoption of industry-specific regulations pursuant to this section.

Labor Code § 432.8

(Added by Statute, Effective 1976.)

The limitations on employers and the penalties provided for in Section 432.7 shall apply to a conviction for violation of subdivision (b) or (c) of Section 11357 of the Health and Safety Code or a statutory predecessor thereof, or subdivision (c) of Section 11360 of the Health and Safety Code, or Section 11364, 11365, or 11550 of the Health and Safety Code as they related to marijuana prior to January 1, 1976, or a statutory predecessor thereof, two years from the date of such a conviction.

Labor Code § 1140

(Added by Statute, Effective 1975.)

This part shall be known and may be referred to as the Alatorre-Zenovich-Dunlap-Berman Agricultural Labor Relations Act of 1975.

Labor Code § 1140.2

(Added by Statute, Effective 1975.)

It is hereby stated to be the policy of the State of California to encourage and protect the right of agricultural employees to full freedom of association, self-organization, and designation of representatives of their own choosing, to negotiate the terms and conditions of their employment, and to be free from the interference, restraint, or coercion of employers of labor, or their agents, in the designation of such representatives or in self-organization or in other concerted activities for the purpose of collective bargaining or other mutual aid or protection. For this purpose this part is adopted to provide for collective-bargaining rights for agricultural employees.

Labor Code § 1140.4

(Amended by Statute, Effective January 1, 1995.)

As used in this part:

(a) The term "agriculture" includes farming in all its branches, and, among other things, includes the cultivation and tillage of the soil, dairying, the production, cultivation, growing, and harvesting of any agricultural or horticultural commodities (including commodities defined as agricultural commodities in Section 1141j(g) of Title 12 of the United States Code), the raising of livestock, bees, furbearing animals, or poultry, and any practices (including any forestry or lumbering operations) performed by a farmer or on a farm as an incident to or in conjunction with such farming operations, including preparation for market and delivery to storage or to market or to carriers for transportation to market.

(b) The term "agricultural employee" or "employee" shall mean one engaged in agriculture, as such term is defined in subdivision (a). However, nothing in this subdivision shall be construed to include any person other than those employees excluded from the coverage of the National Labor Relations Act, as amended, as agricultural employees, pursuant to Section 2(3) of the Labor Management Relations Act (Section 152(3), Title 29, United States Code), and Section 3(f) of the Fair Labor Standards Act (Section 203(f), Title 29, United States Code).

Further, nothing in this part shall apply, or be construed to apply, to any employee who performs work to be done at the site of the construction, alteration, painting, or repair of a building, structure, or other work (as these terms have been construed under Section 8(e) of the Labor Management Relations Act, 29 U.S.C. Sec. 158(e)) or logging or timber-clearing operations in initial preparation of land for farming, or who does land leveling or only land surveying for any of the above.

As used in this subdivision, "land leveling" shall include only major land moving operations changing the contour of the land, but shall not include annual or seasonal tillage or preparation of land for cultivation.

(c) The term "agricultural employer" shall be liberally construed to include any person acting directly or indirectly in the interest of an employer in relation to an agricultural employee, any individual grower, corporate grower, cooperative grower, harvesting association, hiring association, land management group, any association of persons or cooperatives engaged in agriculture, and shall include any person who owns or leases or manages land used for agricultural purposes, but shall exclude any person supplying agricultural workers to an employer, any farm labor contractor as defined by Section 1682, and any person functioning in the capacity of a labor contractor. The employer engaging such labor contractor or person shall be deemed the employer for all purposes under this part.

(d) The term "person" shall mean one or more individuals, corporations, partnerships, limited liability companies, associations, legal representatives, trustees in bankruptcy, receivers, or any other legal entity, employer, or labor organization having an interest in the outcome of a proceeding under this part.

(e) The term "representatives" includes any individual or labor organization.

(f) The term "labor organization" means any organization of any kind, or any agency or employee representation committee or plan, in which employees participate and which exists, in whole or in part, for the purpose of dealing with employers concerning grievances, labor disputes, wages, rates of pay, hours of employment, or conditions of work for agricultural employees.

(g) The term "unfair labor practice" means any unfair labor practice specified in Chapter 4 (commencing with Section 1153) of this part.

(h) The term "labor dispute" includes any controversy concerning terms, tenure, or conditions of employment, or concerning the association or representation of persons in negotiating, fixing, maintaining, changing, or seeking to arrange terms or conditions of employment, regardless of whether the disputants stand in the proximate relation of employer and employee.

(i) The term "board" means Agricultural Labor Relations Board.

(j) The term "supervisor" means any individual having the authority, in the interest of the employer, to hire, transfer, suspend, lay off, recall, promote, discharge, assign, reward, or discipline other employees, or the responsibility to direct them, or to adjust their grievances, or effectively to recommend such action, if, in connection with the foregoing, the exercise of such authority is not of a merely routine or clerical nature, but requires the use of independent judgment.

VII. Penal Code Sections

Penal Code § 182

(Amended by Statute, Effective April 4, 2011, and Operative October 1, 2011.)

(a) If two or more persons conspire:

(1) To commit any crime.

(2) Falsely and maliciously to indict another for any crime, or to procure another to be charged or arrested for any crime.

(3) Falsely to move or maintain any suit, action, or proceeding.

(4) To cheat and defraud any person of any property, by any means which are in themselves criminal, or to obtain money or property by false pretenses or by false promises with fraudulent intent not to perform those promises.

(5) To commit any act injurious to the public health, to public morals, or to pervert or obstruct justice, or the due administration of the laws.

(6) To commit any crime against the person of the President or Vice President of the United States, the Governor of any state or territory, any United States justice or judge, or the secretary of any of the executive departments of the United States.

They are punishable as follows:

When they conspire to commit any crime against the person of any official specified in paragraph (6), they are guilty of a felony and are punishable by imprisonment pursuant to subdivision (h) of Section 1170 for five, seven, or nine years.

When they conspire to commit any other felony, they shall be punishable in the same manner and to the same extent as is provided for the punishment of that felony. If the felony is one for which different punishments are prescribed for different degrees, the jury or court which finds the defendant guilty thereof shall determine the degree of the felony the defendant conspired to commit. If the degree is not so determined, the punishment for conspiracy to commit the felony shall be that prescribed for the lesser degree, except in the case of conspiracy to commit murder, in which case the punishment shall be that prescribed for murder in the first degree.

If the felony is conspiracy to commit two or more felonies which have different punishments and the commission of those felonies constitute but one offense of conspiracy, the penalty shall be that prescribed for the felony which has the greater maximum term.

When they conspire to do an act described in paragraph (4), they shall be punishable by imprisonment in a county jail for not more than one year, or by imprisonment pursuant to subdivision (h) of Section 1170, or by a fine not exceeding ten thousand dollars ($10,000), or by both that imprisonment and fine.

When they conspire to do any of the other acts described in this section, they shall be punishable by imprisonment in a county jail for not more than one year, or pursuant to subdivision (h) of Section 1170, or by a fine not exceeding ten thousand dollars ($10,000), or by both that imprisonment and fine. When they receive a felony conviction for conspiring to commit identity theft, as defined in Section 530.5, the court may impose a fine of up to twenty-five thousand dollars ($25,000).

All cases of conspiracy may be prosecuted and tried in the superior court of any county in which any overt act tending to effect the conspiracy shall be done.

(b) Upon a trial for conspiracy, in a case where an overt act is necessary to constitute the offense, the defendant cannot be convicted unless one or more overt acts are expressly alleged in the indictment or information, nor unless one of the acts alleged is proved; but other overt acts not alleged may be given in evidence.

Penal Code § 290

(Amended by Proposition 35, Effective November 6, 2012.)

(a) Sections 290 to 290.024, inclusive, shall be known and may be cited as the Sex Offender Registration Act. All references to "the Act" in those sections are to the Sex Offender Registration Act.

(b) Every person described in subdivision (c), for the rest of his or her life while residing in California, or while attending school or working in California, as described in Sections 290.002 and 290.01, shall be required to register with the chief of police of the city in which he or she is residing, or the sheriff of the county if he or she is residing in an unincorporated area or city that has no police department, and, additionally, with the chief of police of a campus of the University of California, the California State University, or community college if he or she is residing upon the campus or in any of its facilities, within five working days of coming into, or changing his or her residence within, any city, county, or city and county, or campus in which he or she temporarily resides, and shall be required to register thereafter in accordance with the Act.

(c) The following persons shall be required to register:

Any person who, since July 1, 1944, has been or is hereafter convicted in any court in this state or in any federal or military court of a violation of Section 187 committed in the perpetration, or an attempt to perpetrate, rape or any act punishable under Section 286, 288, 288a, or 289, Section 207 or 209 committed with intent to violate Section 261, 286, 288, 288a, or 289, Section 220, except assault to commit mayhem, subdivision (b) and (c) of Section 236.1, Section 243.4, paragraph (1), (2), (3), (4), or (6) of subdivision (a) of Section 261, paragraph (1) of subdivision (a) of Section 262 involving the use of force or violence for which the person is sentenced to the state prison, Section 264.1, 266, or 266c, subdivision (b) of Section 266h, subdivision (b) of Section 266i, Section 266j, 267, 269, 285, 286, 288, 288a, 288.3, 288.4, 288.5, 288.7, 289, or 311.1, subdivision (b), (c), or (d) of Section 311.2, Section 311.3, 311.4, 311.10, 311.11, or 647.6, former Section 647a, subdivision (c) of Section 653f, subdivision 1 or 2 of Section 314, any offense involving lewd or lascivious conduct under Section 272, or any felony violation of Section 288.2; any statutory predecessor that includes all elements of one of the above-mentioned offenses; or any person who since that date has been or is hereafter convicted of the attempt or conspiracy to commit any of the above-mentioned offenses.

Penal Code § 374.8

(Amended by Statute, Effective April 4, 2011, and Operative October 1, 2011.)

(a) In any prosecution under this section, proof of the elements of the offense shall not be dependent upon the requirements of Title 22 of the California Code of Regulations.

(b) Any person who knowingly causes any hazardous substance to be deposited into or upon any road, street, highway, alley, or railroad right-of-way, or upon the land of another, without the permission of the owner, or into the waters of this state is punishable by imprisonment in the county jail for not more than one year or by imprisonment pursuant to subdivision (h) of Section 1170 for a term of 16 months, two years, or three years, or by a fine of not less than fifty dollars ($50) nor more than ten thousand dollars ($10,000), or by both the fine and imprisonment, unless the deposit occurred as a result of an emergency that the person promptly reported to the appropriate regulatory authority.

(c) For purposes of this section, "hazardous substance" means either of the following:

(1) Any material that, because of its quantity, concentration, or physical or chemical characteristics, poses a significant present or potential hazard to human health and safety or to the environment if released into the environment, including, but not limited to, hazardous waste and any material that the administering agency or a handler, as defined in Chapter 6.91 (commencing with Section 25410) of Division 20 of the Health and Safety Code, has a reasonable basis for believing would be injurious to the health and safety of persons or harmful to the environment if released into the environment.

(2) Any substance or chemical product for which one of the following applies:

(A) The manufacturer or producer is required to prepare a MSDS, as defined in Section 6374 of the Labor Code, for the substance or product pursuant to the Hazardous Substances Information Training Act (Chapter 2.5 (commencing with Section 6360) of Part 1 of Division 5 of the Labor Code) or pursuant to any applicable federal law or regulation.

(B) The substance is described as a radioactive material in Chapter 1 of Title 10 of the Code of Federal Regulations maintained and updated by the Nuclear Regulatory Commission.

(C) The substance is designated by the Secretary of Transportation in Chapter 27 (commencing with Section 1801) of the appendix to Title 49 of the United States Code and taxed as a radioactive substance or material.

(D) The materials listed in subdivision (b) of Section 6382 of the Labor Code.

Penal Code § 667

(Amended by Proposition 36, November 6, 2012. This section was added by Prop. 8, June 8, 1982.)

(a) (1) In compliance with subdivision (b) of Section 1385, any person convicted of a serious felony who previously has been convicted of a serious felony in this state or of any offense committed in another jurisdiction which includes all of the elements of any serious felony, shall receive, in addition to the sentence imposed by the court for the present offense, a five-year enhancement for each such prior conviction on charges brought and tried separately. The terms of the present offense and each enhancement shall run consecutively.

(2) This subdivision shall not be applied when the punishment imposed under other provisions of law would result in a longer term of imprisonment. There is no requirement of prior incarceration or commitment for this subdivision to apply.

(3) The Legislature may increase the length of the enhancement of sentence provided in this subdivision by a statute passed by majority vote of each house thereof.

(4) As used in this subdivision, "serious felony" means a serious felony listed in subdivision (c) of Section 1192.7.

(5) This subdivision shall not apply to a person convicted of selling, furnishing, administering, or giving, or offering to sell, furnish, administer, or give to a minor any methamphetamine-related drug or any precursors of methamphetamine unless the prior conviction was for a serious felony described in subparagraph (24) of subdivision (c) of Section 1192.7.

(b) It is the intent of the Legislature in enacting subdivisions (b) to (i), inclusive, to ensure longer prison sentences and greater punishment for those who commit a felony and have been previously convicted of one or more serious and/or violent felony offenses.

(c) Notwithstanding any other law, if a defendant has been convicted of a felony and it has been pled and proved that the defendant has one or more prior serious and/or violent felony convictions as defined in subdivision (d), the court shall adhere to each of the following:

(1) There shall not be an aggregate term limitation for purposes of con-

secutive sentencing for any subsequent felony conviction.

(2) Probation for the current offense shall not be granted, nor shall execution or imposition of the sentence be suspended for any prior offense.

(3) The length of time between the prior serious and/or violent felony conviction and the current felony conviction shall not affect the imposition of sentence.

(4) There shall not be a commitment to any other facility other than the state prison. Diversion shall not be granted nor shall the defendant be eligible for commitment to the California Rehabilitation Center as provided in Article 2 (commencing with Section 3050) of Chapter 1 of Division 3 of the Welfare and Institutions Code.

(5) The total amount of credits awarded pursuant to Article 2.5 (commencing with Section 2930) of Chapter 7 of Title 1 of Part 3 shall not exceed one-fifth of the total term of imprisonment imposed and shall not accrue until the defendant is physically placed in the state prison.

(6) If there is a current conviction for more than one felony count not committed on the same occasion, and not arising from the same set of operative facts, the court shall sentence the defendant consecutively on each count pursuant to subdivision (e).

(7) If there is a current conviction for more than one serious or violent felony as described in paragraph (6), the court shall impose the sentence for each conviction consecutive to the sentence for any other conviction for which the defendant may be consecutively sentenced in the manner prescribed by law.

(8) Any sentence imposed pursuant to subdivision (e) will be imposed consecutive to any other sentence which the defendant is already serving, unless otherwise provided by law.

(d) Notwithstanding any other law and for the purposes of subdivisions (b) to (i), inclusive, a prior conviction of a serious and/or violent felony shall be defined as:

(1) Any offense defined in subdivision (c) of Section 667.5 as a violent felony or any offense defined in subdivision (c) of Section 1192.7 as a serious felony in this state. The determination of whether a prior conviction is a prior felony conviction for purposes of subdivisions (b) to

(i), inclusive, shall be made upon the date of that prior conviction and is not affected by the sentence imposed unless the sentence automatically, upon the initial sentencing, converts the felony to a misdemeanor. None of the following dispositions shall affect the determination that a prior conviction is a prior felony for purposes of subdivisions (b) to (i), inclusive:

(A) The suspension of imposition of judgment or sentence.

(B) The stay of execution of sentence.

(C) The commitment to the State Department of Health Services as a mentally disordered sex offender following a conviction of a felony.

(D) The commitment to the California Rehabilitation Center or any other facility whose function is rehabilitative diversion from the state prison.

(2) A prior conviction in another jurisdiction for an offense that, if committed in California, is punishable by imprisonment in the state prison shall constitute a prior conviction of a particular serious and/or violent felony if the prior conviction in the other jurisdiction is for an offense that includes all of the elements of a particular violent felony as defined in subdivision (c) of Section 667.5 or serious felony as defined in subdivision (c) of Section 1192.7.

(3) A prior juvenile adjudication shall constitute a prior serious and/or violent felony conviction for purposes of sentence enhancement if:

(A) The juvenile was 16 years of age or older at the time he or she committed the prior offense.

(B) The prior offense is listed in subdivision (b) of Section 707 of the Welfare and Institutions Code or described in paragraph (1) or (2) as a serious and/or violent felony.

(C) The juvenile was found to be a fit and proper subject to be dealt with under the juvenile court law.

(D) The juvenile was adjudged a ward of the juvenile court within the meaning of Section 602 of the Welfare and Institutions Code because the person committed an offense listed in subdivision (b) of Section 707 of the Welfare and Institutions Code.

(e) For purposes of subdivisions (b) to (i), inclusive, and in addition to any other enhancement or punishment provisions which may apply, the following shall apply where a defendant has one or more prior serious and/or violent felony convictions:

(1) If a defendant has one prior serious and/or violent felony conviction as defined in subdivision (d) that has been pled and proved, the determinate term or minimum term for an indeterminate term shall be twice the term otherwise provided as punishment for the current felony conviction.

(2) (A) Except as provided in subparagraph (C), if a defendant has two or more prior serious and/or violent felony convictions as defined in subdivision (d) that have been pled and proved, the term for the current felony conviction shall be an indeterminate term of life imprisonment with a minimum term of the indeterminate sentence calculated as the greatest of:

(i) Three times the term otherwise provided as punishment for each current felony conviction subsequent to the two or more prior serious and/or violent felony convictions.

(ii) Imprisonment in the state prison for 25 years.

(iii) The term determined by the court pursuant to Section 1170 for the underlying conviction, including any enhancement applicable under Chapter 4.5 (commencing with Section 1170) of Title 7 of Part 2, or any period prescribed by Section 190 or 3046.

(B) The indeterminate term described in subparagraph (A) shall be served consecutive to any other term of imprisonment for which a consecutive term may be imposed by law. Any other term imposed subsequent to any indeterminateterm described in subparagraph (A) shall not be merged therein but shall commence at the time the person would otherwise have been released from prison.

(C) If a defendant has two or more prior serious and/or violent felony convictions as defined in subdivision (c) of Section 667.5 or subdivision (c) of Section 1192.7 that have been pled and proved, and the current offense is not a serious or violent felony as defined in subdivision (d), the defendant shall be sentenced pursuant to paragraph (1) of subdivision (e) unless the prosecution pleads and proves any of the following:

(i) The current offense is a controlled substance charge, in which an allegation under Section 11370.4 or 11379.8 of the Health and Safety Code was admitted or found true.

(ii) The current offense is a felony sex offense, defined in subdivision (d) of Section 261.5 or Section 262, or any felony offense that results in mandatory registration as a sex offender pursuant to subdivision (c) of Section 290 except for violations of Sections 266 and 285, paragraph (1) of subdivision (b) and subdivision (e) of Section 286, paragraph (1) of subdivision (b) and subdivision (e) of Section 288a, Section 311.11, and Section 314.

(iii) During the commission of the current offense, the defendant used a firearm, was armed with a firearm or deadly weapon, or intended to cause great bodily injury to another person.

(iv) The defendant suffered a prior serious and/or violent felony conviction, as defined in subdivision (d) of this section, for any of the following felonies:

(I) A "sexually violent offense" as defined in subdivision (b) of Section 6600 of the Welfare and Institutions Code.

(II) Oral copulation with a child who is under 14 years of age, and who is more than 10 years younger than he or she as defined by Section 288a, sodomy with another person who is under 14 years of age and more than 10 years younger than he or she as defined by Section 286, or sexual penetration with another person who is under 14 years of age, and who is more than 10 years younger than he or she, as defined by Section 289.

(III) A lewd or lascivious act involving a child under 14 years of age, in violation of Section 288.

(IV) Any homicide offense, including any attempted homicide offense, defined in Sections 187 to 191.5, inclusive.

(V) Solicitation to commit murder as defined in Section 653f.

(VI) Assault with a machine gun on a peace officer or

firefighter, as defined in paragraph (3) of subdivision (d) of Section 245.

(VII) Possession of a weapon of mass destruction, as defined in paragraph (1) of subdivision (a) of Section 11418.

(VIII) Any serious and/or violent felony offense punishable in California by life imprisonment or death.

(f) (1) Notwithstanding any other law, subdivisions (b) to (i), inclusive, shall be applied in every case in which a defendant has one or more prior serious and/or violent felony convictions as defined in subdivision (d). The prosecuting attorney shall plead and prove each prior serious and/or violent felony conviction except as provided in paragraph (2).

(2) The prosecuting attorney may move to dismiss or strike a prior serious and/or violent felony conviction allegation in the furtherance of justice pursuant to Section 1385, or if there is insufficient evidence to prove the prior serious and/or violent felony conviction. If upon the satisfaction of the court that there is insufficient evidence to prove the prior serious and/or violent felony conviction, the court may dismiss or strike the allegation. Nothing in this section shall be read to alter a court's authority under Section 1385.

(g) Prior serious and/or violent felony convictions shall not be used in plea bargaining as defined in subdivision (b) of Section 1192.7. The prosecution shall plead and prove all known prior felony serious and/or violent convictions and shall not enter into any agreement to strike or seek the dismissal of any prior serious and/or violent felony conviction allegation except as provided in paragraph (2) of subdivision (f).

(h) All references to existing statutes in subdivisions (c) to (g), inclusive, are to statutes as they existed on November 7, 2012.

(i) If any provision of subdivisions (b) to (h), inclusive, or the application thereof to any person or circumstance is held invalid, that invalidity shall not affect other provisions or applications of those subdivisions which can be given effect without the invalid provision or application, and to this end the provisions of those subdivisions are severable.

(j) The provisions of this section shall not be amended by the Legislature except by statute passed in each house by rollcall vote entered in the journal, two-thirds of the membership concurring, or by a statute that becomes effective only when approved by the electors.

Penal Code § 1000

(Amended by Statute, Effective January 1, 2015.)

(a) This chapter shall apply whenever a case is before any court upon an accusatory pleading for a violation of Section 11350, 11357, 11364, or 11365, paragraph (2) of subdivision (b) of Section 11375, Section 11377, or Section 11550 of the Health and Safety Code, or subdivision (b) of Section 23222 of the Vehicle Code, or Section 11358 of the Health and Safety Code if the marijuana planted, cultivated, harvested, dried, or processed is for personal use, or Section 11368 of the Health and Safety Code if the narcotic drug was secured by a fictitious prescription and is for the personal use of the defendant and was not sold or furnished to another, or subdivision (d) of Section 653f if the solicitation was for acts directed to personal use only, or Section 381 or subdivision (f) of Section 647 of the Penal Code, if for being under the influence of a controlled substance, or Section 4060 of the Business and Professions Code, and it appears to the prosecuting attorney that, except as provided in subdivision (b) of Section 11357 of the Health and Safety Code, all of the following apply to the defendant:

(1) The defendant has no conviction for any offense involving controlled substances prior to the alleged commission of the charged offense.

(2) The offense charged did not involve a crime of violence or threatened violence.

(3) There is no evidence of a violation relating to narcotics or restricted dangerous drugs other than a violation of the sections listed in this subdivision.

(4) The defendant's record does not indicate that probation or parole has ever been revoked without thereafter being completed.

(5) The defendant's record does not indicate that he or she has successfully completed or been terminated from diversion or deferred entry of judgment pursuant to this chapter within five years prior to the alleged commission of the charged offense.

(6) The defendant has no prior felony conviction within five years prior to the alleged commission of the charged offense.

(b) The prosecuting attorney shall review his or her file to determine whether or not paragraphs (1) to (6), inclusive, of subdivision (a) apply to the defendant. Upon the agreement of the prosecuting attorney, law enforcement, the public defender, and the presiding judge of the criminal division of the superior court, or a judge designated by the presiding judge, this procedure shall be completed as soon as possible after the initial filing of the charges. If the defendant is found eligible, the prosecuting attorney shall file with the court a declaration in writing or state for the record the grounds upon which the determination is based, and shall make this information available to the defendant and his or her attorney. This procedure is intended to allow the court to set the hearing for deferred entry of judgment at the arraignment. If the defendant is found ineligible for deferred entry of judgment, the prosecuting attorney shall file with the court a declaration in writing or state for the record the grounds upon which the determination is based, and shall make this information available to the defendant and his or her attorney. The sole remedy of a defendant who is found ineligible for deferred entry of judgment is a postconviction appeal.

(c) All referrals for deferred entry of judgment granted by the court pursuant to this chapter shall be made only to programs that have been certified by the county drug program administrator pursuant to Chapter 1.5 (commencing with Section 1211) of Title 8, or to programs that provide services at no cost to the participant and have been deemed by the court and the county drug program administrator to be credible and effective. The defendant may request to be referred to a program in any county, as long as that program meets the criteria set forth in this subdivision.

(d) Deferred entry of judgment for a violation of Section 11368 of the Health and Safety Code shall not prohibit any administrative agency from taking disciplinary action against a licensee or from denying a license. Nothing in this subdivision shall be construed to expand or restrict the provisions of Section 1000.4.

(e) Any defendant who is participating in a program referred to in this section may be required to undergo analysis of his or her urine for the purpose of testing for the presence of any drug as part of the program. However, urine analysis results shall not be admissible as a basis for any new criminal prosecution or proceeding.

Penal Code § 1170(h)

(Added by Statute, Effective 1982.)

(h) (1) Except as provided in paragraph (3), a felony punishable pursuant to this subdivision where the term is not specified in the underlying offense shall be punishable by a term of imprisonment in a county jail for 16 months, or two or three years.

(2) Except as provided in paragraph (3), a felony punishable pursuant to this subdivision shall be punishable by imprisonment in a county jail for the term described in the underlying offense.

(3) Notwithstanding paragraphs (1) and (2), where the defendant (A) has a prior or current felony conviction for a serious felony described in subdivision (c) of Section 1192.7 or a prior or current conviction for a violent felony described in subdivision (c) of Section 667.5, (B) has a prior felony conviction in another jurisdiction for an offense that has all the elements of a serious felony described in subdivision (c) of Section 1192.7 or a violent felony described in subdivision (c) of Section 667.5, (C) is required to register as a sex offender pursuant to Chapter 5.5 (commencing with Section 290) of Title 9 of Part 1, or (D) is convicted of a crime and as part of the sentence an enhancement pursuant to Section 186.11 is imposed, an executed sentence for a felony punishable pursuant to this subdivision shall be served in state prison.

(4) Nothing in this subdivision shall be construed to prevent other dispositions authorized by law, including pretrial diversion, deferred entry of judgment, or an order granting probation pursuant to Section 1203.1.

(5) (A) Unless the court finds that, in the interests of justice, it is not appropriate in a particular case, the court, when imposing a sentence pursuant to paragraph (1) or (2), shall suspend execution of a concluding portion of the term for a period selected at the court's discretion.

(B) The portion of a defendant's sentenced term that is suspended pursuant to this paragraph shall be known as mandatory supervision, and, unless otherwise ordered by the court, shall commence upon release from physical custody or an alternative custody program, whichever is later. During the period of mandatory supervision, the defendant shall be supervised by the county probation officer in accordance with the terms, conditions, and procedures generally applicable to persons placed on probation, for the remaining unserved portion of the sentence imposed by the court. The period of supervision shall be mandatory, and may not be earlier terminated except by court order. Any proceeding to revoke or modify mandatory supervision under this subparagraph shall be conducted pursuant to either subdivisions (a) and (b) of Section 1203.2 or Section 1203.3. During the period when the defendant is under that supervision, unless in actual custody related to the sentence imposed by the court, the defendant shall be entitled to only actual time credit against the term of imprisonment imposed by the court. Any time period which is suspended because a person has absconded shall not be credited toward the period of supervision.

(6) The sentencing changes made by the act that added this subdivision shall be applied prospectively to any person sentenced on or after October 1, 2011.

(7) The sentencing changes made to paragraph (5) by the act that added this paragraph shall become effective and operative on January 1, 2015, and shall be applied prospectively to any person sentenced on or after January 1, 2015.

Penal Code § 12022

(Amended by Statute, Effective January 1, 2014.)

(a) (1) Except as provided in subdivisions (c) and (d), a person who is armed with a firearm in the commission of a felony or attempted felony shall be punished by an additional and consecutive term of imprisonment pursuant to subdivision (h) of Section 1170 for one year, unless the arming is an element of that offense. This additional term shall apply to a person who is a principal in the commission of a felony or attempted felony if one or more of the principals is armed with a firearm, whether or not the person is personally armed with a firearm.

(2) Except as provided in subdivision (c), and notwithstanding subdivision (d), if the firearm is an assault weapon, as defined in Section 30510 or 30515, or a machinegun, as defined in Section 16880, or a .50 BMG rifle, as defined in Section 30530, the additional and consecutive term described in this subdivision shall be three years imprisonment pursuant to subdivision (h) of Section 1170 whether or not the arming is an element of the offense of which the person was convicted. The additional term provided in this paragraph shall apply to any person who is a principal in the commission of a felony or attempted felony if one or more of the principals is armed with an assault weapon, machinegun, or a .50 BMG rifle, whether or not the person is personally armed with an assault weapon, machinegun, or a .50 BMG rifle.

(b) (1) A person who personally uses a deadly or dangerous weapon in the commission of a felony or attempted felony shall be punished by an additional and consecutive term of imprisonment in the state prison for one year, unless use of a deadly or dangerous weapon is an element of that offense.

(2) If the person described in paragraph (1) has been convicted of carjacking or attempted carjacking, the additional term shall be in the state prison for one, two, or three years.

(3) When a person is found to have personally used a deadly or dangerous weapon in the commission of a felony or attempted felony as provided in this subdivision and the weapon is owned by that person, the court shall order that the weapon be deemed a nuisance and disposed of in the manner provided in Sections 18000 and 18005.

(c) Notwithstanding the enhancement set forth in subdivision (a), a person who is personally armed with a firearm in the commission of a violation or attempted violation of Section 11351, 11351.5, 11352, 11366.5, 11366.6, 11378, 11378.5, 11379, 11379.5, or 11379.6 of the Health and Safety Code shall be punished by an additional and consecutive term of imprisonment pursuant to subdivision (h) of Section 1170 for three, four, or five years.

(d) Notwithstanding the enhancement set forth in subdivision (a), a person who is not personally armed with a firearm who, knowing that another principal is personally armed with a firearm, is a principal in the commission of an offense or attempted offense specified in subdivision (c), shall be punished by an additional and consecutive term of imprisonment pursuant to subdivision (h) of Section 1170 for one, two, or three years.

(e) For purposes of imposing an enhancement under Section 1170.1, the enhancements under this section shall count as a single enhancement.

(f) Notwithstanding any other provision of law, the court may strike the additional punishment for the enhancements provided in subdivision (c) or (d) in an unusual case where the interests of justice would best be served, if the court specifies on the record and enters into the minutes the circumstances indicating that the interests of justice would best be served by that disposition.

VIII. Revenue and Taxation Code Sections

Revenue and Taxation Code § 34010

(AUMA, Effective November 9, 2016.)

For purposes of this part:

(a) "Board" shall mean the Board of Equalization or its successor agency.

(b) "Bureau" shall mean the Bureau of Marijuana Control within the Department of Consumer Affairs.

(c) "Tax Fund" means the California Marijuana Tax Fund created by Section 34018.

(d) "Marijuana" shall have the same meaning as set forth in Section 11018 of the Health and Safety Code and shall also mean medical cannabis.

(e) "Marijuana products" shall have the same meaning as set forth in Section 11018.1 of the Health and Safety Code and shall also mean medical concentrates and medical cannabis products.

(f) "Marijuana flowers" shall mean the dried flowers of the marijuana plant as defined by the Board.

(g) "Marijuana leaves" shall mean all parts of the marijuana plant other than marijuana flowers that are sold or consumed.

(h) "Gross receipts" shall have the same meaning as set forth in Section 6012.

(i) "Retail sale" shall have the same meaning as set forth in Section 6007.

(j) "Person" shall have the same meaning as set forth in section 6005.

(k) "Microbusiness" shall have the same meaning as set forth in Section 26070(a)(3) of the Business and Professions Code.

(l) "Nonprofit" shall have the same meaning as set forth in Section 26070.5 of the Business and Professions Code.

Revenue and Taxation Code § 34011

(AUMA, Effective November 9, 2016.)

(a) Effective January 1, 2018, a marijuana excise tax shall be imposed upon purchasers of marijuana or marijuana products sold in this state at the rate of fifteen percent (15%) of the gross receipts of any retail sale by a dispensary or other person required to be licensed pursuant to Chapter 3.5 of Division 8 of the Business and Professions Code or a retailer, microbusiness, nonprofit, or other person required to be licensed pursuant to Division 10 of the Business and Professions Code to sell marijuana and marijuana products directly to a purchaser.

(b) Except as otherwise provided by regulation, the tax levied under this section shall apply to the full price, if non-itemized, of any transaction involving both marijuana or marijuana products and any other otherwise distinct and identifiable goods or services, and the price of any goods or services, if a reduction in the price of marijuana or marijuana products is contingent on purchase of those goods or services.

(c) A dispensary or other person required to be licensed pursuant to Chapter 3.5 of Division 8 of the Business and Professions Code or a retailer, microbusiness, nonprofit, or other person required to be licensed pursuant to Division 10 of the Business and Professions Code shall be responsible for collecting this tax and remitting it to the board in accordance with rules and procedures established under law and any regulations adopted by the board.

(d) The excise tax imposed by this section shall be in addition to the sales and use tax imposed by the state and local governments.

(e) Gross receipts from the sale of marijuana or marijuana products for purposes of assessing the sales and use tax under Part 1 of this division shall include the tax levied pursuant to this section.

(f) No marijuana or marijuana products may be sold to a purchaser unless the excise tax required by law has been paid by the purchaser at the time of sale.

(g) The sales and use tax imposed by Part 1 of this division shall not apply to retail sales of medical cannabis, medical cannabis concentrate, edible medical cannabis products or topical cannabis as those terms are defined in Chapter 3.5 of Division 8 of the Business and Professions Code when a qualified patient (or primary caregiver for a qualified patient) provides his or her card issued under Section 11362.71 of the Health and Safety Code and a valid government-issued identification card.

Revenue and Taxation Code § 34012

(AUMA, Effective November 9, 2016.)

(a) Effective January 1, 2018, there is hereby imposed a cultivation tax on all harvested marijuana that enters the commercial market upon all persons required to be licensed to cultivate marijuana pursuant to Chapter 3.5 of Division 8 of the Business and Professions Code or Division 10 of the Business and Professions Code. The tax shall be due after the marijuana is harvested.

>(1) The tax for marijuana flowers shall be nine dollars and twenty-five cents ($9.25) per dry-weight ounce.

>(2) The tax for marijuana leaves shall be set at two dollars and seventy-five cents ($2.75) per dry-weight ounce.

(b) The board may adjust the tax rate for marijuana leaves annually to reflect fluctuations in the relative price of marijuana flowers to marijuana leaves.

(c) The board may from time to time establish other categories of harvested marijuana, categories for unprocessed or frozen marijuana or immature plants, or marijuana that is shipped directly to manufacturers. These categories shall be taxed at their relative value compared with marijuana flowers.

(d) The board may prescribe by regulation a method and manner for payment of the cultivation tax that utilizes tax stamps or state-issued product bags that indicate that all required tax has been paid on the product to which the tax stamp is affixed or in which the marijuana is packaged.

(e) The tax stamps and product bags shall be of the designs, specifications and denominations as may be prescribed by the board and may be purchased by any licensee under Chapter 3.5 of Division 8 of the Business and Professions Code or under Division 10 of the Business and Professions Code.

(f) Subsequent to the establishment of a tax stamp program, the board may by regulation provide that no marijuana may be removed from a licensed cultivation facility or transported on a public highway unless in a state-issued product bag bearing a tax stamp in the proper denomination.

(g) The tax stamps and product bags shall be capable of being read by a scanning or similar device and must be traceable utilizing the track and trace system pursuant to Section 26170 of the Business and Professions Code.

(h) Persons required to be licensed to cultivate marijuana pursuant to Chapter 3. 5 of Division 8 of the Business and Professions Code or Division 10 of the Business and Professions Code shall be responsible for payment of the tax pursuant to regulations adopted by the board. No marijuana may be sold unless the tax has been paid as provided in this part.

(i) All marijuana removed from a cultivator's premises, except for plant waste, shall be presumed to be sold and thereby taxable under this section.

(j) The tax imposed by this section shall be imposed on all marijuana cultivated in the state pursuant to rules and regulations promulgated by the board, but shall not apply to marijuana cultivated for personal use under Section 11362.1 of the Health and Safety Code or cultivated by a qualified patient or primary caregiver in accordance with the Compassionate Use Act.

(k) Beginning January 1, 2020, the rates set forth in subdivisions (a), (b), and (c) shall be adjusted by the board annually there after for inflation.

Revenue and Taxation Code § 34013

(AUMA, Effective November 9, 2016.)

(a) The board shall administer and collect the taxes imposed by this part pursuant to the Fee Collection Procedures Law (Part 30 (commencing with Section 55001) of Division 2 of the Revenue and Taxation Code). For purposes of this part, the references in the Fee Collection Procedures Law to "fee" shall include the tax imposed by this part, and references to "fee payer" shall include a person required to pay or collect the tax imposed by this part.

(b) The board may prescribe, adopt, and enforce regulations relating to the administration and enforcement of this part, including, but not limited to, collections, reporting, refunds, and appeals.

(c) The board shall adopt necessary rules and regulations to administer the taxes in this part. Such rules and regulations may include methods or procedures to tag marijuana or marijuana products, or the packages thereof, to designate prior tax payment.

(d) The board may prescribe, adopt, and enforce any emergency regulations as necessary to implement, administer and enforce its duties under this division. Any emergency regulation prescribed, adopted, or enforced pursuant to this section shall be adopted in accordance with Chapter 3.5 (commencing with section 11340) of Part 1 of Division 3 of Title 2 of the Government Code, and for purposes of that chapter, including Section 11349.6 of the Government Code, the adoption of the regulation is an emergency and shall be considered by the Office of Administrative Law as necessary for the immediate preservation of the public peace, health and safety, and general welfare. Notwithstanding any other provision of law, the emergency regulations adopted by the board may remain in effect for two years from adoption.

(e) Any person who fails to pay the taxes imposed under this part shall, in addition to owing the taxes not paid, be subject to a penalty of at least one-half the amount of the taxes not paid, and shall be subject to having its license revoked pursuant to Section 26031 of the Business and Professions Code or pursuant to Chapter 3.5 of Division 8 of the Business and Professions Code.

(f) The board may bring such legal actions as are necessary to collect any deficiency in the tax required to be paid, and, upon the board's request, the Attorney General shall bring the actions.

Revenue and Taxation Code § 34014

(AUMA, Effective November 9, 2016.)

(a) All persons required to be licensed involved in the cultivation and retail sale of marijuana or marijuana products must obtain a separate permit from the board pursuant to regulations adopted by the board. No fee shall be charged to any person for issuance of the permit. Any person required to obtain a permit who engages in business as a cultivator, dispensary, retailer, microbusiness or nonprofit pursuant to Chapter 3.5 of Division 8 of the Business and Professions Code or Division 10 of the Business and Professions Code without a permit or after a permit has been canceled, suspended, or revoked, and each officer of any corporation which so engages in business, is guilty of a misdemeanor.

(b) The board may require every licensed dispensary, cultivator, microbusiness, nonprofit, or other person required to be licensed, to provide security to cover the liability for taxes imposed by state law on marijuana produced or received by the cultivator, microbusiness, nonprofit, or other person required to be licensed in accordance with procedures to be established by the board.

Notwithstanding anything herein to the contrary, the board may waive any security requirement it imposes for good cause, as determined by the board. "Good cause" includes, but is not limited to, the inability of a cultivator, microbusiness, nonprofit, or other person required to be licensed to obtain security due to a lack of service providers or the policies of service providers that prohibit service to a marijuana business. A person may not commence or continue any business or operation relating to marijuana cultivation until any surety required by the board with respect to the business or operation have been properly prepared, executed and submitted under this part.

(c) In fixing the amount of any security required by the board, the board shall give consideration to the financial hardship that may be imposed on licensees as a result of any shortage of available surety providers.

Revenue and Taxation Code § 34015

(AUMA, Effective November 9, 2016.)

(a) The marijuana excise tax and cultivation tax imposed by this part is due and payable to the board quarterly on or before the last day of the month following each quarterly period of three months. On or before the last day of the month following each quarterly period, a return for the preceding quarterly period shall be filed with the board by each person required to be licensed for cultivation or retail sale under Divisions 8 or 10 of the Business and Professions Code using electronic media. Returns shall be authenticated in a form or pursuant to methods as may be prescribed by the board. If the cultivation tax is paid by stamp pursuant to section 34012(d) the board may by regulation determine when and how the tax shall be paid.

(b) The board may require every person engaged in the cultivation, distribution or retail sale o f marijuana and marijuana products required to be licensed pursuant to Chapter 3.5 of Division 8 of the Business or Professions Code or Division 10 of the Business and Professions Code to file, on or before the 25th day of each month, a report using electronic media respecting the person's inventory, purchases, and sales during the preceding month and any other information as the board may require to carry out the purposes of this part. Reports shall be authenticated in a form or pursuant to methods as may be prescribed by the board.

Revenue and Taxation Code § 34016

(AUMA, Effective November 9, 2016.)

(a) Any peace officer, or board employee granted limited peace officer status pursuant to paragraph (6) of subdivision (a) of Section 830.11 of the Penal Code, upon presenting appropriate credentials, is authorized to enter any place as described in paragraph (3) and to conduct inspections in accordance with the following paragraphs, inclusive.

(1) Inspections shall be performed in a reasonable manner and at times that are reasonable under the circumstances, taking into consideration the normal business hours of the place to be entered.

(2) Inspections may be at any place at which marijuana or marijuana products are sold to purchasers, cultivated, or stored, or at any site where evidence of activities involving evasion of tax may be discovered.

(3) Inspections shall be requested or conducted no more than once in a 24-hour period.

(b) Any person who fails or refuses to allow an inspection shall be subject to a misdemeanor. Each offense shall be punished by a fine not to exceed five thousand dollars ($5,000), or imprisonment not exceeding one year in a county jail, or both the fine and imprisonment. The court shall order any fines assessed be deposited in the California Marijuana Tax Fund.

(c) Upon discovery by the board or a law enforcement agency that a licensee or any other person possesses, stores, owns, or has made a retail sale of marijuana or marijuana products, without evidence of tax payment or not contained in secure packaging, the board or the law enforcement agency shall be authorized to seize the marijuana or marijuana products. Any marijuana or marijuana products seized by a law enforcement agency or the board shall within seven days be deemed forfeited and the board shall comply with the procedures set forth in Sections 30436 through 30449, inclusive.

(d) Any person who renders a false or fraudulent report is guilty of a misdemeanor and subject to a fine not to exceed one thousand dollars ($1,000) for each offense.

(e) Any violation of any provisions of this part, except as otherwise provided, is a misdemeanor and is punishable as such.

(f) All moneys remitted to the board under this part shall be credited to the California Marijuana Tax Fund.

Revenue and Taxation Code § 34017

(AUMA, Effective November 9, 2016.)

The Legislative Analyst's Office shall submit a report to the Legislature by January 1, 2020, with recommendations to the Legislature for adjustments to the tax rate to achieve the goals of undercutting illicit market prices and discouraging use by persons younger than 21 years of age while ensuring sufficient revenues are generated for the programs identified in Section 34019.

Revenue and Taxation Code § 34018

(AUMA, Effective November 9, 2016.)

(a) The California Marijuana Tax Fund is hereby created in the State Treasury. The Tax Fund shall consist of all taxes, interest, penalties, and other amounts collected and paid to the board pursuant to this part, less payment of refunds.

(b) Notwithstanding any other law, the California Marijuana Tax Fund is a special trust fund established solely to carry out the purposes of the Control, Regulate and Tax Adult Use of Marijuana Act and all revenues deposited into the Tax Fund, together with interest or dividends earned by the fund, are hereby continuously appropriated for the purposes of the Control, Regulate and Tax Adult Use of Marijuana Act without regard to fiscal year and shall be expended only in accordance with the provisions of this part and its purposes.

(c) Notwithstanding any other law, the taxes imposed by this part and the revenue derived therefrom, including investment interest, shall not be considered to be part of the General Fund, as that term is used in Chapter 1 (commencing with section 16300) of Part 2 of Division 4 of the Government Code, shall not be considered General Fund revenue for purposes of Section 8 of Article XVI of the California Constitution and its implementing statutes, and shall not be considered "moneys" for purposes of subdivisions (a) and

(b) of Section 8 of Article XVI of the California Constitution and its implementing statutes.

Revenue and Taxation Code § 34019

(AUMA, Effective November 9, 2016.)

(a) Beginning with fiscal year 2017-2018 the Department of Finance shall estimate revenues to be received pursuant to sections 34011 and 34012 and provide those estimates to the Controller no later than June 15 of each year. The Controller shall use these estimates when disbursing funds pursuant to this section. Before any funds are disbursed pursuant to subdivisions (b), (c), (d), and (e) of this section the Controller shall disburse from the Tax Fund to the appropriate account, without regard to fiscal year, the following:

(1) Reasonable costs incurred by the board for administering and collecting the taxes imposed by this part; provided, however; such costs shall not exceed four percent (4%) of tax revenues received.

(2) Reasonable costs incurred by the Bureau, the Department o f Consumer Affairs, the Department of Food and Agriculture, and the Department of Public Health for implementing, administering, and enforcing Chapter 3.5 of Division 8 of the Business and Professions Code and Division 10 of the Business and Professions Code to the extent those costs are not reimbursed pursuant to Section 26180 of the Business and Professions Code or pursuant to Chapter 3.5 of Division 8 o f the Business and Professions Code. This paragraph shall remain operative through fiscal year 2022-2023.

(3) Reasonable costs incurred by the Department of Fish and Wildlife, the State Water Resources Control Board, and the Department of Pesticide Regulation for carrying out their respective duties under Chapter 3.5 of Division 8 of the Business and Professions Code or Division 10 of the Business and Professions Code to the extent those costs are not otherwise reimbursed.

(4) Reasonable costs incurred by the Controller for performing duties imposed by the Control, Regulate and Tax Adult Use of Marijuana Act, including the audit required by Section 34020.

(5) Reasonable costs incurred by the State Auditor for conducting the performance audit pursuant to Section 26191 of the Business and Pro-

fessions Code.

(6) Reasonable costs incurred by the Legislative Analyst's Office for performing duties imposed by Section 34017.

(7) Sufficient funds to reimburse the Division of Labor Standards Enforcement and Occupational Safety and Health within the Department of Industrial Relations and the Employment Development Department for the costs of applying and enforcing state labor laws to licensees under Chapter 3.5 of Division 8 of the Business and Professions Code and Division 10 of the Business and Professions Code.

(b) The Controller shall next disburse the sum of ten million dollars ($10,000,000) to a public university or universities in California annually beginning with fiscal year 2018-2019 until fiscal year 2028-2029 to research and evaluate the implementation and effect of the Control, Regulate and Tax Adult Use of Marijuana Act, and shall, if appropriate, make recommendations to the Legislature and Governor regarding possible amendments to the Control, Regulate and Tax Adult Use of Marijuana Act. The recipients of these funds shall publish reports on their findings at a minimum of every two years and shall make the reports available to the public. The Bureau shall select the universities to be funded. The research funded pursuant to this subdivision shall include but not necessarily be limited to:

(1) Impacts on public health, including health costs associated with marijuana use, as well as whether marijuana use is associated with an increase or decrease in use of alcohol or other drugs.

(2) The impact of treatment for maladaptive marijuana use and the effectiveness of different treatment programs.

(3) Public safety issues related to marijuana use, including studying the effectiveness of the packaging and labeling requirements and advertising and marketing restrictions contained in the Act at preventing underage access to and use of marijuana and marijuana products, and studying the health-related effects among users of varying potency levels of marijuana and marijuana products.

(4) Marijuana use rates, maladaptive use rates for adults and youth, and diagnosis rates of marijuana-related substance use disorders.

(5) Marijuana market prices, illicit market prices, tax structures and rates, including an evaluation of how to best tax marijuana based on

potency, and the structure and function of licensed marijuana businesses.

(6) Whether additional protections are needed to prevent unlawful monopolies or anti- competitive behavior from occurring in the non-medical marijuana industry and, if so, recommendations as to the most effective measures for preventing such behavior.

(7) The economic impacts in the private and public sectors, including but not necessarily limited to, job creation, workplace safety, revenues, taxes generated for state and local budgets, and criminal justice impacts, including, but not necessarily limited to, impacts on law enforcement and public resources, short and long term consequences of involvement in the criminal justice system, and state and local government agency administrative costs and revenue.

(8) Whether the regulatory agencies tasked with implementing and enforcing the Control, Regulate and Tax Adult Use of Marijuana Act are doing so consistent with the purposes of the Act, and whether different agencies might do so more effectively.

(9) Environmental issues related to marijuana production and the criminal prohibition of marijuana production.

(10) The geographic location, structure, and function of licensed marijuana businesses, and demographic data, including race, ethnicity, and gender, of license holders.

(11) The outcomes achieved by the changes in criminal penalties made under the Control, Regulate, and Tax Adult Use of Marijuana Act for marijuana-related offenses, and the outcomes of the juvenile justice system, in particular, probation-based treatments and the frequency of up-charging illegal possession of marijuana or marijuana products to a more serious offense.

(c) The Controller shall next disburse the sum of three million dollars ($3,000, 000) annually to the Department of the California Highway Patrol beginning fiscal year 2018-2019 until fiscal year 2022-2023 to establish and adopt protocols to determine whether a driver is operating a vehicle while impaired, including impairment by the use of marijuana or marijuana products, and to establish and adopt protocols setting forth best practices to assist law enforcement agencies. The department may hire personnel to establish the protocols specified in this subdivision. In addition, the department may make grants to public and private research institutions for the purpose of developing technology for determining when a driver is operating a vehicle while impaired, including impairment by the use of marijuana or marijuana products.

(d) The Controller shall next disburse the sum o f ten million dollars ($10,000,000) beginning fiscal year 2018-2019 and increasing ten million dollars ($10,000,000) each fiscal year thereafter until fiscal year 2022-2023, at which time the disbursement shall be fifty million dollars ($50,000,000) each year thereafter, to the Governor's Office of Business and Economic Development, in consultation with the Labor and Workforce Development Agency and the Department of Social Services, to administer a Community Reinvestments grants program to local health departments and at least fifty-percent to qualified community-based nonprofit organizations to support job placement, mental health treatment, substance use disorder treatment, system navigation services, legal services to address barriers to reentry, and linkages to medical care for communities disproportionately affected by past federal and state drug policies. The Office shall solicit input from community-based job skills, job placement, and legal service providers with relevant expertise as to the administration of the grants program. In addition, the Office shall periodically evaluate the programs it is funding to determine the effectiveness of the programs, shall not spend more than four percent (4%) for administrative costs related to implementation, evaluation and oversight of the programs, and shall award grants annually, beginning no later than January 1, 2020.

(e) The Controller shall next disburse the sum of two million dollars ($2,000,000) annually to the University of California San Diego Center for Medicinal Cannabis Research to further the objectives of the Center including the enhanced understanding of the efficacy and adverse effects of marijuana as a pharmacological agent.

(f) By July 15 of each fiscal year beginning in fiscal year 2018-2019, the Controller shall, after disbursing funds pursuant to subdivisions (a), (b), (c), (d), and (e), disburse funds deposited in the Tax Fund during the prior fiscal year into sub-trust accounts, which are hereby created, as follows:

(1) Sixty percent (60%) shall be deposited in the Youth Education, Prevention, Early Intervention and Treatment Account, and disbursed by the Controller to the Department of Health Care Services for programs for youth that are designed to educate about and to prevent substance use disorders and to prevent harm from substance use. The Department

of Health Care services shall enter into inter-agency agreements with the Department of Public Health and the Department of Education to implement and administer these programs. The programs shall emphasize accurate education, effective prevention, early intervention, school retention, and timely treatment services for youth, their families and caregivers. The programs may include, but are not limited to, the following components:

(A) Prevention and early intervention services including outreach, risk survey and education to youth, families, caregivers, schools, primary care health providers, behavioral health and substance use disorder service providers, community and faith-based organizations, foster care providers, juvenile and family courts, and others to recognize and reduce risks related to substance use, and the early signs of problematic use and of substance use disorders.

(B) Grants to schools to develop and support Student Assistance Programs, or other similar programs, designed to prevent and reduce substance use, and improve school retention and performance, by supporting students who are at risk of dropping out of school and promoting alternatives to suspension or expulsion that focus on school retention, remediation, and professional care. Schools with higher than average dropout rates should be prioritized for grants.

(C) Grants to programs for outreach, education and treatment for homeless youth and out-of-school youth with substance use disorders.

(D) Access and linkage to care provided by county behavioral health programs for youth, and their families and caregivers, who have a substance use disorder or who are at risk for developing a substance use disorder.

(E) Youth-focused substance use disorder treatment programs that are culturally and gender competent, trauma-informed, evidence-based and provide a continuum of care that includes screening and assessment (substance use disorder as well as mental health), early intervention, active treatment, family involvement, case management, overdose prevention, prevention of communicable diseases related to substance use, relapse management for substance use and other co-occurring behavioral health disorders, vocational services, literacy services, parenting classes, family therapy and counseling services, medication-assisted treatments, psychiatric medication and psychotherapy. When indicated, referrals must be made to other providers.

(F) To the extent permitted by law and where indicated, interventions shall utilize a two-generation approach to addressing substance use disorders with the capacity to treat youth and adults together. This would include supporting the development of family-based interventions that address substance use disorders and related problems within the context of families, including parents, foster parents, caregivers and all their children.

(G) Programs to assist individuals, as well as families and friends of drug using young people, to reduce the stigma associated with substance use including being diagnosed with a substance use disorder or seeking substance use disorder services. This includes peer-run outreach and education to reduce stigma, anti-stigma campaigns, and community recovery networks.

(H) Workforce training and wage structures that increase the hiring pool of behavioral health staff with substance use disorder prevention and treatment expertise. Provide ongoing education and coaching that increases substance use treatment providers' core competencies and trains providers on promising and evidenced-based practices.

(I) Construction of community-based youth treatment facilities.

(J) The departments may contract with each county behavioral health program for the provision of services.

(K) Funds shall be allocated to counties based on demonstrated need, including the number of youth in the county, the prevalence of substance use disorders among adults, and confirmed through statistical data, validated assessments or submitted reports prepared by the applicable county to demonstrate and validate need.

(L) The departments shall periodically evaluate the programs they are funding to determine the effectiveness of the programs.

(M) The departments may use up to four percent (4%) of the moneys allocated to the Youth Education, Prevention, Early Intervention and Treatment Account for administrative costs related to implementation, evaluation and oversight of the programs.

(N) If the Department of Finance ever determines that funding pursuant to marijuana taxation exceeds demand for youth prevention and treatment services in the state, the departments shall provide a plan to the Department of Finance to provide treatment services to adults as well as youth using these funds.

(O) The departments shall solicit input from volunteer health organizations, physicians who treat addiction, treatment researchers, family therapy and counseling providers, and professional education associations with relevant expertise as to the administration of any grants made pursuant to this paragraph.

(2) Twenty percent (20%) shall be deposited in the Environmental Restoration and Protection Account, and disbursed by the Controller as follows:

(A) To the Department of Fish and Wildlife and the Department of Parks and Recreation for the cleanup, remediation, and restoration of environmental damage in watersheds affected by marijuana cultivation and related activities including, but not limited to, damage that occurred prior to enactment of this part, and to support local partnerships for this purpose. The Department of Fish and Wildlife and the Department of Parks and Recreation may distribute a portion of the funds they receive from the Environmental Restoration and Protection Account through grants for purposes specified in this paragraph.

(B) To the Department of Fish and Wildlife and the Department of Parks and Recreation for the stewardship and operation of state-owned wildlife habitat areas and state park units in a manner that discourages and prevents the illegal cultivation, production, sale and use of marijuana and marijuana products on public lands, and to facilitate the investigation, enforcement and prosecution of illegal cultivation, production, sale, and use of marijuana or marijuana products on public lands.

(C) To the Department of Fish and Wildlife to assist in funding the watershed enforcement program and multiagency taskforce established pursuant to subdivisions (b) and (c) of Section 12029 of the

Fish and Game Code to facilitate the investigation, enforcement, and prosecution of these offenses and to ensure the reduction of adverse impacts of marijuana cultivation, production, sale, and use on fish and wildlife habitats throughout the state.

(D) For purposes of this paragraph, the Secretary of the Natural Resources Agency shall determine the allocation of revenues between the departments. During the first five years of implementation, first consideration should be given to funding purposes specified in subparagraph (A).

(E) Funds allocated pursuant to this paragraph shall be used to increase and enhance activities described in subparagraphs (A), (B), and (C), and not replace allocation of other funding for these purposes. Accordingly, annual General Fund appropriations to the Department of Fish and Wildlife and the Department of Parks and Recreation shall not be reduced below the levels provided in the Budget Act of 2014 (Chapter 25 of Statutes of 2014).

(3) Twenty percent (20%) shall be deposited into the State and Local Government Law Enforcement Account and disbursed by the Controller as follows:

(A) To the Department of the California Highway Patrol for conducting training programs for detecting, testing and enforcing laws against driving under the influence of alcohol and other drugs, including driving under the influence of marijuana. The Department may hire personnel to conduct the training programs specified in this subparagraph.

(B) To the Department of the California Highway Patrol to fund internal California Highway Patrol programs and grants to qualified nonprofit organizations and local governments for education, prevention and enforcement of laws related to driving under the influence of alcohol and other drugs, including marijuana; programs that help enforce traffic laws, educate the public in traffic safety, provide varied and effective means of reducing fatalities, injuries and economic losses from collisions; and for the purchase of equipment related to enforcement of laws related to driving under the influence of alcohol and other drugs, including marijuana.

(C) To the Board of State and Community Corrections for making grants to local governments to assist with law enforcement, fire protection, or other local programs addressing public health and safety associated with the implementation of the Control, Regulate and Tax Adult Use of Marijuana Act. The Board shall not make any grants to local governments which have banned the cultivation, including personal cultivation under Section 11362.2(b)(3) of the Health and Safety Code, or retail sale of marijuana or marijuana products pursuant to Section 26200 of the Business and Professions Code or as otherwise provided by law.

(D) For purposes of this paragraph the Department of Finance shall determine the allocation of revenues between the agencies; provided, however, beginning in fiscal year 2022-2023 the amount allocated pursuant to subparagraph (A) shall not be less than ten million dollars ($10,000,000) annually and the amount allocated pursuant to subparagraph (B) shall not be less than forty million dollars ($40,000,000) annually. In determining the amount to be allocated before fiscal year 2022-2023 pursuant to this paragraph, the Department of Finance shall give initial priority to subparagraph (A).

(g) Funds allocated pursuant to subdivision (f) shall be used to increase the funding of programs and purposes identified and shall not be used to replace allocation of other funding for these purposes.

(h) Effective July 1, 2028, the Legislature may amend this section by majority vote to further the purposes of the Control, Regulate and Tax Adult Use of Marijuana Act, including allocating funds to programs other than those specified in subdivisions (d) and (f) of this section. Any revisions pursuant to this subdivision shall not result in a reduction of funds to accounts established pursuant to subdivisions (d) and (f) in any subsequent year from the amount allocated to each account in fiscal year 2027-2028. Prior to July 1, 2028, the Legislature may not change the allocations to programs specified in subdivisions (d) and (f) of this section.

Revenue and Taxation Code § 34020

(AUMA, Effective November 9, 2016.)

The Controller shall periodically audit the Tax Fund to ensure that those funds are used and accounted for in a manner consistent with this part and as otherwise required by law.

Revenue and Taxation Code § 34021

(AUMA, Effective November 9, 2016.)

(a) The taxes imposed by this Part shall be in addition to any other tax imposed by a city, county, or city and county.

Revenue and Taxation Code § 34021.5

(AUMA, Effective November 9, 2016.)

(a)(1) A county may impose a tax on the privilege of cultivating, manufacturing, producing, processing, preparing, storing, providing, donating, selling, or distributing marijuana or marijuana products by a licensee operating under Chapter 3.5 of Division 8 of the Business and Professions Code or Division 10 of the Business and Professions Code.

(a)(2) The board of supervisors shall specify in the ordinance proposing the tax the activities subject to the tax, the applicable rate or rates, the method of apportionment, if necessary, and the manner of collection of the tax. The tax may be imposed for general governmental purposes or for purposes specified in the ordinance by the board of supervisors.

(a)(3) In addition to any other method of collection authorized by law, the board of supervisors may provide for the collection of the tax imposed pursuant to this section in the same manner, and subject to the same penalties and priority of lien, as other charges and taxes fixed and collected by the county. A tax imposed pursuant to this section is a tax and not a fee or special assessment. The board of supervisors shall specify whether the tax applies throughout the entire county or within the unincorporated area of the county.

(a)(4) The tax authorized by this section may be imposed upon any or all of the activities set forth in paragraph (1), as specified in the ordinance, regardless of whether the activity is undertaken individually, collectively, or cooperatively, and regardless of whether the activity is for compensation or gratuitous, as determined by the board of supervisors.

(b) A tax imposed pursuant to this section shall be subject to applicable voter approval requirements imposed by law.

(c) This section is declaratory of existing law and does not limit or prohibit the levy or collection of any other fee, charge, or tax, or a license or service fee or charge upon, or related to, the activities set forth in subdivision (a) as otherwise provided by law. This section shall not be construed as a limitation upon the taxing authority of a county as provided by law.

(d) This section shall not be construed to authorize a county to impose a sales or use tax in addition to the sales and use tax imposed under an ordinance conforming to the provisions of Sections 7202 and 7203 of the Revenue and Taxation Code.

IX. Vehicle Code Sections

Vehicle Code § 23152

(Amended by Statute, Operative January 1, 2014.)

(a) It is unlawful for a person who is under the influence of any alcoholic beverage to drive a vehicle.

(b) It is unlawful for a person who has 0.08 percent or more, by weight, of alcohol in his or her blood to drive a vehicle.

For purposes of this article and Section 34501.16, percent, by weight, of alcohol in a person's blood is based upon grams of alcohol per 100 milliliters of blood or grams of alcohol per 210 liters of breath.

In any prosecution under this subdivision, it is a rebuttable presumption that the person had 0.08 percent or more, by weight, of alcohol in his or her blood at the time of driving the vehicle if the person had 0.08 percent or more, by weight, of alcohol in his or her blood at the time of the performance of a chemical test within three hours after the driving.

(c) It is unlawful for a person who is addicted to the use of any drug to drive a vehicle. This subdivision shall not apply to a person who is participating in a narcotic treatment program approved pursuant to Article 3 (commencing with Section 11875) of Chapter 1 of Part 3 of Division 10.5 of the Health and Safety Code.

(d) It is unlawful for a person who has 0.04 percent or more, by weight, of alcohol in his or her blood to drive a commercial motor vehicle, as defined in Section 15210.

In any prosecution under this subdivision, it is a rebuttable presumption that the person had 0.04 percent or more, by weight, of alcohol in his or her blood at the time of driving the vehicle if the person had 0.04 percent or more, by weight, of alcohol in his or her blood at the time of the performance of a chemical test within three hours after the driving.

(e) It is unlawful for a person who is under the influence of any drug to drive a vehicle.

(f) It is unlawful for a person who is under the combined influence of any alcoholic beverage and drug to drive a vehicle.

(g) This section shall become operative on January 1, 2014.

Vehicle Code § 23222

(Amended by Statute, Effective January 1, 2011.)

(a) No person shall have in his or her possession on his or her person, while driving a motor vehicle upon a highway or on lands, as described in subdivision (b) of Section 23220, any bottle, can, or other receptacle, containing any alcoholic beverage which has been opened, or a seal broken, or the contents of which have been partially removed.

(b) Except as authorized by law, every person who possesses, while driving a motor vehicle upon a highway or on lands, as described in subdivision (b) of Section 23220, not more than one avoirdupois ounce of marijuana, other than concentrated cannabis as defined by Section 11006.5 of the Health and Safety Code, is guilty of an infraction punishable by a fine of not more than one hundred dollars ($100).

Vehicle Code § 40000.15

(Amended by Statute, Effective January 1, 2007.)

A violation of any of the following provisions shall constitute a misdemeanor, and not an infraction:

Subdivision (g), (j), (k), (l), or (m) of Section 22658, relating to unlawfully towed or stored vehicles.

Sections 23103 and 23104, relating to reckless driving.

Section 23109, relating to speed contests or exhibitions.

Subdivision (a) of Section 23110, relating to throwing at vehicles.

Section 23152, relating to driving under the influence.

Subdivision (b) of Section 23222, relating to possession of marijuana.

Subdivision (a) or (b) of Section 23224, relating to persons under 21 years of age knowingly driving, or being a passenger in, a motor vehicle carrying any alcoholic beverage.

Section 23253, relating to directions on toll highways or vehicular crossings.

Section 23332, relating to trespassing.

Section 24002.5, relating to unlawful operation of a farm vehicle.

Section 24011.3, relating to vehicle bumper strength notices.

Section 27150.1, relating to sale of exhaust systems.

Section 27362, relating to child passenger seat restraints.

Section 28050, relating to true mileage driven.

Section 28050.5, relating to nonfunctional odometers.

Section 28051, relating to resetting odometers.

Section 28051.5, relating to devices to reset odometers.

Subdivision (d) of Section 28150, relating to possessing four or more jamming devices.

X. Water Code Sections

Water Code § 25

(Added by Statute, Effective 1967.)

"Board," unless otherwise specified, means the State Water Resources Control Board.

Water Code § 1052

(Amended by Statute, Effective March 1, 2014.)

(a) The diversion or use of water subject to this division other than as authorized in this division is a trespass.

(b) The Attorney General, upon request of the board, shall institute in the superior court in and for any county where the diversion or use is threatened, is occurring, or has occurred an action for the issuance of injunctive relief as may be warranted by way of temporary restraining order, preliminary injunction, or permanent injunction.

(c) Any person or entity committing a trespass as defined in this section may be liable in an amount not to exceed the following:

(1) If the unauthorized diversion or use occurs in a critically dry year immediately preceded by two or more consecutive below normal, dry, or critically dry years or during a period for which the Governor has issued a proclamation of a state of emergency under the California Emergency Services Act (Chapter 7 (commencing with Section 8550) of Division 1 of Title 2 of the Government Code) based on drought conditions, the sum of the following:

(A) One thousand dollars ($1,000) for each day in which the trespass occurs.

(B) Two thousand five hundred dollars ($2,500) for each acre-foot of water diverted or used in excess of that diverter's water rights.

(2) If the unauthorized diversion or use is not described by paragraph (1), five hundred dollars ($500) for each day in which the unauthorized

diversion or use occurs.

(d) Civil liability for a violation of this section may be imposed by the superior court or the board as follows:

(1) The superior court may impose civil liability in an action brought by the Attorney General, upon request of the board, to impose, assess, and recover any sums pursuant to subdivision (c). In determining the appropriate amount, the court shall take into consideration all relevant circumstances, including, but not limited to, the extent of harm caused by the violation, the nature and persistence of the violation, the length of time over which the violation occurs, and the corrective action, if any, taken by the violator.

(2) The board may impose civil liability in accordance with Section 1055.

(e) All funds recovered pursuant to this section shall be deposited in the Water Rights Fund established pursuant to Section 1550.

(f) The remedies prescribed in this section are cumulative and not alternative.

Water Code § 1525

(SB 837, Effective June 27, 2016.)

(a) Each person or entity who holds a permit or license to appropriate water, and each lessor of water leased under Chapter 1.5 (commencing with Section 1020) of Part 1, shall pay an annual fee according to a fee schedule established by the board.

(b) Each person or entity who files any of the following shall pay a fee according to a fee schedule established by the board:

(1) An application for a permit to appropriate water.

(2) A registration of appropriation for a small domestic use, small irrigation use, or livestock stockpond use.

(3) A petition for an extension of time within which to begin construction, to complete construction, or to apply the water to full beneficial use under a permit.

(4) A petition to change the point of diversion, place of use, or purpose

of use, under a permit, license, or registration.

(5) A petition to change the conditions of a permit or license, requested by the permittee or licensee, that is not otherwise subject to paragraph (3) or (4).

(6) A petition to change the point of discharge, place of use, or purpose of use, of treated wastewater, requested pursuant to Section 1211.

(7) An application for approval of a water lease agreement.

(8) A request for release from priority pursuant to Section 10504.

(9) An application for an assignment of a state-filed application pursuant to Section 10504.

(10) A statement of water diversion and use pursuant to Part 5.1 (commencing with Section 5100) that reports that water was used for cannabis cultivation.

(c) The board shall set the fee schedule authorized by this section so that the total amount of fees collected pursuant to this section equals that amount necessary to recover costs incurred in connection with the issuance, administration, review, monitoring, and enforcement of permits, licenses, certificates, and registrations to appropriate water, water leases, statements of water diversion and use for cannabis cultivation, and orders approving changes in point of discharge, place of use, or purpose of use of treated wastewater. The board may include, as recoverable costs, but is not limited to including, the costs incurred in reviewing applications, registrations, statements of water diversion and use for cannabis cultivation, petitions and requests, prescribing terms of permits, licenses, registrations, and change orders, enforcing and evaluating compliance with permits, licenses, certificates, registrations, change orders, and water leases, inspection, monitoring, planning, modeling, reviewing documents prepared for the purpose of regulating the diversion and use of water, applying and enforcing the prohibition set forth in Section 1052 against the unauthorized diversion or use of water subject to this division and the water diversion related provisions of Article 6 (commencing with Section 19331) of Chapter 3.5 of Division 8 of the Business and Professions Code, and the administrative costs incurred in connection with carrying out these actions.

(d) (1) The board shall adopt the schedule of fees authorized under this section as emergency regulations in accordance with Section 1530.

(2) For filings subject to subdivision (b), the schedule may provide for a single filing fee or for an initial filing fee followed by an annual fee, as appropriate to the type of filing involved, and may include supplemental fees for filings that have already been made but have not yet been acted upon by the board at the time the schedule of fees takes effect.

(3) The board shall set the amount of total revenue collected each year through the fees authorized by this section at an amount equal to the amounts appropriated by the Legislature for expenditure for support of water rights program activities from the Water Rights Fund established under Section 1550, taking into account the reserves in the Water Rights Fund. The board shall review and revise the fees each fiscal year as necessary to conform with the amounts appropriated. If the board determines that the revenue collected during the preceding year was greater than, or less than, the amounts appropriated, the board may further adjust the annual fees to compensate for the over or under collection of revenue.

(e) Annual fees imposed pursuant to this section for the 2003–04 fiscal year shall be assessed for the entire 2003–04 fiscal year.

Water Code § 1535

(SB 837, Effective June 27, 2016.)

(a) Any fee subject to this chapter that is required in connection with the filing of an application, registration, request, statement, or proof of claim, other than an annual fee required after the period covered by the initial filing fee, shall be paid to the board.

(b) If a fee established under subdivision (b) of Section 1525, Section 1528, or Section 13160.1 is not paid when due, the board may cancel the application, registration, petition, request, statement, or claim, or may refer the matter to the State Board of Equalization for collection of the unpaid fee.

Water Code § 1831

(MCRSA- SB 837, Effective June 27, 2016.)

(a) When the board determines that any person is violating, or threatening to violate, any requirement described in subdivision (d), the board may issue an order to that person to cease and desist from that violation.

(b) The cease and desist order shall require that person to comply forthwith or in accordance with a time schedule set by the board.

(c) The board may issue a cease and desist order only after notice and an opportunity for hearing pursuant to Section 1834.

(d) The board may issue a cease and desist order in response to a violation or threatened violation of any of the following:

(1) The prohibition set forth in Section 1052 against the unauthorized diversion or use of water subject to this division.

(2) Any term or condition of a permit, license, certification, or registration issued under this division.

(3) Any decision or order of the board issued under this part, Section 275, Chapter 11 (commencing with Section 10735) of Part 2.74 of Division 6, or Article 7 (commencing with Section 13550) of Chapter 7 of Division 7, in which decision or order the person to whom the cease and desist order will be issued, or a predecessor in interest to that person, was named as a party directly affected by the decision or order.

(4) A regulation adopted under Section 1058.5.

(5) Any extraction restriction, limitation, order, or regulation adopted or issued under Chapter 11 (commencing with Section 10735) of Part 2.74 of Division 6.

(6) Any diversion or use of water for cannabis cultivation if any of the following applies:

(A) A license is required, but has not been obtained, under Article 6 (commencing with Section 19331) of Chapter 3.5 of Division 8 of the Business and Professions Code.

(B) The diversion is not in compliance with an applicable limitation or requirement established by the board or the Department of Fish and Wildlife under Section 13149.

(C) The diversion or use is not in compliance with a requirement imposed under subdivision (d) or (e) of Section 19332.2 of the Business and Professions Code.

(e) This article does not alter the regulatory authority of the board under other provisions of law.

Water Code § 1840

(MCRSA- SB 837, Effective June 27, 2016.)

(a) (1) Except as provided in subdivision (b), a person who, on or after January 1, 2016, diverts 10 acre-feet of water per year or more under a permit or license shall install and maintain a device or employ a method capable of measuring the rate of direct diversion, rate of collection to storage, and rate of withdrawal or release from storage. The measurements shall be made using the best available technologies and best professional practices, as defined in Section 5100, using a device or methods satisfactory to the board, as follows:

(A) A device shall be capable of continuous monitoring of the rate and quantity of water diverted and shall be properly maintained. The permittee or licensee shall provide the board with evidence that the device has been installed with the first report submitted after installation of the device. The permittee or licensee shall provide the board with evidence demonstrating that the device is functioning properly as part of the reports submitted at five-year intervals after the report documenting installation of the device, or upon request of the board.

(B) In developing regulations pursuant to Section 1841, the board shall consider devices and methods that provide accurate measurement of the total amount diverted and the rate of diversion. The board shall consider devices and methods that provide accurate measurements within an acceptable range of error, including the following:

(i) Electricity records dedicated to a pump and recent pump test.

(ii) Staff gage calibrated with an acceptable streamflow rating curve.

(iii) Staff gage calibrated for a flume or weir.

(iv) Staff gage calibrated with an acceptable storage capacity curve.

(v) Pressure transducer and acceptable storage capacity curve.

(2) The permittee or licensee shall maintain a record of all diversion monitoring that includes the date, time, and diversion rate at time intervals of one hour or less, and the total amount of water diverted. These records shall be included with reports submitted under the permit or license, as required under subdivision (c), or upon request of the board.

(b) (1) The board may modify the requirements of subdivision (a) upon finding either of the following:

(A) That strict compliance is infeasible, is unreasonably expensive, would unreasonably affect public trust uses, or would result in the waste or unreasonable use of water.

(B) That the need for monitoring and reporting is adequately addressed by other conditions of the permit or license.

(2) The board may increase the 10-acre-foot reporting threshold of subdivision (a) in a watershed or subwatershed, after considering the diversion reporting threshold in relation to quantity of water within the watershed or subwatershed. The board may increase the 10-acre-foot reporting threshold to 25 acre-feet or above if it finds that the benefits of the additional information within the watershed or subwatershed are substantially outweighed by the cost of installing measuring devices or employing methods for measurement for diversions at the 10-acre-foot threshold.

(c) At least annually, a person who diverts water under a registration, permit, or license shall report to the board the following information:

(1) The quantity of water diverted by month.

(2) The maximum rate of diversion by months in the preceding calendar year.

(3) The information required by subdivision (a), if applicable.

(4) The amount of water used, if any, for cannabis cultivation.

(d) Compliance with the applicable requirements of this section is a condition of every registration, permit, or license.

Water Code § 1845

(SB 837, Effective June 27, 2016.)

(a) Upon the failure of any person to comply with a cease and desist order issued by the board pursuant to this chapter, the Attorney General, upon the request of the board, shall petition the superior court for the issuance of prohibitory or mandatory injunctive relief as appropriate, including a temporary restraining order, preliminary injunction, or permanent injunction.

(b) (1) A person or entity who violates a cease and desist order issued pursuant to this chapter may be liable in an amount not to exceed the following:

(A) If the violation occurs in a critically dry year immediately preceded by two or more consecutive below normal, dry, or critically dry years or during a period for which the Governor has issued a proclamation of a state of emergency under the California Emergency Services Act (Chapter 7 (commencing with Section 8550) of Division 1 of Title 2 of the Government Code) based on drought conditions, ten thousand dollars ($10,000) for each day in which the violation occurs.

(B) If the violation is not described by subparagraph (A), one thousand dollars ($1,000) for each day in which the violation occurs.

(2) Civil liability may be imposed by the superior court. The Attorney General, upon the request of the board, shall petition the superior court to impose, assess, and recover those sums.

(3) Civil liability may be imposed administratively by the board pursuant to Section 1055.

Water Code § 1846

(SB 837, Effective June 27, 2016.)

(a) A person or entity may be liable for a violation of any of the following in an amount not to exceed five hundred dollars ($500) for each day in which the violation occurs:

(1) A term or condition of a permit, license, certificate, or registration issued under this division.

(2) A regulation or order adopted by the board.

(b) Civil liability may be imposed by the superior court. The Attorney General, upon the request of the board, shall petition the superior court to impose, assess, and recover those sums.

(c) Civil liability may be imposed administratively by the board pursuant to Section 1055.

Water Code § 1847

(SB 837, Effective June 27, 2016.)

(a) A person or entity may be liable for a violation of any of the requirements of subdivision (b) in an amount not to exceed the sum of the following:

(1) Five hundred dollars ($500), plus two hundred fifty dollars ($250) for each additional day on which the violation continues if the person fails to correct the violation within 30 days after the board has called the violation to the attention of that person.

(2) Two thousand five hundred dollars ($2,500) for each acre-foot of water diverted or used in violation of the applicable requirement.

(b) Liability may be imposed for any of the following violations:

(1) Violation of a limitation or requirement established by the board or the Department of Fish and Wildlife under Section 13149.

(2) Failure to submit information, or making a material misstatement in information submitted, under subdivision (a), (b), or (c) of Section 19332.2 of the Business and Professions Code.

(3) Violation of any requirement imposed under subdivision (e) of Section 19332.2 of the Business and Professions Code.

(4) Diversion or use of water for cannabis cultivation for which a license is required, but has not been obtained, under Article 6 (commencing with Section 19331) of Chapter 3.5 of Division 8 of the Business and Professions Code.

(c) Civil liability may be imposed by the superior court. The Attorney General, upon the request of the board, shall petition the superior court to impose, assess, and recover those sums.

(d) Civil liability may be imposed administratively by the board pursuant to Section 1055.

Water Code § 5100

(Amended by Statute, Effective February 3, 2010.)

As used in this part:

(a) "Best available technologies" means technologies at the highest technically practical level, using flow totaling devices, and if necessary, data loggers and telemetry.

(b) "Best professional practices" means practices attaining and maintaining the accuracy of measurement and reporting devices and methods.

(c) "Diversion" means taking water by gravity or pumping from a surface stream or subterranean stream flowing through a known and definite channel, or other body of surface water, into a canal, pipeline, or other conduit, and includes impoundment of water in a reservoir.

(d) "Person" means all persons whether natural or artificial, including the United States of America, State of California, and all political subdivisions, districts, municipalities, and public agencies.

Water Code § 5101

(Amended by Statute, Effective January 1, 2012.)

Each person who, after December 31, 1965, diverts water shall file with the board, prior to July 1 of the succeeding year, a statement of his or her diversion and use, except that a statement is not required to be filed if the diversion is any of the following:

(a) From a spring that does not flow off the property on which it is located and from which the person's aggregate diversions do not exceed 25 acre-feet in any year.

(b) Covered by a registration for small domestic use, small irrigation use, or livestock stockpond use, or permit or license to appropriate water on file with the board.

(c) Included in a notice filed pursuant to Part 5 (commencing with Section 4999).

(d) Regulated by a watermaster appointed by the department and included in annual reports filed with a court or the board by the watermaster, which reports identify the persons who have diverted water and describe the general purposes and the place, the use, and the quantity of water that has been diverted from each source.

(e) Included in annual reports filed with a court or the board by a watermaster appointed by a court or pursuant to statute to administer a final judgment determining rights to water, which reports identify the persons who have diverted water and give the general place of use and the quantity of water that has been diverted from each source.

(f) For use in compliance with Article 2.5 (commencing with Section 1226) or Article 2.7 (commencing with Section 1228) of Chapter 1 of Part 2.

(g) A diversion that occurs before January 1, 2009, if any of the following applies:

(1) The diversion is from a spring that does not flow off the property on which it is located, and the person's aggregate diversions do not exceed 25 acre-feet in any year.

(2) The diversion is covered by an application to appropriate water on file with the board.

(3) The diversion is reported by the department in its hydrologic data bulletins.

(4) The diversion is included in the consumptive use data for the Delta lowlands published by the department in its hydrologic data bulletins.

Water Code § 5102

(Amended by Statute, Effective 1967.)

The statement may be filed either by the person who is diverting water or, on his behalf, by an agency which he designates and which maintains a record of the water diverted. A separate statement shall be filed for each point of diversion.

Water Code § 5103

(SB 837, Effective June 27, 2016.)

Each statement shall be prepared on a form provided by the board. The statement shall include all of the following information:

(a) The name and address of the person who diverted water and of the person filing the statement.

(b) The name of the stream or other source from which water was diverted, and the name of the next major stream or other body of water to which the source is tributary.

(c) The place of diversion. The location of the diversion works shall be depicted on a specific United States Geological Survey topographic map, or shall be identified using the California Coordinate System, or latitude and longitude measurements. If assigned, the public land description to the nearest 40-acre subdivision and the assessor's parcel number shall also be provided.

(d) The capacity of the diversion works and of the storage reservoir, if any, and the months in which water was used during the preceding calendar year.

(e) (1) (A) At least monthly records of water diversions. The measurements of the diversion shall be made in accordance with Section 1840.

(B) (i) On and after July 1, 2016, the measurement of a diversion of 10 acre-feet or more per year shall comply with regulations adopted by the board pursuant to Article 3 (commencing with Section 1840) of Chapter 12 of Part 2.

(ii) The requirement of clause (i) is extended to January 1, 2017, for any statement filer that enters into a voluntary agreement that is acceptable to the board to reduce the statement filer's diversions during the 2015 irrigation season.

(2) (A) The terms of, and eligibility for, any grant or loan awarded or administered by the department, the board, or the California Bay-Delta Authority on behalf of a person that is subject to paragraph (1) shall be conditioned on compliance with that paragraph.

(B) Notwithstanding subparagraph (A), the board may determine that a person is eligible for a grant or loan even though the person is not complying with paragraph (1), if both of the following apply:

(i) The board determines that the grant or loan will assist the grantee or loan recipient in complying with paragraph (1).

(ii) The person has submitted to the board a one-year schedule for complying with paragraph (1).

(C) It is the intent of the Legislature that the requirements of this subdivision shall complement and not affect the scope of authority granted to the board by provisions of law other than this article.

(f) (1) The purpose of use.

(2) The amount of water used, if any, for cannabis cultivation.

(g) A general description of the area in which the water was used. The location of the place of use shall be depicted on a specific United States Geological Survey topographic map and on any other maps with identifiable landmarks. If assigned, the public land description to the nearest 40-acre subdivision and the assessor's parcel number shall also be provided.

(h) The year in which the diversion was commenced as near as is known.

Water Code § 13149

(MCRSA- SB 837, Effective June 27, 2016.)

(a) (1) (A) The board, in consultation with the Department of Fish and Wildlife, shall adopt principles and guidelines for diversion and use of water for cannabis cultivation in areas where cannabis cultivation may have the potential to substantially affect instream flows. The principles and guidelines adopted under this section may include, but are not limited to, instream flow objectives, limits on diversions, and requirements for screening of diversions and elimination of barriers to fish passage. The principles and guidelines may include requirements that apply to groundwater extractions where the board determines those requirements are reasonably necessary for purposes of this section.

(B) Prior to adopting principles and guidelines under this section, the board shall allow for public comment and hearing, pursuant to Section 13147. The board shall provide an opportunity for the public to review and comment on the proposal for at least 60 days and shall consider the public comments before adopting the principles and guidelines.

(2) The board, in consultation with the Department of Fish and Wildlife, shall adopt principles and guidelines pending the development of long-term principles and guidelines under paragraph (1). The principles and guidelines, including the interim principles and guidelines, shall include measures to protect springs, wetlands, and aquatic habitats from negative impacts of cannabis cultivation. The board may update the interim principles and guidelines as it determines to be reasonably necessary for purposes of this section.

(3) The Department of Fish and Wildlife, in consultation with the board, may establish interim requirements to protect fish and wildlife from the impacts of diversions for cannabis cultivation pending the adoption of long-term princi-

ples and guidelines by the board under paragraph (1). The requirements may also include measures to protect springs, wetlands, and aquatic habitats from negative impacts of cannabis cultivation.

(b) (1) Notwithstanding Section 15300.2 of Title 14 of the California Code of Regulations, actions of the board and the Department of Fish and Wildlife under this section shall be deemed to be within Section 15308 of Title 14 of the California Code of regulations, provided that those actions do not involve relaxation of existing streamflow standards.

(2) The board shall adopt principles and guidelines under this section as part of state policy for water quality control adopted pursuant to Article 3 (commencing with Section 13140) of Chapter 3 of Division 7.

(3) If the Department of Fish and Wildlife establishes interim requirements under this section, it shall do so as emergency regulations in accordance with Chapter 3.5 (commencing with Section 11340) of Part 1 of Division 3 of Title 2 of the Government Code. The adoption of those interim requirements is an emergency and shall be considered by the Office of Administrative Law as necessary for the immediate preservation of the public peace, health, safety, and general welfare. Notwithstanding Chapter 3.5 (commencing with Section 11340) of Part 1 of Division 3 of Title 2 of the Government Code, the emergency regulations shall remain in effect until revised by the Department of Fish and Wildlife, provided that the emergency regulations shall not apply after long-term principles and guidelines adopted by the board under this section take effect for the stream or other body of water where the diversion is located.

(4) A diversion for cannabis cultivation is subject to both the interim principles and guidelines and the interim requirements in the period before final principles and guidelines are adopted by the board.

(5) The board shall have primary enforcement responsibility for principles and guidelines adopted under this section, and shall notify the Department of Food and Agriculture of any enforcement action taken.

Water Code § 13260

(Amended by Statute, Effective March 24, 2011.)

(a) Each of the following persons shall file with the appropriate regional board a report of the discharge, containing the information that may be required by the regional board:

(1) A person discharging waste, or proposing to discharge waste, within any region that could affect the quality of the waters of the state, other than into a community sewer system.

(2) A person who is a citizen, domiciliary, or political agency or entity of this state discharging waste, or proposing to discharge waste, outside the boundaries of the state in a manner that could affect the quality of the waters of the state within any region.

(3) A person operating, or proposing to construct, an injection well.

(b) No report of waste discharge need be filed pursuant to subdivision (a) if the requirement is waived pursuant to Section 13269.

(c) Each person subject to subdivision (a) shall file with the appropriate regional board a report of waste discharge relative to any material change or proposed change in the character, location, or volume of the discharge.

(d) (1) (A) Each person who is subject to subdivision (a) or (c) shall submit an annual fee according to a fee schedule established by the state board.

(B) The total amount of annual fees collected pursuant to this section shall equal that amount necessary to recover costs incurred in connection with the issuance, administration, reviewing, monitoring, and enforcement of waste discharge requirements and waivers of waste discharge requirements.

(C) Recoverable costs may include, but are not limited to, costs incurred in reviewing waste discharge reports, prescribing terms of waste discharge requirements and monitoring requirements, enforcing and evaluating compliance with waste discharge requirements and waiver requirements, conducting surface water and groundwater monitoring and modeling, analyzing laboratory samples, adopting, reviewing, and revising water quality control plans and state policies for water quality control, and reviewing documents prepared for the purpose of regulating the discharge of waste, and administrative costs incurred in connection with carrying out these actions.

(D) In establishing the amount of a fee that may be imposed on a confined animal feeding and holding operation pursuant to this section, including, but not limited to, a dairy farm, the state board shall consider all of the following factors:

(i) The size of the operation.

(ii) Whether the operation has been issued a permit to operate pursuant to Section 1342 of Title 33 of the United States Code.

(iii) Any applicable waste discharge requirement or conditional waiver of a waste discharge requirement.

(iv) The type and amount of discharge from the operation.

(v) The pricing mechanism of the commodity produced.

(vi) Any compliance costs borne by the operation pursuant to state and federal water quality regulations.

(vii) Whether the operation participates in a quality assurance program certified by a regional water quality control board, the state board, or a federal water quality control agency.

(2) (A) Subject to subparagraph (B), the fees collected pursuant to this section shall be deposited in the Waste Discharge Permit Fund, which is hereby created. The money in the fund is available for expenditure by the state board, upon appropriation by the Legislature, solely for the purposes of carrying out this division.

(B) (i) Notwithstanding subparagraph (A), the fees collected pursuant to this section from stormwater dischargers that are subject to a general industrial or construction stormwater permit under the national pollutant discharge elimination system (NPDES) shall be separately accounted for in the Waste Discharge Permit Fund.

(ii) Not less than 50 percent of the money in the Waste Discharge Permit Fund that is separately accounted for pursuant to clause (i) is available, upon appropriation by the Legislature, for expenditure by the regional board with jurisdiction over the permitted industry or construction site that generated the fee to carry out stormwater programs in the region.

(iii) Each regional board that receives money pursuant to clause (ii) shall spend not less than 50 percent of that money solely on stormwater inspection and regulatory compliance issues associated with industrial and construction stormwater programs.

(3) A person who would be required to pay the annual fee prescribed by paragraph (1) for waste discharge requirements applicable to discharges of solid waste, as defined in Section 40191 of the Public Resources Code, at a waste management unit that is also regulated under Division 30 (commenc-

ing with Section 40000) of the Public Resources Code, shall be entitled to a waiver of the annual fee for the discharge of solid waste at the waste management unit imposed by paragraph (1) upon verification by the state board of payment of the fee imposed by Section 48000 of the Public Resources Code, and provided that the fee established pursuant to Section 48000 of the Public Resources Code generates revenues sufficient to fund the programs specified in Section 48004 of the Public Resources Code and the amount appropriated by the Legislature for those purposes is not reduced.

(e) Each person that discharges waste in a manner regulated by this section shall pay an annual fee to the state board. The state board shall establish, by regulation, a timetable for the payment of the annual fee. If the state board or a regional board determines that the discharge will not affect, or have the potential to affect, the quality of the waters of the state, all or part of the annual fee shall be refunded.

(f) (1) The state board shall adopt, by emergency regulations, a schedule of fees authorized under subdivision (d). The total revenue collected each year through annual fees shall be set at an amount equal to the revenue levels set forth in the Budget Act for this activity. The state board shall automatically adjust the annual fees each fiscal year to conform with the revenue levels set forth in the Budget Act for this activity. If the state board determines that the revenue collected during the preceding year was greater than, or less than, the revenue levels set forth in the Budget Act, the state board may further adjust the annual fees to compensate for the over and under collection of revenue.

(2) The emergency regulations adopted pursuant to this subdivision, any amendment thereto, or subsequent adjustments to the annual fees, shall be adopted by the state board in accordance with Chapter 3.5 (commencing with Section 11340) of Part 1 of Division 3 of Title 2 of the Government Code. The adoption of these regulations is an emergency and shall be considered by the Office of Administrative Law as necessary for the immediate preservation of the public peace, health, safety, and general welfare. Notwithstanding Chapter 3.5 (commencing with Section 11340) of Part 1 of Division 3 of Title 2 of the Government Code, any emergency regulations adopted by the state board, or adjustments to the annual fees made by the state board pursuant to this section, shall not be subject to review by the Office of Administrative Law and shall remain in effect until revised by the state board.

(g) The state board shall adopt regulations setting forth reasonable time limits within which the regional board shall determine the adequacy of a report of waste discharge submitted under this section.

(h) Each report submitted under this section shall be sworn to, or submitted under penalty of perjury.

(i) The regulations adopted by the state board pursuant to subdivision (f) shall include a provision that annual fees shall not be imposed on those who pay fees under the national pollutant discharge elimination system until the time when those fees are again due, at which time the fees shall become due on an annual basis.

(j) A person operating or proposing to construct an oil, gas, or geothermal injection well subject to paragraph (3) of subdivision (a) shall not be required to pay a fee pursuant to subdivision (d) if the injection well is regulated by the Division of Oil and Gas of the Department of Conservation, in lieu of the appropriate California regional water quality control board, pursuant to the memorandum of understanding, entered into between the state board and the Department of Conservation on May 19, 1988. This subdivision shall remain operative until the memorandum of understanding is revoked by the state board or the Department of Conservation.

(k) In addition to the report required by subdivision (a), before a person discharges mining waste, the person shall first submit both of the following to the regional board:

(1) A report on the physical and chemical characteristics of the waste that could affect its potential to cause pollution or contamination. The report shall include the results of all tests required by regulations adopted by the board, any test adopted by the Department of Toxic Substances Control pursuant to Section 25141 of the Health and Safety Code for extractable, persistent, and bioaccumulative toxic substances in a waste or other material, and any other tests that the state board or regional board may require, including, but not limited to, tests needed to determine the acid-generating potential of the mining waste or the extent to which hazardous substances may persist in the waste after disposal.

(2) A report that evaluates the potential of the discharge of the mining waste to produce, over the long term, acid mine drainage, the discharge or leaching of heavy metals, or the release of other hazardous substances.

(l) Except upon the written request of the regional board, a report of waste discharge need not be filed pursuant to subdivision (a) or (c) by a user of recycled water that is being supplied by a supplier or distributor of recycled water for whom a master recycling permit has been issued pursuant to Section 13523.1.

Water Code § 13264

(Amended by Statute, Effective January 1, 2004.)

(a) No person shall initiate any new discharge of waste or make any material changes in any discharge, or initiate a discharge to, make any material changes in a discharge to, or construct, an injection well, prior to the filing of the report required by Section 13260 and no person shall take any of these actions after filing the report but before whichever of the following occurs first:

   (1) The issuance of waste discharge requirements pursuant to Section 13263.

   (2) The expiration of 140 days after compliance with Section 13260 if the waste to be discharged does not create or threaten to create a condition of pollution or nuisance and any of the following applies:

      (A) The project is not subject to the California Environmental Quality Act (Division 13 (commencing with Section 21000) of the Public Resources Code).

      (B) The regional board is the lead agency for purposes of the California Environmental Quality Act, a negative declaration is required, and at least 105 days have expired since the regional board assumed lead agency responsibility.

      (C) The regional board is the lead agency for the purposes of the California Environmental Quality Act, and environmental impact report or written documentation prepared to meet the requirements of Section 21080.5 of the Public Resources Code is required, and at least one year has expired since the regional board assumed lead agency responsibility.

      (D) The regional board is a responsible agency for purposes of the California Environmental Quality Act, and at least 90 days have expired since certification or approval of environmental documentation by the lead agency.

   (3) The issuance of a waiver pursuant to Section 13269.

(b) The Attorney General, at the request of a regional board, shall petition the superior court for the issuance of a temporary restraining order, preliminary injunction, or permanent injunction, or combination thereof, as may be appropriate, prohibiting any person who is violating or threatening to violate this section from doing any of the following, whichever is applicable:

(1) Discharging the waste or fluid.

(2) Making any material change in the discharge.

(3) Constructing the injection well.

(c) (1) Notwithstanding any other provision of law, moneys collected under this division for a violation pursuant to paragraph (2) of subdivision (a) shall be deposited in the Waste Discharge Permit Fund and separately accounted for in that fund.

(2) The funds described in paragraph (1) shall be expended by the state board, upon appropriation by the Legislature, to assist regional boards, and other public agencies with authority to clean up waste or abate the effects of the waste, in cleaning up or abating the effects of the waste on waters of the state or for the purposes authorized in Section 13443.

Water Code § 13272

(Amended by Statute, Effective June 20, 2014.)

(a) Except as provided by subdivision (b), any person who, without regard to intent or negligence, causes or permits any oil or petroleum product to be discharged in or on any waters of the state, or discharged or deposited where it is, or probably will be, discharged in or on any waters of the state, shall, as soon as (1) that person has knowledge of the discharge, (2) notification is possible, and (3) notification can be provided without substantially impeding cleanup or other emergency measures, immediately notify the Office of Emergency Services of the discharge in accordance with the spill reporting provision of the California oil spill contingency plan adopted pursuant to Article 3.5 (commencing with Section 8574.1) of Chapter 7 of Division 1 of Title 2 of the Government Code.

(b) The notification required by this section shall not apply to a discharge in compliance with waste discharge requirements or other provisions of this division.

(c) Any person who fails to provide the notice required by this section is guilty of a misdemeanor and shall be punished by a fine of not less than five hundred dollars ($500) or more than five thousand dollars ($5,000) per day for each day of failure to notify, or imprisonment of not more than one year, or both. Except where a discharge to the waters of this state would have occurred but for cleanup or emergency response by a public agency, this subdivision shall not apply to any discharge to land that does not result in a discharge to the waters of this state. This subdivision shall not apply to any person who is fined by the federal government for a failure to report a discharge of oil.

(d) Notification received pursuant to this section or information obtained by use of that notification shall not be used against any person providing the notification in any criminal case, except in a prosecution for perjury or giving a false statement.

(e) Immediate notification to the appropriate regional board of the discharge, in accordance with reporting requirements set under Section 13267 or 13383, shall constitute compliance with the requirements of subdivision (a).

(f) The reportable quantity for oil or petroleum products shall be one barrel (42 gallons) or more, by direct discharge to the receiving waters, unless a more restrictive reporting standard for a particular body of water is adopted.

Water Code § 13276

(MCRSA- AB 243, Effective January 1, 2016.)

(a) The multiagency task force, the Department of Fish and Wildlife and State Water Resources Control Board pilot project to address the Environmental Impacts of Cannabis Cultivation, assigned to respond to the damages caused by marijuana cultivation on public and private lands in California, shall continue its enforcement efforts on a permanent basis and expand them to a statewide level to ensure the reduction of adverse impacts of marijuana cultivation on water quality and on fish and wildlife throughout the state.

(b) Each regional board shall, and the State Water Resources Control Board may, address discharges of waste resulting from medical marijuana cultivation and commercial marijuana cultivation under Division 10 of the Business and Profession Code and associated activities, including by adopting a general permit, establishing waste discharge requirements, or taking action pursuant to Section 13269. In addressing these discharges, each regional board shall include conditions to address items that include, but are not limited to, all of the following:

(1) Site development and maintenance, erosion control, and drainage features.

(2) Stream crossing installation and maintenance.

(3) Riparian and wetland protection and management.

(4) Soil disposal.

(5) Water storage and use.

(6) Irrigation runoff.

(7) Fertilizers and soil.

(8) Pesticides and herbicides.

(9) Petroleum products and other chemicals.

(10) Cultivation-related waste.

(11) Refuse and human waste.

(12) Cleanup, restoration, and mitigation.

Water Code § 13387

(Amended by Statute, Effective April 4, 2011, and Operative October 1, 2011.)

(a) Any person who knowingly or negligently does any of the following is subject to criminal penalties as provided in subdivisions (b), (c), and (d):

(1) Violates Section 13375 or 13376.

(2) Violates any waste discharge requirements or dredged or fill material permit issued pursuant to this chapter or any water quality certification issued pursuant to Section 13160.

(3) Violates any order or prohibition issued pursuant to Section 13243 or 13301, if the activity subject to the order or prohibition is subject to regulation under this chapter.

(4) Violates any requirement of Section 301, 302, 306, 307, 308, 318, 401, or

405 of the Clean Water Act (33 U.S.C. Sec. 1311, 1312, 1316, 1317, 1318, 1328, 1341, or 1345), as amended.

(5) Introduces into a sewer system or into a publicly owned treatment works any pollutant or hazardous substances that the person knew or reasonably should have known could cause personal injury or property damage.

(6) Introduces any pollutant or hazardous substance into a sewer system or into a publicly owned treatment works, except in accordance with any applicable pretreatment requirements, which causes the treatment works to violate waste discharge requirements.

(b) Any person who negligently commits any of the violations set forth in subdivision (a) shall, upon conviction, be punished by a fine of not less than five thousand dollars ($5,000), nor more than twenty-five thousand dollars ($25,000), for each day in which the violation occurs, by imprisonment for not more than one year in a county jail, or by both that fine and imprisonment. If a conviction of a person is for a violation committed after a first conviction of the person under this subdivision, subdivision (c), or subdivision (d), punishment shall be by a fine of not more than fifty thousand dollars ($50,000) for each day in which the violation occurs, by imprisonment pursuant to subdivision (h) of Section 1170 of the Penal Code for 16, 20, or 24 months, or by both that fine and imprisonment.

(c) Any person who knowingly commits any of the violations set forth in subdivision (a) shall, upon conviction, be punished by a fine of not less than five thousand dollars ($5,000), nor more than fifty thousand dollars ($50,000), for each day in which the violation occurs, by imprisonment pursuant to subdivision (h) of Section 1170 of the Penal Code, or by both that fine and imprisonment. If a conviction of a person is for a violation committed after a first conviction of the person under this subdivision or subdivision (d), punishment shall be by a fine of not more than one hundred thousand dollars ($100,000) for each day in which the violation occurs, by imprisonment pursuant to subdivision (h) of Section 1170 of the Penal Code for two, four, or six years, or by both that fine and imprisonment.

(d) (1) Any person who knowingly commits any of the violations set forth in subdivision (a), and who knows at the time that the person thereby places another person in imminent danger of death or serious bodily injury, shall, upon conviction, be punished by a fine of not more than two hundred fifty thousand dollars ($250,000), imprisonment pursuant to subdivision (h) of Section 1170 of the Penal Code for 5, 10, or 15 years, or by both that fine and imprisonment. A person that is an organization shall, upon conviction under this subdivision, be subject to a fine of not more than one million dollars ($1,000,000). If a conviction of a person is for a violation committed after a first conviction of the person under this subdivision, the punishment shall be by a fine of not more than five hundred thousand dollars ($500,000), by imprisonment pursuant to subdivision (h) of Section 1170 of the Penal Code for 10, 20, or 30 years, or by both that fine and imprisonment. A person that is an organization shall, upon conviction for a violation committed after a first conviction of the person under this subdivision, be subject to a fine of not more than two million dollars ($2,000,000). Any fines imposed pursuant to this subdivision shall be in addition to any fines imposed pursuant to subdivision (c).

(2) In determining whether a defendant who is an individual knew that the defendant's conduct placed another person in imminent danger of death or serious bodily injury, the defendant is responsible only for actual awareness or actual belief that the defendant possessed, and knowledge possessed by a person other than the defendant, but not by the defendant personally, cannot be attributed to the defendant.

(e) Any person who knowingly makes any false statement, representation, or certification in any record, report, plan, notice to comply, or other document filed with a regional board or the state board, or who knowingly falsifies, tampers with, or renders inaccurate any monitoring device or method required under this division shall be punished by a fine of not more than twenty-five thousand dollars ($25,000), by imprisonment pursuant to subdivision (h) of Section 1170 of the Penal Code for 16, 20, or 24 months, or by both that fine and imprisonment. If a conviction of a person is for a violation committed after a first conviction of the person under this subdivision, punishment shall be by a fine of not more than twenty-five thousand dollars ($25,000) per day of violation, by imprisonment pursuant to subdivision (h) of Section 1170 of the Penal Code for two, three, or four years, or by both that fine and imprisonment.

(f) For purposes of this section, a single operational upset which leads to simultaneous violations of more than one pollutant parameter shall be treated as a single violation.

(g) For purposes of this section, "organization," "serious bodily injury," "person," and "hazardous substance" shall have the same meaning as in Section 309(c) of the Clean Water Act (33 U.S.C. Sec. 1319(c)), as amended.

(h) (1) Subject to paragraph (2), funds collected pursuant to this section shall be deposited in the State Water Pollution Cleanup and Abatement Account.

(2) (A) Notwithstanding any other provision of law, fines collected for a violation of a water quality certification in accordance with paragraph (2) of subdivision (a) or for a violation of Section 401 of the Clean Water Act (33 U.S.C. Sec. 1341) in accordance with paragraph (4) of subdivision (a) shall be deposited in the Water Discharge Permit Fund and separately accounted for in that fund.

(B) The funds described in subparagraph (A) shall be expended by the state board, upon appropriation by the Legislature, to assist regional boards, and other public agencies with authority to clean up waste or abate the effects of the waste, in cleaning up or abating the effects of the waste on waters of the state, or for the purposes authorized in Section 13443.

Water Code § 13575

(Amended by Statute, Effective January 1, 1999.)

(a) This chapter shall be known and may be cited as the Water Recycling Act of 1991.

(b) As used in this chapter, the following terms have the following meanings:

(1) "Customer" means a person or entity that purchases water from a retail water supplier.

(2) "Entity responsible for groundwater replenishment" means any person or entity authorized by statute or court order to manage a groundwater basin and acquire water for groundwater replenishment.

(3) "Recycled water" has the same meaning as defined in subdivision (n) of Section 13050.

(4) "Recycled water producer" means any local public entity that produces recycled water.

(5) "Recycled water wholesaler" means any local public entity that distributes recycled water to retail water suppliers and which has constructed, or is constructing, a recycled water distribution system.

(6) "Retail water supplier" means any local entity, including a public agency, city, county, or private water company, that provides retail wa-

ter service.

(7) "Retailer" means the retail water supplier in whose service area is located the property to which a customer requests the delivery of reycled water service.

XI. Helpful Charts

Chart: Medical Cannabis License Categories

Established by the Medical Cannabis Regulation and Safety Act

Cultivation:
The Department of Food and Agriculture shall promulgate regulations governing the licensing of cannabis cultivation.

License Category	Description and Restrictions
Type 1 Cultivation; Specialty outdoor; Small	• Outdoor cultivation • No artificial lighting • < 5,000 sq. ft. of total canopy size on one premises • Or up to 50 mature plants on noncontiguous plots
Type 1A Cultivation; Specialty indoor; Small	• Indoor cultivation • Exclusively artificial lighting • Between 501 and 5,000 sq. ft. of total canopy size on one premises
Type 1B Cultivation; Specialty mixed-light; Small	• Combination of natural and supplemental artificial lighting (maximum threshold to be determined by the licensing authority) • Between 2,501 and 5,000 sq. ft. of total canopy size on one premises
Type 1C Cultivation; Specialty cottage	• Combination of natural and supplemental artificial lighting (maximum threshold to be determined by the licensing authority) • < 2,500 sq. ft. of total canopy size for mixed-light cultivation, up to 25 mature plants for outdoor cultivation, or 500 square feet or less of total canopy size for indoor cultivation, on one premises

License Category	Description and Restrictions
Type 2 Cultivation; Outdoor; Small	• Outdoor cultivation • No artificial lighting • Between 5,001 and 10,000 sq. ft. of total canopy size on one premises
Type 2A Cultivation; Indoor; Small	• Indoor cultivation • Exclusively artificial lighting • Between 5,001 and 10,000 sq. ft. of total canopy size on one premises
Type 2B Cultivation; Mixed-light; Small	• Combination of natural and supplemental artificial lighting (maximum threshold to be determined by the licensing authority) • Between 5,001 and 10,000 sq. ft. of total canopy size on one premises
Type 3 Cultivation; Outdoor; Medium	• Outdoor cultivation • No artificial lighting • Between 10,001 sq. ft. to 1 acre of total canopy size on one premises • The Department of Food and Agriculture shall limit the number of licenses allowed of this type
Type 3A Cultivation; Indoor; Medium	• Indoor cultivation • Exclusively artificial lighting • Between 10,001 and 22,000 sq. ft. of total canopy size on one premises • The Department of Food and Agriculture shall limit the number of licenses allowed of this type

License Category	Description and Restrictions
Type 3B Cultivation; Mixed-light; Medium	• Combination of natural and supplemental artificial lighting (maximum threshold to be determined by the licensing authority) • Between 10,001 and 22,000 sq. ft. of total canopy size on one premises • The Department of Food and Agriculture shall limit the number of licenses allowed of this type
Type 4 Cultivation; Nursery	• Cultivation of medical cannabis solely as a nursery • May transport live plants, if the licensee also holds a Type 12 transporter license

Manufacturing and Testing:

The State Department of Public Health shall promulgate regulations governing the licensing of cannabis manufacturers and testing laboratories.

Type 6 Manufacturing Level 1	• Manufacturing sites that produce medical cannabis products using nonvolatile solvents
Type 7 Manufacturing Level 2	• Manufacturing sites that produce medical cannabis products using volatile solvents • The State Department of Public Health shall limit the number of licenses of this type
Type 8 Testing	• Testing of medical cannabis and medical cannabis products • Shall have facilities licensed according to regulations set forth by the division • Shall not hold a license in another license category and shall not own or have ownership interest in another licensed facility

Distributors, Dispensaries, and Transporters:
Licenses to be issued by the Department of Consumer Affairs

License Category	Description and Restrictions
Type 10 Dispensary; General	• Retail of medical cannabis or medical cannabis products • Shall allow for delivery where expressly authorized by local ordinance (pursuant to Section 19340)
Type 10A Producing Dispensary	• Retail of medical cannabis or medical cannabis products • No more than 3 licensed dispensary facilities and wish to hold either a cultivation or manufacturing license or both • Shall allow for delivery where expressly authorized by local ordinance (pursuant to Section 19340)

License Category	Description and Restrictions
Type 11 Distribution	• Distribution of medical cannabis or medical cannabis products from manufacturer to dispensary • Shall hold a Type 12 (transporter) license • Each location where product is stored must be individually licensed • Shall not hold a license in a cultivation, manufacturing, dispensing, or testing license category • Shall not own, or have an ownership interest in, premises licensed in a cultivation, manufacturing, dispensing, or testing license category other than a security interest, lien, or encumbrance on property that is used by a licensee • Shall be bonded and insured at a minimum level established by the licensing authority
Type 12 Transporter	• Transporters of medical cannabis or medical cannabis products between licensees • Shall be bonded and insured at a minimum level established by the licensing authority

Chart: Medical Cannabis Regulation and Safety Act Allowable License Combinations

Find your license type at the top and drop down the column to find other allowable licenses. A licensee may only hold a state license in up to two separate license categories. Some exceptions apply.

Legend:

✓   Allowable cross licensure.

✕   Prohibited cross licensure.

M   Mandatory cross licensure (Type 11 Distributors must also hold a Type 12 Transportation license).

✓+   10A may hold a 6 or a 7 and a 1, 1A, 1B, 1C, 2, 2A, 2B, 3, 3A, 3B, 4 but no more than 4 acres canopy cultivation area throughout the state

1   Allowable, but cultivators shall only transport from a cultivation site to a manufacturer or distributor.

2   Allowable, but manufacturers shall only transport medical cannabis products as follows:

       (i) between a cultivation site and a manufacturing site; (ii) between manufacturing site and manufacturing site; and (iii) between a manufacturing site and a distributor.

3   Type 12 Transporters may also hold a Type 11 Distribution License but it is not mandatory.

N/A   May hold same license.

Medical Cannabis Regulation and Safety Act Allowable License Combinations

License Type	1	1A	1B	1C	2	2A	2B	3	3A
1 Cultivation; Spec. Outdoor; Small	N/A	✓	✓	✓	✓	✓	✓	✓	✓
1A Cultivation; Spec. Indoor; Small	✓	N/A	✓	✓	✓	✓	✓	✓	✓
1B Cultivation; Spec. Mix-light; Small	✓	✓	N/A	✓	✓	✓	✓	✓	✓
1C Cultivation; Spec. Cottage	✓	✓	✓	N/A	✓	✓	✓	✓	✓
2 Cultivation; Outdoor; Small	✓	✓	✓	✓	N/A	✓	✓	✓	✓
2A Cultivation; Indoor; Small	✓	✓	✓	✓	✓	N/A	✓	✓	✓
2B Cultivation; Mix-light; Small	✓	✓	✓	✓	✓	✓	N/A	✓	✓
3 Cultivation; Outdoor; Medium	✓	✓	✓	✓	✓	✓	✓	N/A	✓
3A Cultivation; Indoor; Medium	✓	✓	✓	✓	✓	✓	✓	✓	N/A
3B Cultivation; Mix-light; Medium	✓	✓	✓	✓	✓	✓	✓	✓	✓
4 Cultivation; Nursery	✓	✓	✓	✓	✓	✓	✓	✓	✓
6 Manufacturer 1 nonvolatile solvents	✓	✓	✓	✓	✓	✓	✓	✗	✗
7 Manufacturer 2 volatile solvents	✓	✓	✓	✓	✓	✓	✓	✗	✗
8 Testing Laboratory	✗	✗	✗	✗	✗	✗	✗	✗	✗
10 Dispensary; General	✗	✗	✗	✗	✗	✗	✗	✗	✗
10A Producing Dispensary; Up to 3	✓+	✓+	✓+	✓+	✓+	✓+	✓+	✓+	✓+
11 Distribution	✗	✗	✗	✗	✗	✗	✗	✗	✗
12 Transporter	1	1	1	1	1	1	1	1	1

Medical Cannabis Regulation and Safety Act Allowable License Combinations

License Type	3B	4	6	7	8	10	10A	11	12
1 Cultivation; Spec. Outdoor; Small	✓	✓	✓	✓	×	×	✓+	×	1
1A Cultivation; Spec. Indoor; Small	✓	✓	✓	✓	×	×	✓+	×	1
1B Cultivation; Spec. Mix-light; Small	✓	✓	✓	✓	×	×	✓+	×	1
1C Cultivation; Spec. Cottage	✓	✓	✓	✓	×	×	✓+	×	1
2 Cultivation; Outdoor; Small	✓	✓	✓	✓	×	×	✓+	×	1
2A Cultivation; Indoor; Small	✓	✓	✓	✓	×	×	✓+	×	1
2B Cultivation; Mix-light; Small	✓	✓	✓	✓	×	×	✓+	×	1
3 Cultivation; Outdoor; Medium	✓	✓	×	×	×	×	✓+	×	1
3A Cultivation; Indoor; Medium	✓	✓	×	×	×	×	✓+	×	1
3B Cultivation; Mix-light; Medium	N/A	✓	×	×	×	×	✓+	×	1
4 Cultivation; Nursery	✓	N/A	×	×	×	×	✓+	×	1
6 Manufacturer 1 nonvolatile solvents	×	×	N/A	✓	×	×	✓+	×	2
7 Manufacturer 2 volatile solvents	×	×	✓	N/A	×	×	✓+	×	2
8 Testing Laboratory	×	×	×	×	N/A	×	×	×	×
10 Dispensary; General	×	×	×	×	×	N/A	×	×	×
10A Producing Dispensary; Up to 3	✓+	✓+	✓+	✓+	×	×	N/A	×	×
11 Distribution	×	×	×	×	×	×	×	N/A	M
12 Transporter	1	1	2	2	×	×	×	3	N/A

Chart: Marijuana License Categories

Established by the Adult Use of Marijuana Act
Cultivation: The Department of Food and Agriculture shall promulgate regulations governing the licensing of cannabis cultivation.

License Category	Description and Restrictions
Type 1 Cultivation; Specialty outdoor; Small	• Outdoor cultivation • No artificial lighting • < 5,000 sq. ft. of total canopy size on one premises • Or up to 50 mature plants on noncontiguous plots
Type 1A Cultivation; Specialty indoor; Small	• Indoor cultivation • Exclusively artificial lighting • < 5,000 sq. ft. of total canopy size on one premises
Type 1B Cultivation; Specialty mixed-light; Small	• Combination of natural and supplemental artificial lighting (maximum threshold to be determined by the licensing authority) • < 5,000 sq. ft. of total canopy size on one premises
Type 2 Cultivation; Outdoor; Small	• Outdoor cultivation • No artificial lighting • Between 5,001 and 10,000 sq. ft. of total canopy size on one premises
Type 2A Cultivation; Indoor; Small	• Indoor cultivation • Exclusively artificial lighting • Between 5,001 and 10,000 sq. ft. of total canopy size on one premises

License Category	Description and Restrictions
Type 2B Cultivation; Mixed-light; Small	• Combination of natural and supplemental artificial lighting (maximum threshold to be determined by the licensing authority) • Between 5,001 and 10,000 sq. ft. of total canopy size on one premises
Type 3 Cultivation; Outdoor; Medium	• Outdoor cultivation • No artificial lighting • Between 10,001 sq. ft. to 1 acre of total canopy size on one premises • The Department of Food and Agriculture shall limit the number of licenses allowed of this type
Type 3A Cultivation; Indoor; Medium	• Indoor cultivation • Exclusively artificial lighting • Between 10,001 and 22,000 sq. ft. of total canopy size on one premises • The Department of Food and Agriculture shall limit the number of licenses allowed of this type
Type 3B Cultivation; Mixed-light; Medium	• Combination of natural and supplemental artificial lighting (maximum threshold to be determined by the licensing authority) • Between 10,001 and 22,000 sq. ft. of total canopy size on one premises • The Department of Food and Agriculture shall limit the number of licenses allowed of this type
Type 4 Cultivation; Nursery	• Produces only clones, immature plants, seeds, and other agricultural products used specifically for the planting, propagation, and cultivation of marijuana

License Category	Description and Restrictions
Type 5 Cultivation; Outdoor; Large	• Outdoor cultivation • No artificial lighting • > 1 acre of total canopy size on one premises • May not be issued before January 1, 2023
Type 5A Cultivation; Indoor; Large	• Indoor cultivation • Exclusively artificial lighting • > 22,000 sq. ft. of total canopy size on one premises • May not be issued before January 1, 2023
Type 6 Manufacturing Level 1	• Manufacturing sites that produce marijuana products using nonvolatile solvents, or no solvents
Type 7 Manufacturing Level 2	• Manufacturing sites that produce marijuana products using volatile solvents • Manufacturing sites that produce marijuana products using volatile solvents
Type 8 Testing	• Testing of marijuana and marijuana products • Shall have facilities licensed according to regulations set forth by the department • Shall **not** hold a license in another license category of this division **and** shall **not** own or have ownership interest in a non-testing facility licensed pursuant to this division

Retailers and Distributors:

Licenses to be issued by the Department of Consumer Affairs

License Category	Description and Restrictions
Type 10 Retailer	• Retail sale and delivery of medical or marijuana products to customers
Type 11 Distributor	• Distribution of marijuana and marijuana products • Shall be bonded and insured at a minimum level established by the licensing authority
Type 12 Microbusiness	• Cultivation of marijuana on an area less than 10,000 square feet as well as distribution, Level 1 manufacturing, and retail sale of marijuana • Licensee must comply with all requirements imposed on licensed cultivators, distributors, Level 1 manufacturers, and retailers

Adult Use Marijuana Act Allowable License Combinations

Find your license type at the top and drop down the column to find other allowable licenses.

Legend:

✓   Allowable cross licensure.

✗   Prohibited cross licensure.

N/A   May hold same license.

Note: No Type 5, Type 5A, and Type 5B cultivation licenses may be issued before January 1, 2023.

Adult Use Marijuana Act Allowable License Combinations

License Type	1	1A	1B	2	2A	2B	3	3A	3B
1 Cultivation; Spec. Outdoor; Small	N/A	✓	✓	✓	✓	✓	✓	✓	✓
1A Cultivation; Spec. Indoor; Small	✓	N/A	✓	✓	✓	✓	✓	✓	✓
1B Cultivation; Spec. Mix-light; Small	✓	✓	N/A	✓	✓	✓	✓	✓	✓
2 Cultivation; Outdoor; Small	✓	✓	✓	N/A	✓	✓	✓	✓	✓
2A Cultivation; Indoor; Small	✓	✓	✓	✓	N/A	✓	✓	✓	✓
2B Cultivation; Mix-light; Small	✓	✓	✓	✓	✓	N/A	✓	✓	✓
3 Cultivation; Outdoor; Medium	✓	✓	✓	✓	✓	✓	N/A	✓	✓
3A Cultivation; Indoor; Medium	✓	✓	✓	✓	✓	✓	✓	N/A	✓
3B Cultivation; Mix-light; Medium	✓	✓	✓	✓	✓	✓	✓	✓	N/A
4 Cultivation; Nursery	✓	✓	✓	✓	✓	✓	✓	✓	✓
5 Cultivation; Outdoor; Large	✓	✓	✓	✓	✓	✓	✓	✓	✓
5A Cultivation; Indoor; Large	✓	✓	✓	✓	✓	✓	✓	✓	✓
5B Cultivation; Mix-light; Large	✓	✓	✓	✓	✓	✓	✓	✓	✓
6 Manufacturer 1 nonvolatile solvents	✓	✓	✓	✓	✓	✓	✓	✓	✓
7 Manufacturer 2 volatile solvents	✓	✓	✓	✓	✓	✓	✓	✓	✓
8 Testing Laboratory	✗	✗	✗	✗	✗	✗	✗	✗	✗
10 Retailer	✓	✓	✓	✓	✓	✓	✓	✓	✓
11 Distributor	✓	✓	✓	✓	✓	✓	✓	✓	✓
12 Microbusinesses	✓	✓	✓	✓	✓	✓	✓	✓	✓

Adult Use Marijuana Act Allowable License Combinations

License Type	4	5	5A	5B	6	7	8	10	11	12
1 Cultivation; Spec. Outdoor; Small	✓	✓	✓	✓	✓	✓	✕	✓	✓	✓
1A Cultivation; Spec. Indoor; Small	✓	✓	✓	✓	✓	✓	✕	✓	✓	✓
1B Cultivation; Spec. Mix-light; Small	✓	✓	✓	✓	✓	✓	✕	✓	✓	✓
2 Cultivation; Outdoor; Small	✓	✓	✓	✓	✓	✓	✕	✓	✓	✓
2A Cultivation; ndoor; Small	✓	✓	✓	✓	✓	✓	✕	✓	✓	✓
2B Cultivation; Mix-light; Small	✓	✓	✓	✓	✓	✓	✕	✓	✓	✓
3 Cultivation; Outdoor; Medium	✓	✓	✓	✓	✓	✓	✕	✓	✓	✓
3A Cultivation; Indoor; Medium	✓	✓	✓	✓	✓	✓	✕	✓	✓	✓
3B Cultivation; Mix-light; Medium	✓	✓	✓	✓	✓	✓	✕	✓	✓	✓
4 Cultivation; Nursery	N/A	✓	✓	✓	✓	✓	✕	✓	✓	✓
5 Cultivation; Outdoor; Large	✓	N/A	✓	✓	✓	✓	✕	✓	✓	✓
5A Cultivation; Indoor; Large	✓	✓	N/A	✓	✓	✓	✕	✓	✓	✓
5B Cultivation; Mix-light; Large	✓	✓	✓	N/A	✓	✓	✕	✓	✓	✓
6 Manufacturer 1 nonvolatile solvents	✓	✓	✓	✓	N/A	✓	✕	✓	✓	✓
7 Manufacturer 2 volatile solvents	✓	✓	✓	✓	✓	N/A	✕	✓	✓	✓
8 Testing Laboratory	✕	✕	✕	✕	✕	✕	N/A	✕	✕	✕
10 Retailer	✓	✓	✓	✓	✓	✓	✕	N/A	✓	✓
11 Distributor	✓	✕	✕	✕	✓	✓	✕	✓	N/A	✓
12 Microbusinesses	✓	✕	✕	✕	✓	✓	✕	✓	✓	N/A

www.ingramcontent.com/pod-product-compliance
Lightning Source LLC
Chambersburg PA
CBHW032005180326
41458CB00040B/6527